Dysgu Trwy Lenyddiaeth

CYRIL JONES

Darnau byrion o

lenyddiaeth Gymraeg,

caneuon, cerddi a

detholiadau eraill i'w

defnyddio yn y dosbarth

Cymraeg i Oedolion.

CBAC
WJEC

Dysgu Trwy Lenyddiaeth

Cyhoeddwyd gan CBAC

Cymraeg i Oedolion
CBAC
245 Rhodfa'r Gorllewin
CAERDYDD
CF5 2YX

Argraffwyd gan Wasg Gomer
Argraffiad cyntaf 2010

ISBN 978 1 86085 665 5

Noddwyd gan Lywodraeth Cynulliad Cymru.

Cydnabyddiaeth

Awdur:	Cyril Jones
Golygydd:	Mandi Morse
Dylunydd:	Olwen Fowler
Rheolwr y Project:	Emyr Davies

Darllenwyr ar y CD:
Gareth Roberts, Ellen Salisbury, Nia Elin, Geraint Todd, Huw Euron, Emyr Davies.

Recordiwyd y darnau llafar yn stiwdio CBAC, Caerdydd.

Mae'r cyhoeddwr yn ddiolchgar i'r canlynol am ganiatâd i ddefnyddio'r darnau a nodir:

Diolch i Gyhoeddiadau Sain am gael defnyddio *Dw i eisiau dawnsio* o *Gitâr yn y Twll dan Stâr* gan Meic Stevens; *Lleucu Llwyd* gan Tebot Piws; *Gadael Abertawe* gan Huw Chiswell;
Diolch i label Rasal am gael defnyddio *Coffi Du* gan Gwibdaith Hen Frân;
Diolch i Wasg Gomer am gael defnyddio darn o *Bywyd Blodwen Jones* gan Bethan Gwanas; darnau allan o *Dauwynebog* gan Ceri Wyn Jones; darn allan o *Detholiad o Gerddi* gan TH Parry-Williams;
Diolch i Wasg Carreg Gwalch am gael defnyddio darnau o *Barddoniaeth Boced-Din: Hiwmor Hedd* gan Hedd Bleddyn; darn o *Rhydd fel Aderyn* gan Pat Clayton;
Diolch i Fflach am gael defnyddio *Blwyddyn Mas* gan Einir Dafydd a Ceri Wyn Jones;
Diolch i Wasg y Dref Wen am gael defnyddio darn allan o *Gormod o Win* gan Bob Eynon;
Diolch i Gyhoeddiadau Barddas am gael defnyddio darn allan o *Cadwyni Rhyddid* gan Grahame Davies; darn allan o *Dim Angen Creu Teledu Yma* gan Aled Lewis Evans;
Diolch i Wasg Gee am gael defnyddio darn allan o *Y Lôn Wen* gan Kate Roberts; darn allan o *Croesi Traeth* gan Gwyn Thomas;
Diolch i'r Lolfa am gael defnyddio darn allan o *Budapest* gan Elin Meek; darn allan o *Stori Sydyn: Llais yr Adar Gleision* gan Ali Yassine; darn allan o *Stori Sydyn: Cymru Howard Marks* gan Howard Marks ac Alun Gibbard; darn allan o *Martha, Jac a Sianco* gan Caryl Lewis; darn allan o *Holl Garthion Pen Cymro Ynghyd* gan Ifor ap Glyn; darn allan o *Dirgel Ddyn* gan Mihangel Morgan; darn allan o *Pentigily* gan Hefin Wyn;
Diolch i Wasg Taf am gael defnyddio darn allan o *Hanner Cant* gan Iwan Llwyd;
Diolch i Wasg Addysgol Cymru am gael defnyddio darn allan o *Dyddiadur Ann Frank* gan Eigra Lewis Roberts;
Diolch i Wasg Gwynedd am gael defnyddio darn allan o *Darnau* gan Dylan Iorwerth;
Diolch i Wasg Dinefwr am gael defnyddio darn allan o *Cymru Fydd* gan Saunders Lewis.

Diolch i'r isod am gael defnyddio lluniau:
Mostyn Davies, Marian Delyth, Aneirin Karadog, Y Lolfa, Photolibrary Wales, Einir Dafydd, Cyngor Celfyddydau Cymru, Jaci Taylor, Mark Johnson, Caffi Hoffi Coffi, Mandi Morse, Gwasg Gee ac Olwen Fowler.

Cynnwys

Canllaw i Diwtoriaid

Er mwyn manteisio'n llawn ar y pecyn hwn, dylid defnyddio'r llyfryn a'r cryno-ddisg yn ystod sesiwn. Mae'n bwysig nodi nad oes disgwyl i'r dysgwyr wybod ystyr pob gair na deall popeth yn y darnau a ddewiswyd; mae mwynhau ac ymgyfarwyddo â sŵn a rhythmau iaith yn rhan bwysig o'r broses o ddysgu iaith a gwerthfawrogi ei llenyddiaeth. Awgrymir, felly, bod gwrando ar y darnau ddwy neu dair gwaith yn rhan annatod o bob cyflwyniad. Mae'r 30 darn wedi cael eu recordio ar y cryno-ddisg. Y tiwtor unigol a ŵyr pa ddull sy'n gweddu orau i'w ddosbarth. Does dim rhaid glynu wrth y lefelau a awgrymir 'chwaith; gall ambell ddarn weithio ar fwy nag un lefel. Dyma'r camau a argymhellir ond mae'n bosib newid trefn y tri cham cyntaf:

- Chwarae'r darn ar y cryno-ddisg heb baratoi'r dysgwyr ymlaen llaw drwy eu porthi â geirfa na rhoi sgript iddyn nhw. Ar ôl chwarae'r darn dylid holi'r aelodau am eu dealltwriaeth ohono a gall y tiwtor nodi'r pwyntiau hynny ar y bwrdd gwyn.

- Y tiwtor yn cyflwyno'r darn a'r eirfa i'r dysgwyr. Gall y tiwtor ddefnyddio'r dulliau arferol o gyflwyno geirfa, e.e. cardiau fflach neu adrodd yn uchel. Gellir darllen y darn hefyd. Cyflwynir esboniad a/neu gyfieithiad o'r eirfa anodd gyferbyn â phob llinell neu o dan y darnau rhyddiaith. Pan fo gair wedi'i dreiglo yn y llinell rhoddir ffurf wreiddiol y gair yn yr esboniad. Yn ystod y cam hwn gall y tiwtor gyflwyno peth gwybodaeth am gefndir y darn; gweler y blwch gwybodaeth.

- Chwarae'r darn eto ar y cryno-ddisg. Y tro hwn bydd y dysgwyr yn dilyn y sgript. Ar ôl y gwrandawiad, rhoddir cyfle i'r aelodau gywiro neu ychwanegu at yr wybodaeth a nodwyd ar y bwrdd gwyn ar ôl y cam cyntaf.

- Cyflwyno'r dudalen ymarferion, neu ddetholiad ohoni, i'r dosbarth. Yn ogystal â blwch gwybodaeth, nodir camau clir ar gyfer y tiwtor yn ogystal ag ymarferion yn seiliedig ar batrymau ieithyddol y darnau. Awgrymir gwaith llafar/ysgrifenedig ymestynnol yn ôl gofynion a lefelau'r darnau hefyd. Gall y tiwtor ddefnyddio neu addasu'r ymarferion ar y dudalen hon yn ôl gofynion y grŵp.

- Chwarae'r cryno-ddisg unwaith eto i orffen y sesiwn heb ddilyn y sgript. Trwy ddilyn y camau uchod, bydd y dysgwyr yn adeiladu eu geirfa, eu gwybodaeth a'u dealltwriaeth o'r darnau yn raddol. Dylai'r drefn honno sicrhau bod y dysgwyr yn cael y boddhad o feistroli darnau a oedd y tu hwnt i'w cyrraedd ar y gwrandawiad neu'r darlleniad cyntaf. Mae'n anochel bod rhai patrymau yn y darnau a gyflwynir yn wahanol i'r patrymau sy'n gyfarwydd i'r dysgwyr, yn enwedig y dysgwyr hynny sy'n dal i ddysgu ar y lefelau cyntaf. Dysgu iaith trwy gyfrwng darnau llenyddol yw prif bwrpas y llyfryn a'r cryno-ddisg ond gobeithir hefyd y bydd y dull hwn o gyflwyno llenyddiaeth yn eu sbarduno i ddarllen y llyfrau eu hunain wedyn.

1.   Penillion Mnemonig

Misoedd y flwyddyn

Ionawr, Chwefror, Mawrth ac Ebrill
Dyna bedwar mis mewn pennill;
Mai, Mehefin a Gorffennaf,
Dyna'r misoedd sy'n dod nesaf.

Awst a Medi, Hydref, Tachwedd,
Wedi cyrraedd bron i'r diwedd;
Dim ond Rhagfyr sy'n dod wedyn,
Dyna ni ar ddiwedd blwyddyn.

Y Treiglad Meddal

I gofio'r treiglad meddal:
Mae Ceri o Gaerdydd,
Mae Tom yn dod o Dal-y-bont,
A Pam o Bontypridd.

Mae Gwyn yn dod o _Wynedd,
Mae Dai o Ddinas Brân,
Mae Bob yn dod o Fangor,
A dyna hanner cân.

Mae Mari'n dod o Fargam,
A Llew o Lan-y-bri,
Mae Rhys yn dod o Ryd-y-waun,
Ac wedyn, dyna ni!

Tasgau

Mae hi'n anodd cael hyd i ddarnau o lenyddiaeth sy'n addas i'w defnyddio ar y lefelau cyntaf. Dyfais lafar yw *mnemonig* i helpu'r cof, a gall fod yn ddefnyddiol wrth ddysgu unrhyw beth. Gall fod yn bennill neu odl i gofio rhestr, fel dyddiau'r wythnos, misoedd y flwyddyn, rhifau ac ati. Gall hefyd fod yn ymadrodd neu bennill i helpu cofio rheol neu gyfuniad o eiriau. Dyma'r rheswm y mae cyfuniadau gwirion fel 'hoffi coffi' yn aros yn y cof. Awgrymir:

- Rhoi'r penillion fesul un ar y bwrdd gwyn, neu'r uwch-daflunydd. Gellir gofyn i bawb gydadrodd fwy nag unwaith gyda'r CD. Yna, pawb i ddarllen eto, a'r tiwtor yn dileu geiriau unigol yn raddol.

- Ar ôl ymarfer ychydig, gall y tiwtor ddechrau pob brawddeg, a'r dysgwyr yn gorfod gorffen y llinellau, heb sbardun y bwrdd gwyn.

- Mae amrywiadau niferus ar gael o'r penillion hyn a phenillion tebyg, a llawer o rai defnyddiol o faes dysgu plant bach. Gellir gofyn i bawb gael hyd i ragor neu edrych am benillion syml tebyg, e.e. penillion i gofio dyddiau'r wythnos.

Dyma rai ymarferion hawdd yn seiliedig ar odli. Gellir eu dosbarthu i barau'n gyntaf, yna gofyn i bawb ar lafar gofio ail hanner y llinellau, a'u profi ar lafar.

1.	Dw i'n mwynhau, ar ddydd _____ .	[Iau]
2.	I weld ffrind, rhaid i ti _____ .	[fynd]
3.	Ar ôl saith, dw i'n mynd i'r _____ .	[gwaith]
4.	Yn y tŷ, ga' i goffi _____ .	[du]
5.	Yn yr haf, roedd y tywydd yn _____ .	[braf]
6.	Pwdin da yw/ydy _____ .	[hufen iâ]
7.	Mewn caffi yn y dre, dw i'n hoffi yfed _____ .	[te]
8.	Dw i'n mynd ar y cwrs: dw i'n hoffi cael _____ .	[sgwrs]
9.	Dw i ddim yn credu beth dw i'n weld ar y _____ .	[teledu]
10.	Yn y dydd dw i'n dysgu, yn y nos dw i'n _____ .	[cysgu]

Mae'n anodd rhoi tasgau ychwanegol gan fod cyn lleied o eirfa gan y dysgwyr i'w defnyddio ar y lefel hon. Fodd bynnag, mae'n ymarfer da creu ymadroddion neu benillion mnemonig i fod yn broc i'r cof, e.e. meddwl am gyfuniadau fel Tom Davies, Penny Black ac ati, i gofio'r treiglad meddal. Mae gan bob dysgwr a thiwtor stôr o'r rhain, ond mae'n dda atgoffa dysgwyr fod angen help ar y cof weithiau.

2. **Rap Cwestiynau** gan Aneirin Karadog

Ble wyt ti'n byw; O ble wyt ti'n dod?
Cwestiwn ar ôl cwestiwn, dyna beth sy'n bod.
Oes gen ti rywbeth i fi, neu rywbeth i ni?
Beth sy'n mynd drwy dy feddwl di?
Sut mae'r tywydd? Ydy hi'n braf?
Ydy hi'n oer yng nghanol yr haf?
Wyt ti eisiau coffi neu de neu gwrw?
Wyt ti'n hoffi mynd am dro os ydy hi'n bwrw... glaw, glaw.
Pedwar, pump, chwech, saith, wyth a naw, naw...
Wyt ti'n mynd am dro, i ble wyt ti'n mynd?
Wyt ti'n mynd â'r ci am dro, neu wyt ti'n mynd â ffrind?
Oes rhaid i ti fynd i Aberaeron,
Abertawe, neu dre Caernarfon?
Bangor, Y Rhyl neu dre Tregaron?
Dw i'n dechrau mynd yn wirion.
Beth wnest ti ddoe? Dwyt ti ddim yn cofio.
Darllen, gweithio, canu neu nofio.
Dwyt ti ddim yn gwybod, dwyt ti ddim yn gwrando,
Dydd Sadwrn, dydd Sul... wyt ti wedi blino?
Dydd Mercher, dydd Iau...
Wyt ti'n mwynhau?
Mae gormod o gwestiynau. Dw i wedi cael digon.
Y broblem yw hyn: does dim atebion!

Gwybodaeth
Aneirin Karadog sy'n canu, neu'n rapio. Mae e'n dod o ardal Pont-y-pridd yn
wreiddiol. Mae ei dad yn Gymro, ac mae ei fam yn dod o Lydaw. Mae Aneirin
yn siarad pum iaith, yn cynnwys Llydaweg. Mae e'n canu gyda'r grwpiau
hip-hop *Y Diwygiad* a *Genod Droog*.

Tasgau

Dyma gân yn arddull 'rap', ac mae nifer o ffyrdd i'w defnyddio. Does dim geiriau tu hwnt i lefel Mynediad yn y gân hon. Y jôc yw bod tiwtoriaid yn croesholi dysgwyr â chwestiynau drwy'r amser. Awgrymir gwrando am gategorïau gwahanol o eiriau bob tro, gan wrando eto rhwng pob un os oes angen:

- Gofyn i bawb wrando ar y gân gan restru pob rhif yng nghanol y gân. Pawb i gymharu rhestri ar ôl gwrando. [Atebion: pedwar, pump, chwech, saith, wyth, naw]

- Gofyn i bawb wrando ar y gân gan restru pob un o'r lleoedd a enwir yng nghanol y gân. Pawb i gymharu rhestri ar ôl gwrando.
  [Aberaeron, Abertawe, Caernarfon, Bangor, Y Rhyl, Tregaron]

- Gofyn i bawb wrando ar y gân gan restru pob un o ddyddiau'r wythnos a enwir ar ddiwedd y gân. Pawb i gymharu rhestri ar ôl gwrando. [Atebion: dydd Mercher, dydd Iau, dydd Sadwrn, dydd Sul]

- Gofyn i bawb restru'r diddordebau neu weithgareddau a enwir yn y gân.
  Pawb i gymharu rhestri ar ôl gwrando.
  [Atebion: darllen, gweithio, canu, nofio]

- Gofyn i bawb restru'r holl gwestiynau sy'n codi. Pawb i gymharu rhestri ar ôl gwrando. Y tiwtor i'w rhoi ar y bwrdd gwyn a rhannu pawb yn barau i ofyn y cwestiynau i'w gilydd a'u hateb.

Pwyntiau Iaith
Mae'n bosib y bydd rhai amrywiadau tafodieithol yn codi, e.e. Oes gen ti... (nid *Oes ...* *'da ti*), neu Y broblem yw (nid *Y broblem ydy*). Does dim angen sôn llawer am hyn, dim ond nodi bod amrywiadau fel hyn yn codi'n aml, ac i beidio â phoeni amdanynt.

Sgwrsio Pellach
Rhoi rhestr o atebion i'r dosbarth ar bapur (neu ar y bwrdd gwyn). Rhaid i bawb feddwl am gwestiwn addas i sbarduno'r ateb hwnnw.

1. Ydw, dw i'n mynd â Rover i'r parc.
2. Mae hi'n wyntog iawn.
3. Dw i eisiau te, os gwelwch chi'n dda.
4. Ddoe? Wnes i ddim byd, dim ond dysgu Cymraeg.
5. Oes, rhaid i fi/mi fynd i Gaerdydd.
6. Dw i'n byw yn Llanaber.
7. Dw i'n dod o Langollen.
8. Nac ydw, dw i ddim yn hoffi nofio.

Gyda dosbarth dyfeisgar, gofyn iddyn nhw lunio rap gan ddefnyddio brawddegau o'r llyfrau cwrs yn unig.

3.   **Dw i eisiau dawnsio** gan Meic Stevens

Dw i eisiau dawnsio,
Dw i eisiau neidio,
Dw i eisiau hedfan,
Dw i eisiau cneifio,   *cneifio - to shear (sheep!)*
Dw i eisiau rhedeg ar dy ôl,   *ar dy ôl - after you*
Gwneud y pethau ffôl...   *ffôl - foolish*

Dw i eisiau dawnsio.
Dw i eisiau nofio,
Dw i eisiau dringo,   *dringo - to climb*
Dw i eisiau caru,   *caru - to make love*
Dw i eisiau cyri,
Dw i eisiau rhedeg ar dy ôl,
Gwneud y pethau ffôl i ti,
Ie.

Dw i eisiau ... llinell,
Dw i eisiau gwyneb,   *(g)wyneb - face*
Dw i eisiau Llinos,
Mae gen i eos,   *eos - nightingale*
Dw i jyst eisiau rhedeg ar dy ôl,
Gwneud y pethau ffôl,
Dw i eisiau dawnsio,
Efo chdi... come on 'te...   *efo chdi - gyda ti*

Dw i eisiau morio,   *morio - to sail on the sea*
Dw i eisiau morwyn,
Sdim eisiau angor,   *angor - anchor*
Sdim eisiau cadwyn,   *cadwyn - chain*
Dw i eisiau rhedeg ar dy ôl,
Gwneud y pethau ffôl,
Dw i eisiau dawnsio efo Sue...
Dw i eisiau dawnsio...
Dw i eisiau bwyta,
Ie, mae gen i gitâr.

Dw i eisiau mefus, hufen,   *mefus - strawberries   hufen - cream*
Dw i eisiau gwefus,   *gwefus - lip*
Dw i eisiau rhedeg ar dy ôl,
Gwneud y pethau ffôl,
Dw i eisiau dawnsio...

Gwybodaeth

Mae'r gân yma'n dod o'r albwm *Gitâr yn y Twll dan Stâr*. Y canwr yw Meic Stevens.
Mae e'n dod o Sir Benfro. Mae e'n canu caneuon gwerin a roc a rôl. Mae 25 albwm
gyda fe, a daeth yr albwm yma allan yn 1983.

Tasgau

Mae hon yn gân sy'n ailadrodd yr un patrwm ac mae'n addas i'w defnyddio ar ôl cyflwyno 'eisiau' yn y cwrs. Wrth reswm, bydd nifer o eiriau dieithr yma, a nifer o eiriau anarferol, fel 'cneifio.' Awgrymir:

- Chwarae'r darn ddwywaith ar y CD a gofyn i bawb yn y dosbarth ysgrifennu cymaint o'r pethau sy'n dod ar ôl 'eisiau'. Does dim ots os nad ydyn nhw'n deall y geiriau hynny.

- Rhannu pawb yn barau i gymharu'r rhestri a thrafod mewn parau.

- Chwarae'r gân eto, gan wasgu'r botwm oedi ar ôl pob pennill. Dylid gofyn i'r dysgwyr ddweud beth mae e eisiau / be' mae o isio yn y trydydd person, e.e. Mae e eisiau hedfan / Mae o isio nofio.

- Os ydy'r dysgwyr yn gwybod ystyr y gair, rhaid iddyn nhw feimio'r gair i weddill y dosbarth. Bydd rhaid i'r tiwtor feimio'r geiriau sy'n ddieithr i bawb.

- Dosbarthu'r geiriau ar ochr arall y ddalen a chwarae'r darn unwaith eto, ac os yw'n ddosbarth hwyliog, gofyn iddyn nhw feimio wrth fynd ymlaen!

- Dosbarthu'r fersiwn ysgrifenedig sydd ar y CD, ond gyda'r enwau a'r berfenwau ar ôl 'eisiau' wedi eu dileu, gan ofyn i bawb lenwi'r bylchau wrth wrando ar y gân.

Pwyntiau Iaith

Does dim **yn** gydag **eisiau/isio** - camgymeriad cyffredin!
Mae'n gyfle i ymarfer troi o'r person cyntaf: Dw i eisiau > Mae e eisiau. Dylai tiwtoriaid yn y gogledd ymarfer **Mae o isio...** Ni ddylid gwneud môr a mynydd o'r eirfa newydd yn y gân, na disgwyl i neb gofio'r geiriau tafodieithol neu ddieithr. Dim ond ychydig o hwyl yw'r darn i roi amrywiaeth yn y dysgu.

Sgwrsio Pellach

Ar ôl gorffen â'r gân, dyma gyfle i holi pawb *Beth wyt ti eisiau wneud heno?* Yna, rhoi'r geiriau: *heno, yfory, nos yfory, dydd Sadwrn* a *dydd Sul* ar y bwrdd gwyn. Rhaid i bawb holi'i gilydd mewn parau:

> *Beth wyt ti eisiau wneud nos yfory?*
> *Be' wyt ti isio wneud ddydd Sul?*

Dylai'r tiwtor fynd o gwmpas i helpu a sbarduno.

4. **Englynion** gan Cyril Jones

Dw i'n hoff o de a choffi, - dw i eisiau
dwy deisen; mae Wali   *teisen - cacen*
eisiau 'Brains' gyda chaws Brie,
a Meirion eisiau Mari.

Dwy gadair ond dau gwdyn - ie, dau fwrdd   *cwdyn - sack*
ond dwy ford, dwy delyn;   *bord/bwrdd - table   telyn - harp*
dau dad, dwy ddafad, dau ddyn
a dwy bêl rhwng dau bolyn.   *polyn - pole*

Dw i'n byw 'da Fal yn y Bala - a Bob
yn byw yn y Rhondda;
Dai a Rhys yng Ngwlad yr Ha'   *Gwlad yr Haf - Somerset*
a Lois yn Efail Isa'.

Gwybodaeth
Tri *englyn* sy yma - hen fesur Cymraeg.
Maen nhw mewn cynghanedd, sef patrwm
o odlau a chytseinedd, sy'n unigryw i'r
iaith Gymraeg.

Tasgau

Gellir cyflwyno'r englynion syml hyn pan fo'r dysgwyr yn gyfarwydd â phatrymau fel *Dw i'n hoff..., Dw i eisiau/isio... a Dw i'n byw yn...* Prif bwrpas eu cyflwyno yw rhoi ymarfer gwrando, ynganu a dysgu ar y cof i'r dysgwyr. Dylai eco'r cytseiniaid (dyna beth yw cynghanedd) mewn llinell eu helpu i wneud hyn. Awgrymir:

- Ar ôl gwrando ar yr englynion ar y CD, annog y dosbarth i'w hadrodd yn uchel ddwy neu dair gwaith er mwyn ymgyfarwyddo â rhythm y mesur.

- Rhannu'r dosbarth yn barau a gofyn iddyn nhw ddweud yr englynion wrth ei gilydd a nodi pa eiriau sy'n odli, neu sy'n diweddu â'r un sain, ymhob englyn. Er enghraifft, mae *Wali, coffi, Brie a Mari* yn odli yn yr englyn cyntaf.

- Rhoi'r englynion heb y geiriau sy'n odli ar y bwrdd gwyn a rhannu'r dosbarth i grwpiau bach a gofyn iddyn nhw eu hadrodd gan geisio cofio'r geiriau yn y bylchau heb edrych ar y sgript.

- Eu rhannu yn barau eto a chynnal cystadleuaeth cofio englyn a'i adrodd heb gymorth sgript.

Pwyntiau Iaith

Gyda grwpiau sy'n hoff o ramadeg, dyma gyfle i adolygu'r syniad bod geiriau'n gallu bod yn wrywaidd neu'n fenywaidd yn Gymraeg. Hefyd, mae ffurfiau benywaidd i'r rhifolion dau, tri a phedwar. Awgrymir rhoi dwy golofn ar y bwrdd gwyn a gofyn i bawb benderfynu a ydy'r geiriau yn y penillion yn wrywaidd neu'n fenywaidd:

Gwrywaidd: te, coffi, caws, cwdyn, bwrdd, tad, dyn, polyn.
Benywaidd: teisen, cadair, bord, telyn, dafad, pêl.

Gellir ychwanegu geiriau mwy cyfarwydd i'w hychwanegu at y rhestri, e.e. cath, ci, pen, coes, tywydd, llyfr, gwraig. Bydd angen eu hatgoffa bod treiglad meddal ar ôl *dau* neu *dwy*, a gofyn iddynt fynd drwy'r rhestri gan roi *dau/dwy* o flaen y gair priodol. Mae rhai llyfrau cwrs yn defnyddio'r talfyriadau *eg* ac *eb* i ddynodi enwau gwrywaidd a benywaidd. Mae hefyd yn gyfle i bwysleisio mai enwau unigol sy'n dod ar ôl rhifau yn Gymraeg, yn wahanol i'r Saesneg.

Sgwrsio Pellach

Ar ôl ymarfer dweud yr englyn olaf nifer o weithiau, gellir rhannu pawb yn grwpiau i feddwl am gymaint o gwestiynau â phosibl yn seiliedig ar yr wybodaeth sy ynddo, e.e.

Ble/Lle mae Fal yn byw?
Pwy sy'n byw yn y Rhondda?
Yn Efail Ucha mae Lois yn byw? Nage/Naci
Gyda phwy/ Efo pwy mae Rhys?

Gellir mynnu brawddeg lawn yn ateb bob tro.

5. Hen Benillion

(Traddodiadol)

Tri pheth sy'n anodd 'nabod,
Dyn, derwen a diwrnod;   *derwen - oak tree*
Mae'r dydd yn troi, y pren yn gou   *cou* - cau, *hollow*
A'r dyn yn ddouwynebog.   *douwynebog* - dauwynebog, *two-faced*

Mynd i'r ardd i dorri pwysi,   *pwysi - poses (of flowers)*
Pasio'r lafant, pasio'r lili,   *lafant - lavender*
Pasio'r pincs a'r rhosys cochion,   *rhosys cochion - red roses*
Torri pwysi o ddanadl poethion.   *danadl poethion* - dail poethion, *nettles*

Ym Mhontypridd mae 'nghariad,   *'nghariad* - fy nghariad
Ym Mhontypridd mae 'mwriad,   *'mwriad* - fy mwriad, *my intention*
Ym Mhontypridd mae merch fach lân   *merch fach lân* - merch fach bert/ddel
Os caf hi o fla'n y ffeirad.   *os caf hi - if I get her to the church*
                                           ffeirad - the vicar

Mi fûm yn gweini tymor   *gweini tymor* - gweithio am flwyddyn
Yn ymyl Tŷ'n-y-coed,
A dyna'r lle difyrraf   *difyrraf* - mwyaf difyr/hapusaf
Y bûm i ynddo erioed.   *y bûm i* - y bues i

Yr adar bach yn canu
A'r coed yn suo ynghyd;   *suo* - sibrwd/*to murmur*
Fy nghalon fach a dorrodd
Ar waetha'r rhain i gyd.   *ar waetha - in spite of*

Gwybodaeth

Does neb yn gwybod pwy gyfansoddodd
yr hen benillion. Enw arall arnyn nhw ydy
penillion telyn achos bod pobl yn arfer
canu'r penillion gyda'r delyn. Penillion syml
ydyn nhw ac roedd pobl yn gallu eu cofio
yn hawdd. Maen nhw'n sôn am fyd natur,
am gariad, siom a gwaith. Maen nhw'n
sôn am bobl yn byw yn y wlad fel arfer.

Tasgau

Mae'r rhain yn benillion addas ar gyfer dysgwyr sydd ar fin cyrraedd safon Canoladd, ond wrth gwrs bydd nifer o eiriau dieithr ac anghyffredin yma. Does dim dilyniant, na chysylltiad arall rhwng y penillion, a does dim angen cyflwyno pob un. Awgrymir:

- Gwrando ar y penillion hyn yn unigol er mwyn rhoi cyfle i'r dysgwyr i'w gwerthfawrogi'n well. Ar ôl gwrando ar y pennill awgrymir bod y dosbarth yn darllen y pennill gyda'i gilydd, a mynd drwy'r eirfa newydd.

- Ar ôl darllen y penillion, gofyn iddynt weithio mewn parau i lenwi'r bylchau isod:

  Yn y pennill cyntaf mae'r _____ (coeden, dyn, diwrnod) yn ddauwynebog.

  Mae'n anodd 'nabod y diwrnod am ei fod yn _____ (hir, byr, troi).

  Mae'r bardd yn mynd i'r _____ (parc, gardd, cae) i dorri pwysi.

  Mae'r bardd yn pasio'r _____ (chwyn, lafant, rhosys gwynion).

  Mae'n torri pwysi o _____ (rhosys cochion, lili, danadl poethion).

  Mae cariad y bardd yn byw ym _____ (Bangor, Pentraeth, Pontypridd).

  Mae e/o eisiau gweld ei gariad o flaen y ffeirad achos mae eisiau ei _____ (priodi, caru, gadael).

  Buodd y bardd yn gweithio yn ymyl _____ (Tŷ Coch, Tŷ Canol, Tŷ'n-y-coed) yn y pennill olaf.

- Annog y dysgwyr i drafod y penillion mewn grwpiau bach, gan roi pennill yr un i bob grŵp. Beth mae'r bardd yn trïo'i ddweud? Oes stori tu ôl i'r pennill? Ydyn nhw'n hoffi'r pennill?

Pwyntiau Iaith

Ceir llawer o ferfenwau yn y ddau bennill cyntaf, e.e. troi, mynd, torri, pasio. Gallwch egluro'r gwahaniaeth rhwng berfenw a berf, e.e. dydy *troi* ddim yn dweud pwy sy'n troi na phryd mae rhywun yn troi; mae *troiodd hi'r cornel* yn dweud pwy a phryd. Ambell waith byddwn yn ymateb i gwestiwn trwy ddefnyddio berfenwau yn unig, e.e.

Beth dych chi'n wneud yn y dre fel arfer?
Be' dach chi'n wneud yn y dre fel arfer?
ATEB: Siopa, mynd am dro yn y parc, gwylio'r gêm a gweld fy ffrindiau.

Beth dych chi'n wneud ar ôl codi yn y bore?
Be' dach chi'n wneud ar ôl codi yn y bore?

Beth/Be' fyddwch chi'n wneud amser cinio yn y gwaith?

Beth dych chi'n wneud ar nos Wener fel arfer?
Be' dach chi'n wneud ar nos Wener fel arfer?

Beth dych chi'n hoffi ei wneud ar eich gwyliau?
Be' dach chi'n hoffi ei wneud ar eich gwyliau?

Pa waith dych/dach chi ddim yn hoffi ei wneud yn y tŷ?

Sgwrsio Pellach

Gellir defnyddio *Cardiau Fflach CBAC* i ymarfer ateb y cwestiynau hyn, ac fel sbardunau i siarad yn estynedig, gan ymhelaethu ar yr atebion.

6.   **Coffi Du** gan Gwibdaith Hen Frân

Dw i angen coffi yn y bora   *bora* - bore
I ddeffro llygaid trwm,
Os (na) ga i goffi yn y bora
Mae (fy) mhen i'n teimlo'n llwm.   *teimlo'n llwm* - *feels bare*
Dw i'n disgyn allan o (fy) ngwely,   *disgyn* - cwympo (De)
Rhoi'r tegell mlaen yn syth,
Agor paced ffres o goffi:
Arogl hynny'n wych.   *arogl hynny* - *that aroma*

Cytgan

Coffi du, coffi du, tyrd â choffi du i mi,   *tyrd â* - dere â (De)
Coffi du, coffi du, dw i isho coffi du cryf.
Dw i'n hedio trwy'r drws   *hedio* - *heading*
Â mwg o goffi yn fy llaw,
Rhaid (i) fi yfed yn y car,
Dw i fod yn (y) gwaith erbyn naw
Mae'r coffi yn fy ngwaed
Am fod y mwg yn dod i ben,   *because I have finished the mug*
Mae o'n cylchredeg at fy nhraed,   *cylchredeg* - *circulate*
Ac yn carlamu i fy mhen.   *carlamu* - *gallop*

Cytgan

Dw i'n eistedd wrth fy ngwaith,
Mae'r effaith yn lleihau,   *lleihau* - *lessens*
Hen bryd cael coffi arall   *hen bryd* - *high time*
I gadw'r cysglyd fi ar fai;   *cysglyd* - *sleepy*
Dw i'n hedio lawr i'r gegin gefn
Rhaid bod 'na goffi - genna i ffydd   *genna i* - mae gen i/mae gyda fi
'Neith hi goffi neu ddau arall,   *neith* - gwneith/gwnaiff
Cyn i fi weld diwedd y dydd.

Cytgan

Dydd 'di dod i ben   *dod i ben* - gorffen
A dw i'n methu dod i lawr,   *dod i lawr* - *relax*
Dw i'n troi a throsi yn fy ngwely,
Dydi cysgu ddim yn hawdd.
Dw i'n goro deffro yn y bora,   *dw i'n goro* - mae rhaid i fi
Dw i'n goro mynd yn ôl i 'ngwaith
Ond diolch byth genna i goffi,
I yfed ar y daith.   *fy nhaith* - *my journey*

Gwybodaeth

Mae'r gân yma'n dod o'r albwm *Cedors Hen Wrach*. Mae'r band *Gwibdaith Hen Frân* yn dod o Ben Llŷn ac yn canu caneuon ysgafn. Enwau rhai o'r caneuon hynny ydy *Trôns dy Dad, Carots* a *Cyri*.

Tasgau

Cân ddoniol sy'n cynnwys llawer o ailadrodd. Cyn ei chyflwyno byddai'n syniad da i sôn am rai ffurfiau gogleddol a ffurfiau mwy llafar, e.e. *bora* yn lle *bore, mae genna i* yn lle *mae gyda fi, dw i'n goro* (gorfod) yn lle *rhaid i fi* ac yn y blaen. Awgrymir:

- Chwarae'r darn ar y CD heb ddilyn y sgript y tro cyntaf ac wrth ddilyn y sgript yr ail dro.

- Chwarae'r darn eto ac oedi rhwng pob pennill, am fod llawer o eiriau anodd yma. Ar ôl y pennill cyntaf, er enghraifft, gellir gofyn cwestiynau fel:

    Beth mae e eisiau yn y bore? / Be' mae o isio yn y bore?
    Beth mae e'n wneud ar ôl cwympo mas o'r gwely? / Be' mae o'n wneud
                                         ar ôl disgyn allan o'r gwely?
    Beth mae e'n wneud wedyn? / Be' mae o'n wneud wedyn?

    Ac yn y blaen drwy'r penillion.

- Eu rhannu'n grwpiau bach a gofyn iddyn nhw gyfrif sawl paned o goffi mae e'n yfed yn y gân. Gall y tiwtor holi'r grwpiau yn eu tro wedyn:
    Pryd mae e'n/o'n yfed coffi yn y bore? Yn y prynhawn? Ble/Lle mae e'n/o'n yfed coffi yn y bore ac yn y prynhawn?

- Gofyn i'r dosbarth am eu hoff eiriau neu hoff linellau yn y gân, a rhoi rheswm dros hynny. Er enghraifft, gall y tiwtor ddechrau trwy ddweud 'Dw i'n hoffi *hen bryd cael coffi arall* achos dw i'n yfed coffi yn ddi-stop.'

- Dosbarthu'r fersiwn ysgrifenedig gan adael bylchau yn lle rhai o'r geiriau sy'n odli a gofyn iddyn nhw lenwi'r bylchau wrth eu hadrodd i'w gilydd mewn parau.

Pwyntiau Iaith

Gan fod llawer o eiriau yn treiglo'n drwynol ar ôl **fy** yn y gân, e.e. *fy ngwely, fy ngwaed, fy nhraed, fy mhen, fy ngwaith a fy nhaith,* gellir cyplysu'r gân ag ymarferion eraill sy'n gysylltiedig â'r treiglad trwynol. Awgrymir llenwi'r bwrdd gwyn â geiriau sy'n gallu treiglo'n drwynol, a phawb yn dyfalu pa air y mae'r tiwtor wedi'i ddewis, e.e. Wyt ti wedi gweld fy _____ i?

Sgwrsio Pellach

Rhannu'r dosbarth yn barau i greu deialog, drwy chwarae rôl. Mae un partner yn gweithio yng nghaffi *Hoffi Coffi* a'r llall yn gwsmer. Wrth greu'r sgwrs, bydd rhaid iddyn nhw gynnwys y pwyntiau canlynol:
• coffi gwyn neu goffi du? Coffi gwan neu goffi cryf?
• pa fath - latte, cappucino?
• mwg neu gwpan?
• siwgwr neu ddim?
• teisen/cacen? Pa fath?
• talu - beth am y pris?

Ysgrifennu

Gellir rhoi sgript *Coffi Du* i'r dosbarth unwaith eto gan ofyn iddynt ysgrifennu dyddiadur *Ar ôl codi...*
Gallant ddechrau fel hyn:

    Deffrais i/Dihunais i y bore 'ma tua _____ o'r gloch.
    Es i i'r gawod ac wedyn _____ .

7. Darn o **Bywyd Blodwen Jones** gan Bethan Gwanas

Chwefror 9fed nos Fercher

Diwrnod cyntaf dyddiadur Cymraeg Blodwen Jones.

Mae'r tiwtor Cymraeg, Llew (hyfryd hyfryd) Morgan wedi gofyn i bawb gadw dyddiadur. Felly dyma fi, a dyma fo. Dwedodd Llew ei fod o'n syniad da. Dw i'n cytuno. Bydd cadw dyddiadur yn gwella fy iaith i, ac yn gwneud i mi feddwl yn Gymraeg. Gobeithio.

Iawn, felly helô Ddyddiadur!

Ym... dw i ddim yn siŵr iawn beth i sgwennu rŵan.

Beth am gyflwyno fy hunan?

Enw:	Blodwen Jones
Oed:	38
Taldra:	5' 9'
Pwysau:	Preifat!
	Dibriod
Cyfeiriad:	Rose Cottage - ond dw i'n mynd i newid yr enw i 'Y Bwthyn', Rachub ger Bethesda, Gwynedd.
Gwaith:	Llyfrgellydd
Diddordebau:	Llyfrau (wrth gwrs), teithio, Llew Morgan
Dymuniadau ar gyfer eleni:	Dysgu Cymraeg yn iawn, tyfu fy llysiau fy hunan, newid fy swydd i, bachu, (dw i'n hoffi'r gair 'na!) bachu Llew Morgan.

Dw i newydd feddwl - gobeithio na fydd Llew eisiau darllen y dyddiaduron...

Iawn, beth ddigwyddodd heddiw? Dim llawer. Codais i am 8.00 fel arfer, rhoiais i fwyd i'r gath a ches i frecwast. Ond roedd y llefrith *off*. Dw i newydd chwilio yn y geiriadur - 'wedi troi' ydi'r term cywir. Ond roedd y llefrith wedi troi, felly roedd y te fel cawl efo croûtons caws. Ych a fi. Felly bwytais i fy *Weetabix* yn sych. Doedd dim post.
Es i i'r gwaith yn y Llyfrgell erbyn 9.00. Roedd llawer o bost yno ond dim byd diddorol.

Ces i frechdan gaws a phicl i ginio.

Ceisiais i ffonio dyn sy'n cadw geifr, ond ches i ddim ateb. O mae'n ddrwg gen i, mae'n rhaid i mi egluro: dw i eisiau prynu gafr. Pam? Pam ddim? Dw i eisiau gallu byw yn dda, fel Felicity Kendal yn *The Good Life*. Dyna pam dw i wedi prynu hadau: ffa, moron, tatws, nionod a bresych. A dw i wedi prynu llyfr *Grow Your Own Vegetables*. Dw i'n edrych ymlaen! A bydd gafr yn bwyta'r gwair i gyd, felly fydd dim angen prynu peiriant torri gwair. Dw i ddim yn ddwl!

Ro'n i adre erbyn 6.00. Prynais i flawd yn *Spar* yn gynta. Dw i eisiau pobi fy mara fy hunan hefyd, ond ddim heno. Heno, es i i'r wers Gymraeg. Dw i'n mynd bob nos Lun a nos Fercher, a dw i wrth fy modd yno.

bachu - to hook/pull
gafr/geifr - goat/s
gwair - hay/grass
blawd - flour
pobi - to bake

Gwybodaeth

Bethan Gwanas ydy'r awdur. Enw'r fferm lle cafodd hi ei geni ydy Gwanas yn ymyl Dolgellau ac mae hi wedi ysgrifennu nifer o lyfrau poblogaidd. Bu'n gweithio fel athrawes gyda'r Gwasanaeth Tramor Gwirfoddol (VSO) ac ysgrifennodd hanes ei chyfnod yno yn y llyfr *Dyddiadur Gbara*. Mae hi'n enwog fel cyflwynydd y rhaglen deledu *Ar y Lein* hefyd.

Tasgau

Mae hwn yn ddyddiadur doniol am ddysgwraig yn dechrau cadw dyddiadur. Mae'n gyflwyniad difyr i ryddiaith Gymraeg. Awgrymir:

- Gofyn i'r dosbarth cyfan am gynnwys y dyddiadur, ar ôl gwrando ar y darn yn cael ei ddarllen ddwy waith. Nodwch y pethau maen nhw'n eu cofio ar y bwrdd gwyn.

- Annog y dysgwyr i lunio 'geiriadur bach' o'r geiriau newydd maen nhw wedi dod ar eu traws yn y darn, gan fod Blodwen Jones ei hun yn chwilio yn y geiriadur am ystyr gair. Dylid eu hannog i'w gosod yn nhrefn yr wyddor.

- Gofyn iddynt gymharu eu rhestri trwy ddweud 'Do'n i ddim wedi clywed y gair llyfrgellydd o'r blaen.' Gall aelod arall gytuno neu anghytuno: 'Ro'n i wedi clywed y gair achos mae fy ffrind yn llyfrgellydd' neu 'do'n i ddim wedi clywed y gair chwaith.'

- Ymarfer y patrwm 'Ceisiais i ffonio dyn sy'n cadw geifr ond ches i ddim ateb' mewn parau. Er enghraifft: 'Ceisiais i ffonio fy chwaer neithiwr ond ches i ddim ateb' ac yn y blaen. Wedyn gellir gofyn iddyn nhw adrodd yn ôl i'r dosbarth cyfan a gofyn iddyn nhw ddefnyddio'r trydydd person hefyd: 'Ceisiodd Siân ffonio ei chwaer ond chafodd hi ddim ateb.'

- Siarad am gymeriad Blodwen Jones mewn parau. Rhoi rhestr o ansoddeiriau ar y bwrdd gwyn a gofyn iddyn nhw ddewis yr ansoddeiriau sy'n ei disgrifio orau o blith y rhestr a dweud pam mewn brawddeg. Eu hannog eto i roi'r ansoddeiriau yn eu 'geiriaduron bach' os nad ydyn nhw'n gwybod eu hystyron. Dyma restr bosib: tal, tew, clyfar, ymarferol (practical), hipïaidd (hippy-like), trefnus (organised), diflas (boring), caredig (kind), canol oed, ifanc, hoffus (likeable)... Eu hannog i ddweud pam ar ôl defnyddio ansoddair. Er enghraifft: 'Mae B.J yn hipïaidd achos mae hi eisiau prynu gafr!' Anogwch yr aelodau eraill i gytuno neu anghytuno hefyd: e.e. 'Dydy pob hipi ddim yn prynu gafr...' ac yn y blaen.

Pwyntiau Iaith
Awgrymir tynnu'r paragraff olaf o'r darn, (o *Ceisiais i ffonio dyn sy'n cadw geifr...*), rhoi copïau i bob pâr yn y grŵp, a gofyn iddyn nhw droi'r cyfan i sôn amdani *hi*, hynny yw, troi'r cyfan i'r 3ydd person. Does dim angen ailysgrifennu'r paragraff, dim ond ei wneud ar lafar. Mae rhai grwpiau'n mwynhau gweithgareddau fel hyn, ond eraill yn eu cael yn anodd.

Sgwrsio Pellach
Gofyn i'r dosbarth siarad am gymeriadau maen nhw'n eu hadnabod sy'n debyg i Blodwen, neu gellir trafod rhaglenni teledu sy'n annog pobl i dyfu llysiau a choginio bwyd cartref.

Ysgrifennu
Gellir gosod tasg ysgrifennu dyddiadur gan ddefnyddio rhai brawddegau allan *o Bywyd Blodwen Jones*. Er enghraifft:

> *Codais i am...*
> *Es i i'r gwaith erbyn... o'r gloch.*
> *Ces i ginio gyda/efo...*
> *Wedyn...*
> *O, anghofiais i...*
> *Ro'n i wedi blino ond roedd rhaid...*
> *Ceisiais i ymlacio trwy...*
> *'Fory bydda i'n...*

8.   Darn o **Budapest** gan Elin Meek

Roedd Gwyn wedi treulio'r prynhawn yn ymweld â thair fflat:

Fflat 1:   Un ystafell fawr, gwely mewn un cornel, cegin a lolfa yn y cornel arall. Ystafell ymolchi fel cwpwrdd. Dim lle i gadw dim. Un ffenestr fawr. Golygfa dros heol brysur.

Fflat 2:   Fflat dwy ystafell wely. Llawer o fetel a marmor. Popeth yn wyn. Ffenestri bach. Dim golygfa - wal a tho adeilad arall.

Fflat 3:   Fflat un ystafell wely. Digon o olau. Llawr pren. Balconi'n edrych dros yr afon. Yn costio ffortiwn.

Doedd Gwyn ddim yn hoffi un o'r fflatiau. Roedd yr asiant tai wedi bod yn canmol pob fflat. Yn canmol pethau bach. Yn gwrthod gweld yr anfanteision. Doedd Gwyn ddim yn hoffi hynny. Oedd e'n edrych fel dyn hawdd ei dwyllo? Beth bynnag, doedd dim rhaid penderfynu mewn prynhawn. Doedd Gwyn ddim yn hoffi gwneud penderfyniadau cyflym. Yn enwedig penderfyniadau busnes. Roedd e eisiau pwyso a mesur cyn gwario ceiniog. Oedd, roedd angen fflat arno. Ond roedd eisiau gwneud arian ar y fflat hefyd, os oedd hi'n bosibl. Dyn busnes oedd e, wedi'r cyfan.

Canodd ei ffôn symudol. András.
"Popeth yn iawn?" gofynnodd y cyfreithiwr. "Wedi dod o hyd i fflat?"
"Na, ddim eto," meddai Gwyn. "Dw i wedi gweld tair. Ond doedd dim un yn plesio."
"Wel, dw i wedi ffonio'r asiant werthodd y fflat i mi," meddai András. "Mae rhai fflatiau ar gael o hyd. Ddim y rhai gorau, efallai. Mae'r rheiny wedi mynd. Ond basai'n werth i iti edrych ar un neu ddwy."
Cafodd Gwyn rif ffôn yr asiant. Ffoniodd, a threfnu cwrdd wrth y fflatiau mewn dwy awr.

Doedd Gwyn ddim yn mwynhau edrych ar y fflatiau. Roedd e'n casáu'r holl beth. Roedd y cyfan yn dod yn ôl ag atgofion iddo. Atgofion am y gorffennol. Atgofion chwerw.

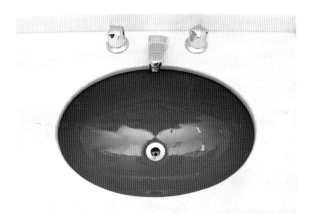

treulio - to spend (time)
marmor - marble
asiant - agent
canmol - to praise
twyllo - to deceive
pwyso a mesur - to consider carefully
atgofion - memories

Gwybodaeth
Mae Elin Meek yn byw yn Abertawe, ac yn gweithio fel cyfieithydd ac awdur. Yn y stori, mae Gwyn yn mynd i ddinas Budapest ar wyliau, ac yn gweld Margit, hen gariad iddo. Yn y darn yma, mae Gwyn yn meddwl prynu fflat yn y ddinas, gan fod rhaid iddo deithio yno'n aml.

Tasgau

Rhan o stori a geir yn y darn hwn. Er mwyn amrywio ychydig ar y dull cyflwyno, gellir rhoi'r cwestiynau isod ar y bwrdd gwyn cyn chwarae rhan gynta'r darn ar gryno-ddisg (tan *Roedd yr asiant tai...*).

1. O ba fflat oedd yr olygfa orau?   [Fflat 3]
2. Ym mha fflat doedd dim cypyrddau?   [Fflat 1]
3. Pa fflat oedd â'r nifer mwya o ystafelloedd?   [Fflat 2]
4. Pa fflat oedd y mwya modern?   [Fflat 2]
5. Pa fflat oedd y druta?   [Fflat 3]
6. Pa fflat oedd yn un ystafell?   [Fflat 1]
7. Pa fflat oedd yn agos i'r ffordd fawr?   [Fflat 1]
8. Pa fflat roedd Gwyn yn ei hoffi?   [Dim un]

- Yna, trafod y cwestiynau mewn parau cyn rhoi'r atebion.

- Gwrando ar y stori wrth ddarllen y sgript. Yna, trafod pam doedd Gwyn ddim yn hoffi edrych ar fflatiau. Pam roedd atgofion chwerw'n codi wrth wneud hyn? Does dim atebion yn y darn hwn, ond dyma gyfle i ddyfalu beth sy'n dod nesa, neu beth yw'r stori sy'n arwain at y sefyllfa hon.

Pwyntiau Iaith
Mae ffurfio cystrawen cwestiwn yn dechrau â *Pa...* yn gallu achosi problemau, yn enwedig wrth roi arddodiad o'i flaen. Y tro hwn, rhaid ffurfio cwestiwn *Pa...* gan holi ymhellach am y gair mewn print tywyll, e.e.

Mae John yn mynd i **goleg** Aberystwyth = I ba goleg mae John yn mynd?

1. Mae Mair yn byw ym **mhentre** Llangrannog = Ym mha bentre mae Mair yn byw?
2. Mae Spiro'n dod o **wlad** Groeg = O ba wlad mae Spiro'n dod?
3. Roedd y tiwtor yn sôn am y **rheol** = Am ba reol roedd y tiwtor yn sôn?
4. Mae'r **plant** yn perthyn i deulu'r Owens = I ba deulu mae'r plant yn perthyn?
5. Mae hi'n methu ateb y **cwestiynau** cynta = Pa gwestiynau mae hi'n methu eu hateb?
6. Mae Gwen yn gweithio i **fanc** Lloyds = I ba fanc mae Gwen yn gweithio?
7. Roedd Tom yn edrych ar **raglen** Dai Jones = Ar ba raglen roedd Tom yn edrych?
8. Aeth Mair â **pharsel** y plant i'r tŷ = Â pha barsel aeth Mair i'r tŷ?

Sgwrsio Pellach
Ydyn nhw wedi bod yn chwilio am dŷ neu fflat erioed?
Oedd yr asiant wedi dweud y gwir am y lle?
Oedd symud tŷ'n brofiad anodd o gwbl?
Sut mae byw mewn fflat yn gallu bod yn wahanol i fyw mewn tŷ?

9. Lleucu Llwyd gan Tebot Piws

Lleucu Llwyd, rwyt ti'n hardd
Lleucu Llwyd, rwyt ti'n werth y byd i mi,
Lleucu Llwyd, rwyt ti'n angel,
Lleucu Llwyd, rwy'n dy garu di, di, di.

gwerth y byd - mean the world

O! Rwy'n cofio cwrdd â thi,
Ac rwy'n cofio'r glaw.
Ydy'r eos yn y goedwig?
Ydy'r blodau yn y maes gerllaw?
Yn yr afon mae cyfrinach:
Dy gusan cyntaf di,
Yn y goedwig mae y blodau
Yn sibrwd dy enw di.

eos - nightingale
maes - cae
cyfrinach - secret

sibrwd - whispering

O, mae'r oriau mân yn pasio,
Fel eiliaid ar adain y gwynt;
O, gorweddaf ar fy ngwely,
Efallai daw'r freuddwyd yn gynt.
O, mae rhywun yn agosáu,
Mi glywaf wichian y glwyd,
Ac rwy'n nabod sŵn yr esgid
Mae'n perthyn i Lleucu Llwyd.

awr/oriau - hour/s
eiliad/eiliaid - second/s

breuddwyd - dream
agosáu - dod yn agos
gwichian - to squeak

perthyn i - belongs to

Gwybodaeth

Cân werin yw Lleucu Llwyd ac mae'r fersiwn hwn yn dod o ail albwm
y band Tebot Piws a ddaeth allan yn 1970. Dyma un o'r bandiau
poblogaidd Cymraeg cyntaf. Yn wreiddiol roedd Lleucu Llwyd wedi
syrthio mewn cariad â bardd o'r enw Llywelyn Goch ym Mhennal.

Tasgau

Bydd nifer o eiriau dieithr yn y gân hon a dylid atgoffa'r dysgwyr nad oes disgwyl iddynt ddeall pob gair. Awgrymir:

- Annog y dysgwyr i wrando ar y darn ddwywaith ar y CD. Gofyn iddyn nhw nodi tri pheth y mae'r canwr yn eu dweud wrth Lleucu Llwyd mewn parau. Gall y parau gymharu eu hatebion. Does dim ots os nad ydyn nhw'n deall y geiriau hynny. Hynny yw, *Lleucu Llwyd, rwyt ti'n...*

- Gwrando ar y gân eto, a'r tiwtor yn gwasgu'r botwm oedi ar ôl y pennill cyntaf. Gellir trafod y tywydd a'r lle: Oedd hi'n braf? Oedden nhw allan yn y wlad? Pa gliwiau sy'n dweud eu bod nhw allan yn y wlad?

- Oedi eto ar ddiwedd yr ail bennill a gofyn ble mae'r canwr y tro hwn. Gofyn am y cliwiau sy'n dweud bod y canwr yn y tŷ. Gellir eu holi am ble mae Lleucu Llwyd hefyd. Ydy hi yn y tŷ? Beth mae hi'n wneud?

- Rhestru rhai o'r geiriau newydd/idiomau sy yn y gân neu eu rhoi ar gardiau fflach. Er enghraifft: agosáu, oriau mân, werth y byd, breuddwyd, cyfrinach, angel. Yna, gofyn i'r grŵp lunio eu brawddegau eu hunain i gynnwys y geiriau newydd, mewn parau.

Pwyntiau Iaith
Mae angen adolygu'r rhagenwau a'r rhagenwau sy'n codi drwy'r amser, e.e. dy gusan di, fy ngwely i. Mae'n werth cael hyd i ddisiau rhagenwau (disiau â'r rhagenwau *fi, ti, fe/fo, ni, chi, nhw* arnynt). I gyflawni'r dasg, rhaid rhoi nifer o eiriau treigladwy ar y bwrdd gwyn, yn cynnwys geiriau o'r gân o bosib. Yna, pawb yn ei dro i daflu'r dis, a chreu brawddeg yn cynnwys y gair nesaf ar y rhestr, e.e. gwely + fi = Dw i'n hoffi aros yn fy ngwely i.

Sgwrsio Pellach
Ydyn nhw'n hoffi'r gân?
Ydy'r gân yn eu hatgoffa o rywun neu ryw ddigwyddiad?
Ydy'r gân yn eu hatgoffa o gân arall?
Pa ddarlun sy'n dod i'r meddwl wrth glywed y gân?
Ydyn nhw'n cofio sut roedd y tywydd ar adeg arbennig, e.e. wrth gwrdd â chariad am y tro cynta?

Ysgrifennu
Gellir gofyn i'r dysgwyr ysgrifennu disgrifiad o bartner, ffrind neu unrhyw gydnabod. Rhaid iddyn nhw ddechrau â'r geiriau: *Y tro cynta i mi gwrdd â / cyfarfod...*

10.   Limrigau gan Hedd Bleddyn

I slimio, cafodd gwraig o Gwm-ann
Dabledi drwy'r post o Japan,
A nawr yn y gwely
Mae'i gŵr hi yn methu
Ei ffeindio, er chwilio 'mhob man.

Mi es i 'Werddon mewn dingi   *'Werddon - Iwerddon*
A hynny bob cam o Gaergybi,   *bob cam - all the way*
Ro'n i'n teimlo'n reit saff
'Rôl gafael mewn rhaff   *gafael - to hold (a rope)*
Tu ôl i gwch mawr Irish Ferry.

Bues wrthi am oesoedd yn sgwennu,   *bues wrthi - I've been at it (for ages)*
Limrigau, caneuon ac ati,   *ac ati - and so on*
Ond dw i ddim yn siŵr
A oes gwraig neu ŵr
Am ddarllen y rwtsh 'ma sy gen i.

Gwybodaeth

Daw'r limrigau hyn o lyfr *Hiwmor Hedd* (2006) gan Hedd Bleddyn. Mae limrigau doniol
yn boblogaidd ym mhob iaith. Bu Hedd Bleddyn yn aelod o dîm Talwrn y Beirdd Bro
Ddyfi am flynyddoedd. Cystadleuaeth boblogaidd ar y radio rhwng gwahanol dimau yw'r
Talwrn. Ystyr gwreiddiol y gair 'talwrn' oedd y man lle'r roedd pobl yn ymladd ceiliogod.

Tasgau

Tipyn o hwyl a geir yma. Mae'n bwysig bod y dosbarth yn deall yr ergyd sydd ymhob limrig, felly byddai'n syniad da i'r tiwtor egluro pob gair anodd cyn i'r dysgwyr wrando ar y limrigau, un ar y tro. Wrth gwrs, y tiwtor a ŵyr orau pa eiriau fydd yn anodd i'r grŵp. Awgrymir:

- Oedi'r cryno-ddisg ar ôl gwrando ar bob limrig ac ailchwarae os bydd angen.

- Rhannu'r dosbarth yn barau ac ymarfer adrodd neu ddarllen y limrigau heb golli'r ystyr neu'r ergyd.

- Gofyn i aelodau'r dosbarth p'un yw eu hoff limrig a pham.

- Rhannu'r dosbarth yn barau a gofyn i bob aelod lunio cwestiynau i'w gilydd yn seiliedig ar y limrigau, e.e. O ble roedd y wraig yn y limrig (cyntaf) yn dod? O ble daeth y tabledi? Sut aeth e/o i Iwerddon? Gall y dosbarth cyfan wrando ar y cwestiynau a'r atebion wedyn.

Pwyntiau Iaith

Canolbwyntio ar batrymau'r gorffennol yw'r nod yma. Awgrymir rhoi'r rhestr isod ar y bwrdd gwyn:

> Es i ...
> Ces i...
> Gwelais i...
> Prynais i...
> Anghofiais i...
> Clywais i...
> Des i...
> Teimlais i...
> Cyrhaeddais i...

Gellir defnyddio'r ffurfiau cwmpasog, os nad yw'r grŵp yn gyfarwydd â'r ffurfiau cryno, e.e. Mi wnes i weld..., mi wnes i brynu... Rhaid mynd o gwmpas mewn cadwyn, a phawb yn ychwanegu cymal, a chan gofio'r hyn a ddywedwyd ynghynt, fel bod y frawddeg yn mynd yn hirach.

Sgwrsio Pellach

Cyfansoddi limrig ar y cyd. Mae'n bosib cael hwyl trwy gyfansoddi limrig yn y dosbarth. Bydd rhaid dewis odlau syml fel 'au' ac 'o' yn y lle cyntaf. Gellir trefnu 'talwrn limrigau' wrth i'r cynigion wella!

Gellir rhoi enghraifft i ddechrau:

> Aeth dysgwr i siop yn Llandudno
> I brynu Mars Bar a dwy feiro,
> Fe gafodd pawb sioc
> Pan ddaeth allan toc
> Wedi prynu _____ (gair ar yr odl 'o')

11.   Blwyddyn Mas gan Einir Dafydd a Ceri Wyn Jones

Mae'n iawn i ti gael blwyddyn mas a theithio i bedwar ban;   *pedwar ban - four corners*
Mae'n iawn i ti gael byw yn fras yn bell o'r un hen fan;   *yn fras - in style, live well*
Mae'n iawn i ti gael mynd tu hwnt i stryd ein bywyd bach,   *tu hwnt - beyond*
A chwrso sêr a chroesi swnt i flasu'r awyr iach.   *cwrso - dilyn, swnt - strait*

Cytgan:
Ond beth, beth amdana i ers i ti fynd fy nghâr?   *câr - cariad*
Mor grwn yw'r ddaear lle'r ei di,
Mor sgwâr fy milltir sgwâr, mor sgwâr fy milltir sgwâr.

Mae'n iawn i ti gael blwyddyn mas a chael dy draed yn rhydd.
Mae'n iawn i ti gael profi ias gwahanol bob un dydd.   *ias - thrill*
Mae'n iawn i ti gael troi dy gefn ar gwmni'r pentre gwag,
A'r un wynebau gwag drachefn a'r un hen sgwrs Gymrâg.   *gwag - empty*

Cytgan:

Ond mae hi'n flwyddyn mas i fi wrth aros gartre weth,   *weth - hefyd/eto (Sir Benfro)*
A falle dof fi hebddot ti i ddeall beth yw beth.
A falle bydd y filltir sgwâr yn cynnig rhyw help llaw
Am fod fan hyn, fan gwyn a gwâr, mor wyn â'r un man draw.   *man gwyn - the grass is greener*
    gwâr - civilised

Cytgan:

Ond beth, beth amdanat ti ers i ti fynd fy nghâr?
Gobeithio bod y ddaear gron   *daear gron - the round earth*
Mor grwn â'r filltir sgwâr, mor grwn â'r filltir sgwâr.

Gwybodaeth
Daw'r gân hon o gryno-ddisg Einir Dafydd, *Ffeindia Fi*. Enillodd y gân hon gystadleuaeth Cân i Gymru. Roedd hi'n fyfyrwraig yng Ngholeg y Drindod, Caerfyrddin pan enillodd hi'r gystadleuaeth.

Tasgau

Ceir digon o ailadrodd yn y gân hon a nifer o idiomau newydd addas i lefel Canolradd neu Uwch o bosib. Awgrymir:

- Cyflwyno idiomau newydd y gân i'r dosbarth cyn chwarae'r cryno-ddisg, a'u trafod:

    Y filltir sgwâr *(Beth yw eu milltir sgwâr nhw?)*
    Man gwyn man draw *(Oes ganddyn nhw fan gwyn fan draw?)*
    I bedwar ban y byd *(Pwy sydd wedi teithio i bedwar ban yn y dosbarth?)*
    Byw yn fras *(Hoffen nhw fyw yn fras?)*
    Help llaw *(Ydyn wedi nhw rhoi help llaw i rywun?)*
    Mynd tu hwnt i *(Ydyn nhw wedi bod tu hwnt i Ewrop ar wyliau?)*

- Chwarae'r gân drwyddi heb ddilyn y sgript. Holi'r dosbarth a rhoi pwyntiau ar y bwrdd gwyn.

- Chwarae'r gân eto gan ddilyn y sgript a defnyddio'r botwm oedi ar ddiwedd pob pennill er mwyn gwneud yn siŵr eu bod yn ei deall.

- Rhannu'r dosbarth yn grwpiau bach a gofyn iddyn nhw drafod y gân. Ydyn nhw'n hoffi'r gân neu beidio? Mae'n bwysig eu bod yn rhoi rhesymau.

- Pob grŵp yn adrodd yn ôl i'r dosbarth cyfan a gwrando ar y gân unwaith eto.

- Gofyn iddyn nhw baratoi cyflwyniad byr am y llefydd y maen nhw wedi ymweld â nhw yng Nghymru, ym Mhrydain neu yn y byd gan ddefnyddio rhai o'r idiomau uchod, e.e. 'Dw i ddim wedi teithio i bedwar ban y byd. Mae'n well 'da fi / Mae'n well gen i fy milltir sgwâr...'

Pwyntiau Iaith
Dyma gyfle i siarad am idiomau Cymraeg gwahanol. Byddant wedi dod ar draws nifer yn barod, e.e. gwneud eu gorau glas, wrth fy modd, cael llond bol ac ati. Gellir gofyn am ragor gan y grŵp, a'u rhoi ar y bwrdd gwyn. Mae nifer o lyfrau defnyddiol am idiomau Cymraeg, yn cynnwys *Y Geiriau Bach* gan Cennard Davies.

Sgwrsio Pellach
Mae'r person yn y gân yn genfigennus am fod ei chariad/gariad yn teithio'r byd. Pryd maen nhw'n teimlo'n genfigennus?

Ydyn nhw'n fodlon yn eu milltir sgwâr? Ydyn nhw eisiau teithio'r byd?

Ysgrifennu
Ysgrifennu'r cyflwyniadau byr fel gwaith cartref. Gellir dechrau'r darn â: *Dw i'n cofio'r tro cynta i ni ymweld â...*

12. Darn o **Rhydd Fel Aderyn** gan Pat Clayton

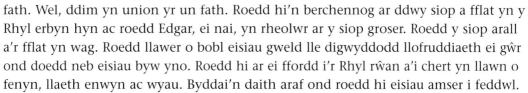

Trioleg yr Aderyn Brith

Roedd Myfanwy Jones yn ddynes siomedig. Roedd pum mis
wedi mynd heibio ers i'w gŵr gael ei ladd ac roedd hi wedi
disgwyl gweld newid yn ei bywyd. Ond roedd popeth yr un
fath. Wel, ddim yn union yr un fath. Roedd hi'n berchennog ar ddwy siop a fflat yn y
Rhyl erbyn hyn ac roedd Edgar, ei nai, yn rheolwr ar y siop groser. Roedd y siop arall
a'r fflat yn wag. Roedd llawer o bobl eisiau gweld lle digwyddodd llofruddiaeth ei gŵr
ond doedd neb eisiau byw yno. Roedd hi ar ei ffordd i'r Rhyl rŵan a'i chert yn llawn o
fenyn, llaeth enwyn ac wyau. Byddai'n daith araf ond roedd hi eisiau amser i feddwl.

'Beth sy'n dy boeni di, Myfanwy?' gofynnodd iddi'i hun yn uchel. 'Wel, a dweud y
gwir, mae Huw wedi fy siomi i,' atebodd. 'Pam? Does arno fo ddim byd i ti.' 'Dw i
wedi rhoi pedair blynedd ar hugain iddo fo,' 'A beth arall fyddet ti wedi ei wneud efo
dy fywyd?' 'Wn i ddim. Teithio'r byd, efallai.' 'Wel, dim ond pedair a deugain oed wyt
ti. Dos i deithio'r byd - mae gen ti ddigon o bres.' 'Dw i eisiau bod efo Huw.' 'Callia,
Myfanwy! Paid â bod yn wirion, nid merch ifanc wyt ti!'

Roedd hynny'n wir, beth bynnag. Roedd hi wedi bod mewn cariad efo Huw ers pan
oedd hi'n bymtheg mlwydd oed, a Huw mewn cariad efo hi. Wrth gwrs, doedd teulu
Huw erioed wedi rhoi sêl eu bendith ar y cariad hwnnw. Roedd hyd yn oed tad Huw,
Syr Mansel, oedd yn meddwl y byd o Myfanwy, wedi gyrru Huw i Rydychen i'w cadw
nhw ar wahân. Pan ddeallodd Myfanwy ei bod hi'n feichiog, aeth ei rhieni yn wallgof.
Mynnon nhw ei bod hi'n priodi Robert Wyn Jones, y gwas ffarm, ar unwaith. Dim
ond ei rhieni a Huw, ymhen misoedd wedyn, oedd yn gwybod mai merch Huw oedd
Megan. Pan ddaeth Huw yn ôl fel ficer Eglwys Sant Elidir, cytunodd Myfanwy ar
unwaith i ofalu am y ficerdy ac roedd y ddau wedi bod yn ffrindiau mawr, a dim
byd arall, am fwy nag ugain mlynedd... ond rŵan dylai pethau fod yn wahanol.

siomedig - disappointed	perchennog - owner
llofruddiaeth - murder	llaeth enwyn - buttermilk
arno fo - he doesn't owe	callia - get a grip
gwirion - dwl	sêl eu bendith - seal of approval
hyd yn oed - even	beichiog - pregnant
gwallgof - mad	ficerdy - vicarage

Gwybodaeth

Mae Pat Clayton wedi ysgrifennu nifer o lyfrau i ddysgwyr. Dyma gefndir y stori'n bras:
Ym 1919, ar ôl dianc o Wersyll Parc Cinmel, cafodd Danny ei guddio gan Megan,
ei wraig, yn seler hen ficerdy. Roedd pawb yn meddwl ei fod wedi boddi. Cafodd
lawer o anturiaethau *(adventures)*. Ar ddamwain, lladdodd Robert Wyn Jones, a
oedd wedi agor siop groser yn y Rhyl. Yn y darn hwn cawn wybod pwy yw
Myfanwy Jones a Robert - darnau eraill yn jig-so'r stori...

Tasgau

Mae'r darn hwn yn addas ar gyfer dysgwyr sydd wedi dechrau cael blas ar ddarllen llyfrau Cymraeg, fel llyfrau Bob Eynon. Cafodd y nofel ei gosod yng ngogledd ddwyrain Cymru ar ddechrau'r ugeinfed ganrif. Dyma ddechrau'r drydedd nofel mewn trioleg.

- Mae'r stori'n ddigon cymhleth! Awgrymir rhoi enwau'r holl gymeriadau ar y bwrdd gwyn cyn y gwrandawiad cyntaf:
  - Myfanwy Jones
  - Edgar
  - Huw
  - Syr Mansel
  - Robert Wyn Jones

- Ar ôl gwrando ar y stori eto, rhaid trafod pwy yw'r cymeriadau hyn, a sut maen nhw'n perthyn i'w gilydd. Dyma'r atebion:
  - Myfanwy Jones sy'n dweud y stori.
  - Edgar yw / ydy ei nai hi, sy'n rhedeg y siop groser.
  - Huw oedd ei charad hi, a fe yw / fo ydy ficer Eglwys Sant Elidir.
  - Syr Mansel oedd tad Huw.
  - Robert Wyn Jones oedd gŵr Myfanwy, ond sy wedi cael ei ladd.

- Ar ôl dosbarthu'r darn ei hun, gellir gofyn i'r dosbarth beth maen nhw'n feddwl sy'n mynd i ddigwydd nesa yn y stori, a thrafod y posibiliadau mewn parau, wedyn fel grŵp.

Pwyntiau Iaith
Dyma gyfle i adolygu neu gyflwyno'r hen ddull o gyfrif yn seiliedig ar yr enghreifftiau yn y darn: pedair blynedd ar hugain; pedair a deugain oed; pymtheg mlwydd oed, ac yn y blaen. Fel arfer, dim ond mewn llenyddiaeth a Chymraeg ffurfiol y defnyddir yr hen ddull o rifo bellach. Awgrymir rhoi enghreifftiau ar y bwrdd gwyn, a gofyn i bawb 'drosi' yr hen rifau i rifau'r dull cyfoes:

1.	Deunaw oed	- Un deg wyth oed
2.	Un mlynedd ar hugain	- Dau ddeg un o flynyddoedd
3.	Deuddeg a thrigain	- Saith deg dau
4.	Pymtheg	- Un deg pump
5.	Deg ar hugain	- Tri deg
6.	Saith a deugain	- Pedwar deg saith
7.	Pedwar ugain a naw	- Wyth deg naw
8.	Cant namyn un	- Naw deg naw

Sgwrsio Pellach
Fyddan nhw'n siarad â'u hunain weithiau? Pryd?
Ydyn nhw'n nabod rhywun neu'n cofio rhywun oedd yn siarad â'i hun?
Ydyn nhw'n nabod *aderyn brith*? (teitl y gyfres o nofelau).
Ydyn nhw'n gallu meddwl am *aderyn brith* mewn llyfr neu ffilm?

Ysgrifennu
Gellir gofyn i bawb ysgrifennu deialog â nhw'u hunain, fel yn ail baragraff y darn.
Gallant ddarllen y darn yn uchel yn y dosbarth wedyn.

13. Darn o **Gormod o Win** gan Bob Eynon

'Dyn ni yn mynd i ddathlu dy ben-blwydd di mewn steil eleni,' meddai Jean Jones wrth ei gŵr Graham tra oedden nhw'n cael brecwast un bore. Edrychodd Graham i fyny o'i bapur newydd. 'Mewn steil - pam?' gofynnodd e. 'Achos fe fyddi di yn chwe deg pum mlwydd oed,' atebodd ei wraig. 'Dw i am i ni gael gwyliau da cyn i ni fynd yn rhy hen.'

Gwenodd Graham arni. 'Beth am Ibiza?' meddai e. 'Dw i ddim wedi bod mewn disco ers i'r plant briodi.' 'Twpsyn!' meddai Jean. 'Mae cwmnïau teithio arbennig ar gael sy'n trefnu gwyliau i bobl fel ni, pobl sy am ymweld â hen leoedd diddorol yn hytrach na lleoedd swnllyd fel Calella a Lloret.' Aethon nhw i'r swyddfa deithio yn y dref a dewis taith mewn bws trwy ganol Sbaen. Y mis canlynol roedden nhw ar eu ffordd i Southampton mewn trên; yna aethon nhw mewn cwch i Santander, lle'r oedd bws yn aros amdanyn nhw.

Roedd y teithwyr ar y bws i gyd yn eu chwedegau neu saithdegau. Ond roedd yr arweinydd yn ei dridegau; Miguel oedd ei enw, ac roedd e'n siarad Saesneg yn rhugl. 'Ardderchog,' meddai Graham gyda gwên fach. 'Fe fydd e'n gwybod am bob disco ar y ffordd!' Ond bachgen nerfus ac ofnus oedd Miguel. Reit o'r dechrau rhoddodd e reolau i'r teithwyr fel y byddai athro wrth siarad â phlant bach.

'Peidiwch â mynd allan ar eich pennau eich hunain yn ystod y gwyliau,' meddai wrthyn nhw. 'Fe fydda i'n trefnu i ni fynd allan mewn grŵp bob tro. Mae Sbaen yn lle peryglus i deithwyr: mae Madrid yn llawn giangsters, mae Granada'n llawn lladron.' Felly, ym mhob dinas, roedd y teithwyr yn dilyn Miguel i bobman fel defaid. Os byddai rhywrai yn ceisio dianc am ychydig oddi wrth y grŵp, byddai'r arweinydd yn sylwi arnyn nhw, a'u galw nhw'n ôl. 'Fe fyddwch chi'n mynd ar goll,' byddai e'n dweud wrthyn nhw. 'Ydych chi eisiau difetha'r gwyliau i bawb arall?'

Roedd rhai o'r teithwyr yn cwyno dan eu hanadl, ond doedd neb yn cwyno yn uchel; doedden nhw ddim hyd yn oed yn prynu dim byd yn y siopau heb ofyn i'r arweinydd am ei gyngor e. Ond roedd Jean a Graham yn fwy annibynnol. Cyn diwedd y gwyliau roedden nhw wedi cael digon ar Miguel...

dathlu - celebrate
lleidr/lladron - thief/thieves
cwyno - to complain

arweinydd - courier
rhywrai - some people
cyngor - advice

rhugl - fluent
difetha - to spoil
annibynnol - independent

Gwybodaeth

Dyma ddechrau'r stori *Gormod o Win* (Gwasg y Dref Wen 2003) gan Bob Eynon o'r gyfrol o storïau byrion o'r un teitl. Cyhoeddodd Bob Eynon, sy'n dod o Dreorci ac sy'n ddysgwr ac yn ieithydd ei hun, lawer o straeon ar gyfer dysgwyr. Maen nhw'n addas ar gyfer dysgwyr o bob oedran - storïau antur, ffug-wyddonol, straeon am y gorllewin gwyllt yn ogystal â llyfrau dirgelwch yng nghyfres Debra Craig.

Tasgau

Awgrymir bod y dysgwyr yn gwrando ar y darn yn gyntaf. Gellir mynd ymlaen i ddarllen gweddill y stori o'r gyfrol wreiddiol.

- Dechrau'r stori sydd yma. Gellir gofyn i bawb ddyfalu mewn parau beth sy'n digwydd wrth i'r stori ddatblygu. Ar ôl rhoi rhai munudau i drafod hyn, rhaid esbonio sut gallai'r plot ddatblygu wrth weddill y dosbarth.

- Mae'r rhan fwyaf o storïau Bob Eynon yn cynnwys naratif yn y trydydd person, a digwyddiadau yn y gorffennol. Gellir gofyn i'r dosbarth ailadrodd y stori o safbwynt arall, e.e. o safbwynt Graham neu Jean gyda'r darn hwn. Does dim angen ailysgrifennu'r darn, dim ond gwneud y dasg ar lafar.

Pwyntiau Iaith

Gellir defnyddio'r darn i ymarfer lluosi enwau. Dosbarthwch y darn gyda'r geiriau isod wedi eu tanlinellu:

gŵr, plant, gwraig, cwmnïau, athro, lleoedd, teithwyr, arweinydd, papur, rheolau, swyddfa, mis, lleidr, siopau.

Rhaid i bawb benderfynu a ydy'r gair yn unigol neu'n lluosog. Wedyn, gofynnwch i bawb drafod beth yw ffurf unigol y geiriau lluosog, a ffurf luosog y geiriau unigol.

Sgwrsio Pellach

Mae gwyliau'n destun sgwrsio da a difyr. Gofynnwch i bawb ddod â hen luniau gwyliau i'r dosbarth, a dewch â chyflenwad o hen gardiau post eich hun. Rhaid i bawb yn ei dro basio'r lluniau o gwmpas a dweud hanes y gwyliau hynny. Gall fod yn wir neu'n ffrwyth dychymyg.

I sbarduno'r meddwl, gellir rhoi dechrau'r brawddegau isod ar y bwrdd gwyn:

> Es i ar fy ngwyliau i...
> Es i mewn bws i... ac mewn awyren i...
> Gwelais i...
> Sylwais i ar...
> Cawson ni/Gaethon ni...
> Hedfanon ni...
> Mwynheuon ni achos...

14. **Blues Pontcanna** gan Grahame Davies

Mi alwodd rhywun 'yuppie' ar fy ôl i,
Wrth ddod yn ôl o'r deli gyda'r gwin;
Rwy'n methu ffeindio'r fowlen guacamole,
Ac nawr rwy'n ofni y bydd fy ffrindiau'n flin.
Anghofion nhw fy nghredit ar y sgrin.
Does neb yn gwybod fy nhrafferthion i gyd,   *trafferthion - troubles*
Does neb i nghanmol heblaw fi fy hun.   *canmol - praise   heblaw - apart from*
Mae blues Pontcanna yn diflasu 'myd.   *diflasu - to bore*

Rhaid mynd i'r ddinas, ond y trwbwl yw
Mae'n beryg parcio'n rhywle heblaw'r gwaith,
Rhag ofn i'r iobiau grafu'r BMW
Ac i ugain mil o gar ddioddef craith.   *dioddef craith - to suffer a scar*
Dim byrddau yn *Le Gallois* ar ôl saith.
Baglais dros ddyn digartref ar y stryd.   *digartref - homeless*
Dyw 'nynes llnau ddim yn medru'r iaith.   *dynes llnau* (glanhau) *- cleaning lady*
Mae blues Pontcanna yn diflasu 'myd.

Does 'run o'm ffrindiau wedi gweld fy lluniau
Yn *Barn*, er imi'i roi'n y stafell fyw.   *er i mi - although I*
Y bore 'ma, mi glywais ddyn y biniau
Yn dweud ystrydeb hiliol yn fy nghlyw.   *ystrydeb hiliol - racist cliché*
Mae rhywbeth mawr yn bod ar fy feng shui.
Mae'r gath 'di bwyta'r anchovies i gyd.
Mae *Golwg* wedi 'mrifo i i'r byw.   *i'r byw - to the quick*
Mae blues Pontcanna yn diflasu 'myd.

Mae'n artaith bod yn berson creadigol   *artaith - torture, agony*
Ac Es Ffôr Si yn talu'r biliau i gyd,
A neb 'di galw ar fy ffôn symudol.
Mae blues Pontcanna yn diflasu 'myd.

Gwybodaeth
Daw'r gerdd hon o'r gyfrol *Cadwyni Rhyddid* gan Grahame Davies. Mae'n
enedigol o ardal Coedpoeth, Wrecsam ac yn byw yng Nghaerdydd yn awr.
Y gyfrol hon oedd Llyfr y Flwyddyn yn 2001. Mae'r gerdd hon yn dychanu
(*satirise*) y Cymry Cymraeg sy'n byw yng Nghaerdydd.

Tasgau

Mae hon yn gerdd gyfoes, ysgafn sy'n dychanu aelodau'r dosbarth canol yn ardal Pontcanna yng Nghaerdydd. Efallai mai'r disgrifiad gorau o'r person yn y gerdd yw 'cyfryngi' (*a typical media person*). Awgrymir:

- Gofyn i'r dosbarth wrando ar y gerdd ddwy waith a nodi beth maen nhw'n ei gofio. Bydd nifer o gyfeiriadau at sefydliadau neu bethau Cymreig a fydd yn ddieithr iddyn nhw. Awgrymir eu rhoi ar y bwrdd gwyn, a gofyn i'r dosbarth ddyfalu beth ydyn nhw, neu ddweud wrth bawb, os ydyn nhw'n gwybod:

  Le Gallois

  Barn

  Golwg

  Es Ffôr Si

- Gellir ei rhannu'n benillion a gofyn i grwpiau bach lunio cwestiynau am bob pennill. Er enghraifft, ar ôl y pennill cyntaf: Ble buodd e'n prynu gwin? Beth anghofion nhw ar y sgrin?

- Paru dau grŵp a gofyn iddyn nhw ofyn cwestiynau i'w gilydd gan symud ymlaen i'r grŵp / pennill nesaf ar ôl gorffen.

- Trafod y cwestiynau fel dosbarth a rhoi detholiad ohonyn nhw ar y bwrdd gwyn i'w hateb fel gwaith cartref.

- Gofyn i bob dysgwr ddewis llinell o'r gerdd ac i ddweud pam mae'n ei hoffi neu ddim yn ei hoffi.

- Gyda grŵp da gellir gofyn: Beth mae'r bardd yn ei ddychanu yma? Ydy'r dychanu'n effeithiol?

Pwyntiau Iaith

Cofier bod ystyr negyddol i 'yr un' mewn brawddeg fel 'Does yr un o'r bobl...'. Dyma gyfle i ymarfer brawddegau negyddol symlach hefyd. Y dasg yw trosi'r brawddegau cadarnhaol hyn i fod yn rhai negyddol:

1. Mae rhywun yn gwybod fy nhrafferthion.
2. Mae fy nynes glanhau'n medru'r iaith.
3. Roedd rhywbeth yn bod arni.
4. Mae byrddau yn *Le Gallois* heno.
5. Baglais i dros y dyn digartref.
6. Rhaid i mi fynd i'r ddinas.
7. Arnat ti roedd y bai.
8. Mi glywais i ddyn y biniau.

Sgwrsio Pellach

Beth yw ystyr 'dosbarth canol' erbyn heddiw?

Ydy Cymry Caerdydd yn wahanol i ardaloedd eraill?

Ydy hi'n beth da fod dosbarth cyfoethog o Gymry Cymraeg yn byw ac yn gweithio yn y brifddinas?

Beth yw nodweddion (*features*) y bobl yma, yn ôl y gerdd?

Ysgrifennu

Gofynnwch i bawb ysgrifennu portread o berson 'dosbarth canol'. Gellir defnyddio'r syniadau sy yn y gerdd, neu greu portread cwbl ddychmygol.

15. Addasiad o **Darluniau** allan o **Y Lôn Wen** gan Kate Roberts

1. Dw i'n saith a hanner oed, yn eistedd yn y lôn wrth ymyl y llidiart. Mae carreg fawr wastad yno, a dyna lle'r eisteddaf yn magu fy mrawd ieuengaf, Dafydd, mewn siôl. Dw i'n eistedd gymaint yno fel fy mod wedi gwneud twll hwylus i fy nhraed. Mae'n ddiwrnod braf. O fy mlaen mae Sir Fôn ac Afon Menai... Mae llongau hwyliau gwynion yn mynd drwy Afon Menai a thywod Niwbwrch yn disgleirio fel croen ebol melyn yn yr haul. Does neb yn mynd ar hyd y ffordd, mae'n berffaith dawel... Mae gwyddau Jane Roberts, Glanrafon yn pori ar y dorlan ac yn ymestyn eu gyddfau allan wrth fynd heibio er mwyn dangos eu hawdurdod. Ond mae fy mrawd bach a finnau'n berffaith dawel ac yn hapus, yn gwneud dim ond edrych i lawr ar y môr a synfyfyrio. Rydym yn synfyfyrio am hir er mwyn i mam gael gyrru ymlaen efo'i gwaith... mae mor braf yn y tawelwch. Mae gwallt fy mrawd bach yn cosi fy nhalcen, ac mor hyfryd yw ei groen tyner ar fy moch.

llidiart - giât
magu - nursing
hwylus - convenient
gwyddau - geese

dorlan - bank
synfyfyrio - meditating
cosi - tickle

2. Dw i'n naw oed yn eistedd wrth y ddesg yn yr ysgol yn gwneud sỳms. Mae'r athro wedi dangos i ni sut i wneud sỳms newydd, a chawsom lyfrau gydag enghreifftiau, rhyw ddwsin i'r tudalen. Yn awr mae'n rhaid i ni weithio'r problemau hyn yn ein llyfrau ysgrifennu. Mae'r hanner dwsin cyntaf yn hollol yr un fath â'i gilydd ac yn ddigon rhwydd. Mae'r seithfed yn wahanol a dydw i ddim yn gwybod beth i'w wneud. Mae arnaf ofn troi oddi wrth ffordd yr hanner dwsin cyntaf, rhag ofn i fi wneud camgymeriad, dw i mewn penbleth mawr. Mae fy rheswm yn dweud nad yw'r sỳm hon yr un fath â'r lleill, ond methaf weld pam roedd yn rhaid rhoi sỳm wahanol yng nghanol pethau yr un fath. Penderfynaf ddilyn fy rheswm er bod arnaf ofn. Y fi oedd yr unig un i gael y sỳm hon yn iawn. Dw i'n falch, nid oherwydd hyn ond oherwydd i fi benderfynu dilyn fy rheswm am y tro cyntaf erioed a chael fy mod yn iawn.

hollol - entirely
penbleth - quandary

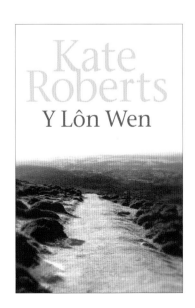

Gwybodaeth

Daw *Darluniau* o'r *Lôn Wen*, hunangofiant Kate Roberts (1891-1985). Ysgrifennodd hi lawer o storïau byrion a nofelau a chafodd hi'r teitl 'brenhines ein llên' gan rai beirniaid llenyddol. Cafodd y brawd 'bach' yn y darn cyntaf ei ladd yn y Rhyfel Mawr. Y digwyddiad trist hwn a symbylodd Kate Roberts i ysgrifennu ei straeon a'i nofelau.

Tasgau

Mae'r *Darluniau* hyn wedi'u hysgrifennu yn y person cyntaf, felly gellir eu cyflwyno ar ddechrau cyfnod dysgu grwpiau Uwch, neu ar ddiwedd cyfnod dysgu Canolradd gydag ambell grŵp. Awgrymir:

- Amrywio'r gwrando y tro hwn trwy oedi'r CD ar ôl y 'darlun' cyntaf. Rhannu'r dosbarth yn barau a'u hannog i ddarllen y darn bob yn ail frawddeg.

- Annog y parau i holi'r cwestiynau canlynol i'w gilydd bob yn ail: Faint ydy oed Kate Roberts yn y 'darlun' hwn? Ydy hi'n hŷn/henach neu yn iau/ifancach na'i brawd? Disgrifiwch y tywydd yn y 'darlun.' Beth mae hi'n gallu'i weld? Beth mae'r gwyddau'n ei wneud? Pam mae hi'n hapus? Pryd byddwch chi'n synfyfyrio fel arfer?

- Gwrando ar yr ail 'ddarlun' a'i ddarllen fel yr uchod, mewn parau gwahanol.

- Annog y parau i geisio cofio cynnwys y darn a'i adrodd i'w gilydd trwy ddweud brawddeg ar y tro.

- Rhannu'r dosbarth a chwarae darn y 'darlun' cyntaf i un grŵp a darn yr ail 'ddarlun' i'r grŵp arall. Wedyn gellir rhannu'r dosbarth cyfan yn barau - un o bob un o'r grwpiau uchod - a'u hannog i adrodd cynnwys y darnau wrth ei gilydd cyn chwarae'r darn i gyd i'r dosbarth cyfan.

Pwyntiau Iaith
Ysgrifennwyd y darnau yn y person cyntaf. Gofynnwch i'r grŵp droi'r darn cyntaf i'r trydydd person ac i'r gorffennol hefyd. Felly, bydd y darn yn cychwyn fel hyn: 'Roedd hi'n saith a hanner oed...' Gellir tynnu sylw at rai enghreifftiau o Gymraeg llenyddol yn y darnau:

> eisteddaf - dw i'n eistedd
> Rydym - 'Dyn ni / 'Dan ni
> Cawsom - Gaethon / Mi gaethon ni
> Mae arnaf ofn - Mae arna i ofn
> Penderfynaf - Dw i'n penderfynu

Sgwrsio Pellach
Roedd Kate Roberts yn blentyn dros gan mlynedd yn ôl. Pa bethau yn y darnau sy'n eu dyddio i'r cyfnod hwnnw?
Mae Kate Roberts yn creu awyrgylch trwy ddefnyddio'r pum synnwyr. Oes enghreifftiau o sut mae hi'n gwneud hyn?
Ydyn nhw'n cofio gofalu am rywun arall pan oedden nhw'n blant?
Ydyn nhw'n cofio treulio amser ar eu pen eu hunain? Beth maen nhw'n ei gofio?

Ysgrifennu
Ysgrifennwch baragraff yn dechrau â'r geiriau:
Dw i'n saith oed...

16. Darn o **Stori Sydyn: Llais yr Adar Gleision** gan Ali Yassine

2001. Roedd cysylltiad Bobby Gould, y rheolwr, â chlwb pêl-droed Caerdydd wedi dod i ben ar ôl un tymor yn unig. Doedd dim llawer o ffans yr Adar Gleision yn flin wrth ei weld yn gadael, yn enwedig fi. Wrth i'r drws gau yn ei wyneb e, arweiniodd hynny at ddrws arall yn agor i fi. Dyma roddodd y cyfle i fi adael terasau'r Grange End a bod yn rhan o holl gyffro diwrnod y gêm fel un o'r staff. Sut digwyddodd hynny? Wel fe wnes i ysgrifennu llythyr digon haerllug.

Ysgrifennes i lythyr yn dweud mai fi ddylai fod yn rheolwr newydd ar dîm pêl-droed Caerdydd! Fel hyn roedd e'n dechrau:
> Gan fy mod yn gwybod cyn lleied am bêl-droed a heb unrhyw gymwysterau o gwbl, dw i'n credu mai fi yw'r boi i'r job!

Roedd gen i fwy o syniadau:
> Dw i'n awgrymu ein bod yn newid enwau'r chwaraewyr i gyd i Jones. Bydd hynny'n ei gwneud yn anodd i'r dyfarnwyr wybod pwy yw pwy. Yr un enw fydd ar gefn pob crys! Bydd hynny hefyd yn gwneud fy ngwaith i fel rheolwr yn rhwydd gan mai'r cyfan fydd gen i i'w ddweud mewn sesiwn ymarfer fydd 'Hey Jonesy!' 'Do this Jonesy' ac ati.

Roedd gen i awgrymiadau eraill hefyd.
> Gan mai Sam Hammam yw perchennog y clwb, dw i'n credu y dylen ni gael sesiwn karaoke yn ystod hanner amser pob gêm gartre'. Gallwn i ei alw fe yn Sing-a-long-a-Sam.

Roeddwn am weld bwydlen y garfan yn newid hefyd er mwyn cynnwys Balti arni bob dydd. Ar ddiwedd y llythyr, dywedais os nad oedden nhw am i fi fod yn rheolwr, fod gen i syniad arall. Beth am adael i fi wneud y cyhoeddiadau ar y *tannoy* ar ddiwrnod y gêm? Anfonais y llythyr draw i Barc Ninian. Fyddwn i'n cael ateb, tybed? Go brin. Ond os cawn ateb, beth fydden nhw'n debygol o ddweud wrtha i?

Ymhen llai nag wythnos, daeth yr ateb. Roedden nhw am siarad 'da fi! Swydd rheolwr, tybed? Draw â fi i Barc Ninian i gael gwybod, na, nid swydd rheolwr - dim syrpreis fanna! - ond roedd ganddyn nhw ddiddordeb mewn trafod fy awgrym i ynglŷn â gwneud gwaith ar y tannoy.

Roedd Julian Jenkins, sy'n dal i weithio gyda'r clwb, ishe gweld sut y byddwn i'n perfformio ar y tannoy. 'Nawr?' holais i. 'Ie, nawr!' Felly i fyny â fi i'r sied fechan a oedd yng nghefn y stand. Agorais y meic a dechrau siarad â Pharc Ninian gwag!

haerllug - digywilydd *cheeky*
cymhwyster/cymwysterau - *qualification/s*
dyfarnwr/dyfarnwyr - *referee/s*
tannoy - uchelseinydd
rheolwr - *manager*

Gwybodaeth
Dyma ddyfyniad o'r llyfr sy'n amlinellu cefndir yr awdur. 'Mae fy ngwreiddiau yn yr Aifft a Somalia. Daeth fy nhad-cu i Brydain a setlo yn Lerpwl, cyn symud i Gaerdydd yn y pumdegau. Fy agwedd i, wedi i mi dyfu, oedd ei bod yn anodd i mi ystyried fy hun yn Gymro yn byw yng Nghymru os nad oeddwn yn gwybod rhywbeth am iaith y wlad. Mae'r ffordd y des i siarad Cymraeg yn stori ddigon difyr...'

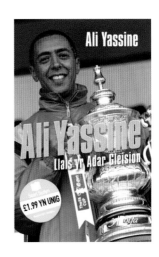

Tasgau

Darn ysgafn agoriadol llyfr Ali Yassine yn y gyfres *Stori Sydyn* yw hwn. Gall fod yn addas ar gyfer grŵp Canolradd da hefyd. Awgrymir y tasgau canlynol:

- Gan fod hwn yn ddarn dealladwy ar y darlleniad cyntaf gellid gwrando ar y CD heb gyflwyno'r eirfa ymlaen llaw.

- Byddai'n bosib trafod rhagor am gefndir yr awdur a'r cyfeiriad ato'n dysgu Cymraeg. Ceir yr wybodaeth ym mhennod 8 y llyfr.

- Mae'r awdur yn adrodd yr hanes amdano'n cael gwaith fel cyhoeddwr ar y tannoy ac mae'n ddarn storïol iawn a cheir llawer o frawddegau byrion ynddo. Gellid annog y grŵp i ddarllen y darn yn uchel fesul brawddeg a gofyn iddyn nhw sylwi ar y modd y mae cychwyn y brawddegau'n cael eu hamrywio, e.e. Roedd... Doedd dim... Wrth i'r... Dyma roddodd... ac yn y blaen.

- Eu hannog i ddweud hanesyn byr, hunagofiannol wrth eu partneriaid, gan eu hannog i gadw'r brawddegau'n fyr ac amrywio'r patrymau. Gallent ailadrodd y straeon wrth weddill y grŵp wedyn.

Pwyntiau Iaith

Awgrymir dechrau â'r ddwy ffurf isod:

> - Fe wnes i ysgrifennu llythyr
> - Ysgrifennes i lythyr

Dyma gyfle i adolygu'r ffurfiau cwmpasog a chryno. Mae'r geiryn rhagferfol 'fe' ('mi' yn y gogledd) yn ddewisol, a ffurf lafar yw'r terfyniad '–es' ar ddiwedd 'ysgrifennes'. Gellir gofyn i'r dosbarth drosi'r brawddegau canlynol:

1.	Dyna beth wnaeth ddigwydd	[Dyna beth ddigwyddodd]
2.	Mi wnes i ddweud wrthyn nhw	[Dwedais i wrthyn nhw]
3.	Wnest ti anfon y llythyr?	[Anfonaist ti'r llythyr?]
4.	Fe wnaeth e roi anrheg i fi	[Rhoddodd e anrheg i mi/fi]
5.	Mi wnaeth y plant fwynhau'n fawr	[Mwynheuodd y plant yn fawr]
6.	Wnaeth y gêm ddechrau ar amser?	[Ddechreuodd y gêm ar amser?]
7.	Wnaeth yr ateb ddim cyrraedd am wyth	[Chyrhaeddod yr ateb ddim am wyth]
8.	Wnes i mo'i weld o yn y gêm	[Welais i mohono fo/fe yn y gêm]

Sgwrsio Pellach

Ydyn nhw'n hoffi pêl-droed?
Beth maen nhw'n wybod am y gêm yng Nghymru?
Ydy pêl-droed yn well na rygbi?

Ysgrifennu

Ysgrifennu llythyr ysgafn, cellweirus - tebyg i lythyr Ali - yn gofyn am swydd bwysig, e.e. prif weinidog Cymru, hyfforddwr tîm rygbi Cymru ac yn y blaen.

17. Darn o **Cymru Howard Marks** gan Howard Marks

I fi, mae yna ddwy Gymru. Yn gyntaf, y Gymru roeddwn am wneud popeth posib i ddianc ohoni. Cymru fy ieuenctid oedd honno yn fwy na dim. Ac yna'r Gymru rydw i wedi trio dod 'nôl i mewn iddi. Dwi wedi cael llawer o bleser yn ailddarganfod Cymru dros y blynyddoedd diwetha. Dyma'r Gymru mae dyn wrth nesu at ei saithdegau yn ei gweld yn gliriach ac yn gliriach. Dyma'r Gymru dwi am wneud fy ngorau glas i ddod 'nôl yn rhan ohoni. Stori'r ddwy Gymru, a'r daith o'r naill i'r llall sydd yn y llyfr yma.

Carchar yn America yw man cychwyn y daith. Dyna lle dechreuodd y daith yn ddaearyddol beth bynnag. Ar y pryd roeddwn yn wynebu 25 mlynedd dan glo ac wedi bod am flynyddoedd yn un o'r dynion roedd heddlu Prydain yn fwya awyddus i'w ddal. Roedd heddlu nifer o wledydd drwy'r byd wedi bod yn gweithio gyda'i gilydd i'm dal ar gyhuddiadau'n ymwneud â phrynu a gwerthu cyffuriau rhyngwladol. Yn ôl yr awdurdodau, fi oedd prif smyglwr cyffuriau'r byd. Cefais fy nal, a'm rhoi yn un o garchardai gwaetha America...

Ond yna, un diwrnod, daeth Tee Bone Taylor i siarad â fi. Roedd e yn y carchar am ladd plisman a dosbarthu crac cocên. Dywedodd ei fod wedi bod yn gwrando ar y radio a'i fod wedi clywed rhaglen am Gymru. Dysgodd fod Hilary Clinton yn dod o deulu Cymreig... Roedd ganddi deulu o Gymru ar y ddwy ochr. Dywedodd Tee Bone nad oedd yn cofio fawr ddim am weddill y rhaglen, dim ond rhai tameidiau. Roedd mam Bob Hope, ei hoff ddigrifwr, yn Gymraes, a phump o chwech Arlywydd cynta America, gan gynnwys Thomas Jefferson, yn Gymry. Roedd 18 o'r rhai oedd wedi arwyddo Datganiad Annibyniaeth America hefyd o deuluoedd Cymreig. A Jesse James, y lleidr banciau, Pretty Boy Floyd, a Murray "the Camel" Humphries, y gangster.

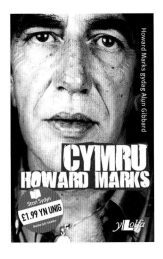

ailddarganfod - *rediscover*
daearyddol - *geographically*
cyhuddiad/cyhuddiadau - *accusation/s*
tameidiau - *bits*
carchardai - *prisons*
(carchar + tŷ = carchardy; carchar + tai = carchardai)
digrifwr - *comedian*
Arlywydd - *President*
Datganiad Annibyniaeth - *Declaration of Independence*

Gwybodaeth

Daw'r darn hwn o ddechrau hunangofiant Howard Marks, *Cymru Howard Marks*. Cafodd ei fagu yn Gymro Cymraeg ym Mynydd Cynffig, ger Penybont-ar-Ogwr a'i addysgu yn Rhydychen. Bu'n enwog fel smyglwr cyffuriau ond bellach mae'r un mor enwog fel diddanwr ac awdur yr hunagofiant Saesneg, *Mr Nice.*

Tasgau

Mae'r gyfrol hon yn rhan o'r gyfres Stori Sydyn a gobeithir y bydd hi'n tanio diddordeb y darllenwyr a'u hannog i ddarllen rhagor o lyfrau yn y gyfres hon yn ogystal â llyfrau eraill. Gellir:

- Cyflwyno'r eirfa yn gyntaf a gwrando ar y CD. Dylai'r darn hwn fod yn gwbl ddealladwy i'r myfyrwyr ar ôl un darlleniad.

- Trafod y darn gyda phartneriaid. Ydyn nhw eisiau darllen rhagor am y cymeriad? Pam? Ydyn nhw'n gwybod rhai ffeithiau eraill amdano?

- Adrodd yn ôl i weddill y dosbarth ar sail y drafodaeth uchod.

Pwyntiau Iaith

Ceir sawl enghraifft o osod elfen fel ansoddair o flaen yr enw yn y darn hwn, e.e. ailddarganfod, hoff ddigrifwr, prif smyglwr cyffuriau. Gofyn iddyn nhw sylwi ar y treiglad meddal yn y ddwy enghraifft gyntaf. Weithiau bydd y treiglad yn digwydd y tu mewn i'r gair, (gelwir geiriau fel hyn yn eiriau cyfansawdd), e.e. prifddinas, prifathro, prifardd. Dro arall ceir dau air ar wahân ond bydd yn dal i dreiglo'n feddal, e.e. prif leisydd, prif weinidog.

Awgrymir gofyn iddyn nhw lunio brawddegau yn cynnwys yr enghreifftiau hyn mewn parau cyn adrodd yn ôl a'u dweud wrth y dosbarth cyfan. Gellir rhoi canllawiau iddyn nhw. Er enghraifft, defnyddio'r ansoddeiriau *ail, prif, gor* a *hoff*. Gan ddibynnu ar safon y grŵp, gellir eu helpu trwy roi geiriau ar y bwrdd gwyn. Er enghraifft:

ail - adrodd [ailadrodd], byw [ail-fyw], meddwl [ailfeddwl], cynnig [ailgynnig], sefyll [ailsefyll], ystyried [ailystyried], llenwi [ail-lenwi].

prif - dinas [prifddinas], canwr [prif ganwr], diddordeb [prif ddiddordeb], siaradwr [prif siaradwr], cyflwynydd [prif gyflwynydd].

gor - bwyta [gorfwyta], yfed [goryfed], canmol [gorganmol], gweithio [gorweithio], dweud [gor-ddweud], hoff [gor-hoff], actio [goractio], ymateb [gorymateb], pwysleisio [gorbwysleisio].

hoff - pryd bwyd [hoff bryd bwyd], rhaglen [hoff raglen], canwr [hoff ganwr].

Sgwrsio Pellach

Ydy hi'n iawn fod pobl fel Howard Marks yn ennill ei fywoliaeth trwy siarad ac ysgrifennu am ei fywyd yn gwerthu a phrynu cyffuriau?
Oes perygl i ni ramantu hanes bywydau cymeriadau fel hyn?
Beth yw eu barn am y cyffur cannabis?

Ysgrifennu

Fel gwaith cartref, gellir gofyn iddynt ysgrifennu portread o berson drwg-hoffus tebyg i Howard Marks, naill ai o lyfr, ffilm neu fywyd go iawn.

18. Carreg Cennen gan Iwan Llwyd

Roedd yn arfer gwarchod y briffordd,
yn un o gadwyn o gestyll
ar hyd glannau Tywi:

gwarchod – amddiffyn, *to defend*
cadwyn - *chain*
glan/nau - *shore/s*

y Dryslwyn, Dinefwr ac yma ym mhen y dyffryn
yr uchaf ohonyn nhw i gyd,
yn cadw llygad barcud ar y byd:

llygad barcud - *a kite's eye view*

erbyn heddiw rhaid gadael y briffordd,
dilyn y lonydd troellog, diarffordd,
y cefnffyrdd sydd wedi hen adael y map,

troellog - *winding, anghysbell* - *remote*
cefnffyrdd - *back roads*

sy'n cuddio yn y pantiau y tu hwnt i Trap,
lle mae'n rhaid oedi
i adael i dractor neu fws fynd heibio:

pant/iau - *hollow/s*

ac yna gadael y cerbyd a dringo
heibio'r hwyaid a'r defaid corniog,
cyn cyrraedd â'n dyrnau'n llawn gwynt:

defaid corniog - *horned sheep*
dwrn/dyrnau - *fist/s*

dim ond bref y gwartheg a chwiban sigl-di-gwt,
ac ymhell, bell uwchben
awyren a'i chynffon wen

sigl-di-gwt - *wagtail*

ar y briffordd i'r byd newydd:
yna un arall, ac un arall wrth ei chwt,
yn hedfan drwy'r machlud ar Dywi:

cwt/cynffon - *tail*
machlud - *sunset*

Roedd yr Arglwydd Rhys wedi'i gweld hi -
mae ei gastell yn dal ar y briffordd o hyd,
y briffordd aruchel i ben pella'r byd.

aruchel - *majestic*

Cefndir hanesyddol

Un o gestyll Yr Arglwydd Rhys oedd castell Carreg Cennen. Roedd Rhys ap Gruffydd (1132-97) yn llywodraethwr y Deheubarth, sef de Cymru. Gyda'i frodyr fe lwyddodd i ddinistrio awdurdod y Normaniaid yn y Deheubarth. Bu castell Dinefwr - un o'r tri chastell sy'n cael eu henwi yn y gerdd - yn gartref iddo. Mae'r Arglwydd Rhys yn enwog hefyd fel noddwr yr eisteddfod gyntaf a gynhaliwyd yng Nghastell Aberteifi yn 1176.

Gwybodaeth

Daw'r gerdd hon o'r gyfrol *Hanner Cant*. Ysgrifennodd Iwan Llwyd lawer o gerddi am lefydd yng Nghymru a ledled y byd. Enillodd y goron yn Eisteddfod Genedlaethol Cwm Rhymni 1989. Bu farw'n ifanc yn 2010.

Tasgau

Cyn gwrando ar y gerdd hon, neu ar ôl gwrando arni unwaith, byddai'n fuddiol petai'r dysgwyr yn darllen am gefndir hanesyddol y gerdd yn y troednodyn iddi. Dydy'r eirfa na'r thema ddim yn anodd a gellir ei chyflwyno ar gychwyn cyfnod safon Uwch. Awgrymir:

● Gwrando ar y gerdd a chyflwyno'r hanes. Gweler isod.

● Ar ôl gwrando arni unwaith eto gellir rhannu'r dosbarth yn barau a'u hannog i'w darllen i'w gilydd. Ar ôl ymgyfarwyddo â'i chynnwys gallant holi'r cwestiynau canlynol i'w gilydd bob yn ail mewn parau:

> Beth ydy enwau cestyll yr Arglwydd Rhys?
> Ar lannau pa afon yr adeiladodd yr Arglwydd y cestyll?
> P'un ydy'r castell uchaf?
> Ydy'r castell uchaf ar y briffordd heddiw?
> Trwy ba bentref rydych chi'n teithio ar y ffordd i'r castell?
> Pam mae'r daith yn un araf?
> Ydy hi'n bosib gyrru'r car yr holl ffordd at y castell?
> Pa aderyn a pha anifail welodd y bardd ar y ffordd i'r castell?
> Pa briffordd arall mae'r bardd yn sôn amdani?
> Pa adeg o'r dydd yw hi yn y gerdd?

● Cynnal trafodaeth gyffredinol ynghylch y disgrifiadau neu'r llinellau maen nhw'n eu hoffi ynddi a nodi'r rheswm dros eu dewis.

● Gwrando ar y gerdd yn cael ei darllen unwaith eto, heb edrych ar y sgript. Yn ychwanegol at hynny, mae'n bosib trefnu taith yn ystod yr haf i lefydd o bwys hanesyddol fel y cestyll a enwir yn y gerdd hon. Yna, gall y dysgwyr gymharu eu profiadau nhw o ymweld â'r lle â phrofiadau'r bardd.

Pwyntiau Iaith
Mae'r gerdd yn llawn idiomau defnyddiol, ac awgrymir eu tanlinellu neu eu hysgrifennu ar y bwrdd gwyn: llygad barcud (sôn am y barcud coch yn dychwelyd i'r ardal); tu hwnt i (y tu draw i); hen adael (wedi gadael ers amser - ei gymharu â newydd adael); â'n gwynt yn ein dyrnau (mae'n golygu 'llawn cyffro' yn ogystal ag anadlu'n drwm ar ôl dringo); un arall ar ei chwt (wrth ei chynffon); wedi'i gweld hi (wedi'i deall hi/deall pethau). Dylid annog parau i lunio brawddegau sy'n cynnwys yr idiomau hyn eu hunain ac adrodd rhai o'r brawddegau hyn yn ôl i'r dosbarth cyfan.

Sgwrsio Pellach
Ar ôl ymweld â rhywle o bwys hanesyddol:
Beth maen nhw'n gofio am yr ymweliad?
Beth maen nhw'n gofio am y safle a'r awyrgylch?
Oedd y lle'n wahanol i'r disgwyl?

Ysgrifennu
Annog y dosbarth i ysgrifennu dyddiadur, gan ddychmygu mai nhw ac nid y bardd sydd wedi ymweld â'r castell. Gallant ddefnyddio rhai manylion o'r gerdd wrth gwrs ond dylent geisio defnyddio eu geiriau eu hunain hefyd.

19. **Gadael Abertawe** gan Huw Chiswell

Gadael Abertawe, gyrru fel ffŵl
Rhywbeth wedi digwydd, methu cadw'n cŵl
Distaw yn y dref,
Gwaedu yn fy sedd,
Dylwn wybod gwell
Na mynd i ganol pethau dwl.
Yn syth drwy sgwâr Dyfaty, cymryd hewl y cwm,   *hewl* - ffordd
Sbardun ar y llawr yn awr,   *sbardun* - throttle
Dechrau plygu'n grwm;   *crwm* - crooked
Sant Pedr, Pontardawe
Yn oren yn y niwl,
A'r lôn yn llifo tano i a'r car yn canu'i diwn.   *llifo tano i*
                                                  - flowing underneath me

W, ces i 'nghodi yn y capel, ar air yr Ysgol Sul,
A dw i'n canu'r hen emynau
Bob cyfle rownd y rîl;   *rownd y rîl* - o hyd
Ddim yn ddyn crefyddol   *crefyddol* - religious
Ond mae angen rhywun ar y whîl.
Nawr Hosanna, Iesu, rho dy law ar fy mhen.
Credu 'mod i'n mynd,
Dw i'n credu 'mod i'n mynd.

Munud ar ôl Ystrad, cyrraedd Craig y Nos,
Llygaid ar y troeon bûm yn trafod gydol oes.   *troeon* - bends
Rhywbeth yn y gwrych,   *gwrych* - clawdd, *hedge*
Rhywun estron yn y drych,   *estron* - dieithr
A rhwng y ddau mae'r olwyn 'tai   *'tai* - fel petai
Yn tynnu am y ffos.   *olwyn* - steering wheel
                                                  ffos - ditch

W, ces i 'nghodi yn y capel, ar air yr Ysgol Sul,
A dw i'n canu'r hen emynau
Bob cyfle rownd y rîl,
Efalle bydd e'n ddigon
Pan ddaw e at y dîl.   *dîl* - deal
Nawr Hosanna, Iesu, rho dy law ar fy mhen.
Credu 'mod i'n mynd.

Dw i wedi colli 'nghrefydd
Ond dal i ddisgwyl Duw,
Ac mae gen i bwt o hunan-barch   *hunan-barch* - self respect
Er i fywyd fynd ar sgiw.
Nawr yn awr y gadael
Angen rhywun wrth y llyw.
Nawr Hosanna, Iesu, rho dy law ar fy mhen.
Meddwl 'mod i'n mynd,
Dw i'n meddwl 'mod i'n mynd.
Dw i'n meddwl 'mod i'n mynd.

Gwybodaeth

Ysgrifennodd Huw Chiswell nifer o ganeuon poblogaidd iawn fel *Y Cwm* sy'n sôn
am ei ardal enedigol yng Nghwm Tawe. Daw'r gân hon o *Goreuon Huw Chiswell*.

Tasgau

- Mae hon yn un o ganeuon gorau Huw Chiswell ac yn addas i'w chyflwyno am fod digon o gyfle i'r dysgwyr drafod pam mae'r canwr yn mynd ar y daith yn y gân.

Awgrymir:

- Gwrando ar y gân a gofyn i'r aelodau am eu hargraffiadau cyntaf ohoni. Pa fath o gân yw hi? Ydyn nhw'n mwynhau caneuon fel hyn?

- Gwrando arni eto gan ddilyn y sgript a nodi rhai pwyntiau ar y bwrdd gwyn.

- Rhannu'r dosbarth yn grwpiau bach a gofyn iddyn nhw drafod pam mae'r canwr yn gadael. Gofyn iddyn nhw drafod pa gliwiau a geir yn y gân a dyfalu pam mae'n gadael Abertawe.

- Uno'r grwpiau yn ddosbarth a gofyn i bob grŵp roi eu fersiynau nhw o stori'r canwr. Beth yw ystyr 'pan ddaw hi at y dîl?'

- Annog y dysgwyr i adrodd stori'r gân trwy droi rhai o'r berfenwau a geir yn y gân yn ferfau yn y trydydd person. Dylid eu hannog i amrywio'r ffurfiau cryno a'r ffurfiau cwmpasog, e.e. Gadawodd y canwr Abertawe a gyrrodd e fel ffŵl... Cafodd e ei fagu...'

Pwyntiau Iaith
Gan dynnu sylw at y frawddeg 'W, ces i 'nghodi yn y capel', gellir ymarfer troi i'r 3ydd person. Cofier defnyddio ffurfiau sy'n gyfarwydd i'r dysgwyr, e.e. *Gaeth / Mi gaeth* yn lle *cafodd*, lle bo'n briodol.

1.	*Ces i fy nal gan y plant.*	[Cafodd e/o ei ddal...]
2.	*Ces i fy ngadael ar y platffform.*	[Cafodd e/o ei adael...]
3.	*Ces i fy rhoi ar ben ffordd.*	[Cafodd e/o ei roi...]
4.	*Ces i fy anfon i'r lle anghywir.*	[Cafodd e/o ei anfon...]
5.	*Ces i fy nharo gan y car.*	[Cafodd e/o ei daro...]
6.	*Ces i fy nghopïo gan yr ymgeisydd.*	[Cafodd e/o ei gopïo...]
7.	*Ces i fy mhenodi i'r swydd newydd.*	[Cafodd e/o ei benodi...]
8.	*Ces i fy nghosbi gan yr athro.*	[Cafodd e/o ei gosbi...]

Yna, gofyn i bawb sôn am Mair, e.e. Cafodd hi ei dal... gan dreiglo fel bo'r angen.

Sgwrsio Pellach
Ceir llawer o themâu yn y gân a all fod yn sail i sgwrsio pellach, e.e. 'Ces i 'nghodi yn y capel.' Gawson nhw gefndir crefyddol o gwbl? Ydy crefydd yn bwysig iddyn nhw o hyd? Gawson nhw gefndir gwledig neu drefol? Mae'n sôn am adael dinas Abertawe hefyd. Ydyn nhw'n cofio gadael rhywle arbennig a oedd yn agos at eu calon neu rywle doedden nhw ddim yn hoff ohono?

Ysgrifennu
Fel gwaith cartref gellir annog y dysgwyr i ysgrifennu dyddiadur y canwr y noson y gadawodd Abertawe a rhoi eu fersiwn dychmygol nhw o'r hyn ddigwyddodd.

20. **Croesi Traeth** gan Gwyn Thomas

Yr oedd hi, y diwrnod hwnnw,
Yn ail o Fedi.
A dyma ni fel teulu,
Yn penderfynu mynd i lan y môr.

Yr oedd hi, y diwrnod hwnnw,
Yn heulog ond fymryn yn wyntog.   *mymryn - ychydig*
Dros y traeth mawr, gwag
Ysgydwai'r gwynt loywderau'r haul,   *glowyderau - brightnesses*
Chwibanai ei felyn dros y tywod,
A disgleiriai'r dŵr ar ei drai pell.   *trai - ebb*

A dyma ddechrau gwneud y pethau
Y bydd pobol yn eu gwneud ar draethau -
Rhawio tywod;   *rhawio - rhofio, to shovel*
Rhoi babi i eistedd yn ei ryfeddod   *rhyfeddod - syndod*
Hallt; codi cestyll; cicio pêl.   *hallt - salty*
Mi aeth yr hogiau o gydwybod,   *o gydwybod - out of conscience*
Hyd yn oed i ymdrochi, yn garcus.   *carcus - gofalus*
Ond yr oedd hi y diwrnod hwnnw,
Yn rhy oer i aros yn hir yn y dŵr.
Safwn innau yn edrych.

Daethant o'r môr yn sgleinio a rhincian   *sgleinio - shining*
A chwerthin a sblasio;   *rhincian - gnashing of teeth*
Ac wedyn dyma nhw'n rhedeg o 'mlaen i
Ar draws y traeth maith   *maith - hir*
At eu mam, at eu chwaer,
At ddiddosrwydd a thyweli.   *diddosrwydd - snugness*

Dilynais innau o bell.
Ond wrth groesi'r traeth, tua'r canol,
Dyma fo'n fy nharo i yn ysgytwol   *ysgytwol - yn gryf, fel sioc*
Mai un waith y mae hyn yn digwydd;
'Ddaw'r weithred hon byth, byth yn ôl.   *gweithred - digwyddiad*
Mae'r eiliadau sydd newydd fynd heibio
Mor dynn â'r Oes Haearn o fewn tragwyddoldeb: *tragwyddoldeb - eternity*
Peth fel 'ma ydi ein marwoldeb.   *marwoldeb - mortality*
A theimlais braidd yn chwith yn fan'no -   *chwith - awkward*
Ddigwyddith y peth hwn byth eto.

Ond dal i gerdded a wneuthum
A chyn bo hir fe ddeuthum yn ôl   *deuthum - des i*
At y teulu,
At y sychu stryffaglus a'r newid,   *stryffaglus - trafferthus*

At sŵn y presennol.
A rhwng tyllu tywod
A chrensian drwy frechdan domato   *crensian - to crunch*
A cheisio cysuro'r babi   *cysuro - to comfort*
Fe aeth y chwithdod hwnnw heibio.

Yr oeddwn i, fel yr oedd hi'n digwydd,
Y diwrnod hwnnw yn cael fy mhen blwydd
Yn ddeugain ac un.

Y mae hen ddihareb Rwsiaidd sy'n dweud,   *dihareb - proverb*
'Nid croesi cae yw byw.'
Cywir: croesi traeth ydyw.

Gwybodaeth
Daw'r gerdd hon o'r
gyfrol o'r un teitl a
gyhoeddwyd yn 1978.
Gwyn Thomas oedd
Bardd Cenedlaethol
Cymru rhwng 2005
a 2007. Cafodd Gwyn
Thomas ei fagu ym
Mlaenau Ffestiniog
a bu'n ddarlithydd ac
yn Athro yng Ngholeg
y Brifysgol Bangor tan
iddo ymddeol.

Tasgau

Mae hon yn gerdd ar gyfer grŵp eithaf rhugl sy'n astudio ar lefel Uwch. Awgrymir:

- Rhoi cefndir y gerdd yn fras i'r aelodau gan nodi ei bod wedi cael ei hysgrifennu pan oedd y bardd yn iau ac ar drothwy canol oed. Wedyn gellir chwarae'r darn ar y CD.

- Trafod cynnwys y gerdd a nodi argraffiadau cyntaf ohoni ar y bwrdd gwyn.

- Cyflwyno'r sgript a'r eirfa cyn gwrando ar y gerdd eto.

- Fel gweithgaredd dosbarth, gellir gofyn iddyn nhw ystyried y gerdd fel nifer o olygfeydd a nodi'r golygfeydd ar y bwrdd gwyn, e.e. mae'r olygfa gyntaf yn disgrifio'r teulu yn cyrraedd y traeth; yn yr ail olygfa mae'r bardd yn dilyn y bechgyn ac yn sylweddoli rhywbeth pwysig wrth groesi'r traeth; ac yn yr olygfa olaf, mae'n ailymuno â'r teulu.

- Gofyn i wahanol grwpiau ystyried y gwahanol olygfeydd a thrafod yn fanwl beth sy'n digwydd ynddyn nhw. Wedyn gall y grwpiau adrodd yn ôl i'r dosbarth cyfan.

Pwyntiau Iaith

Mae nifer o ffurfiau cryno yn y gerdd, sy'n nodweddu'r iaith lenyddol, ac efallai'n ddieithr i'r dysgwyr:

Safwn	- ro'n i'n sefyll
Ysgydwai	- roedd (y gwynt) yn ysgwyd
Chwibanai	- roedd (y gwynt) yn chwibanu
Disgleiriai	- roedd (y dŵr) yn disgleirio

Dyma gyfle i esbonio'r rhain: bod angen ychwanegu terfyniad at ferf, yn debyg i'r gorffennol, e.e.

Chwibanodd hi - *she whistled*

Chwibanai hi - *she was whistling*

Gellir gwneud ychydig o ymarferion syml gyda berfau cyfarwydd, rheolaidd i ffurfio brawddegau tebyg, e.e. dilyn, gweithio, siarad, darllen, cofio. Awgrymir tynnu sylw at y rhain wrth ddarllen darnau eraill o lenyddiaeth.

Sgwrsio Pellach

Gellir tynnu eu sylw at y llinell: 'Ddigwyddith y peth hwn byth eto.'
Oes digwyddiadau bach tebyg i hyn yn fyw yn eu cof nhw?
Ydy diwrnodau ar y traeth yn rhan o'u plentyndod nhw?

Ysgrifennu

Fel gwaith cartref gellir gofyn iddyn nhw ysgrifennu eu hymateb nhw i'r gerdd.
Ydy'r gerdd yn effeithiol? Beth yw 'neges' y gerdd, os oes neges?

21. Darn o **Dyddiadur Anne Frank**, addasiad gan Eigra Lewis Roberts

*Mae Anne Frank yn disgrifio'i chuddfan (hiding place) hi a'i chwaer, Margot,
mewn llythyr at ei ffrind, Kitty - dydd Iau, Gorffennaf 9, 1942.*

Roedden ni'n cerdded i lawr y stryd cyn i Dad a Mam ddechrau datgelu, fesul tipyn, beth oedd
y cynllun. Am fisoedd, roedden ni wedi bod yn symud gymaint ag oedd bosibl o'n dodrefn a'n
heiddo allan o'r tŷ. Y cytundeb oedd y bydden ni'n mynd i guddio ar Orffennaf 16. Oherwydd
bod Margot wedi cael ei galw i fyny, bu'n rhaid gweithredu'r cynllun ddeg diwrnod ynghynt,
ac roedd hynny'n golygu y byddai'n rhaid i ni geisio dygymod ag ystafelloedd llai trefnus.

Mae'r guddfan wedi'i lleoli yn yr adeilad lle mae swyddfa Dad. Efallai bod hynny braidd yn
anodd i ddieithriaid ei ddeall, felly mae'n well i mi egluro. Ychydig o bobl oedd yn gweithio
yn y swyddfa, dim ond Mr Kugler, Mr Kleiman, Miep a theipydd tair ar hugain oed o'r enw
Bep Voskuijl, ac roedden nhw i gyd wedi eu hysbysu ein bod ni ar ein ffordd. Ni chafodd
tad Mr Voskuijl, tad Bep, sy'n gweithio yn y warws, a'i ddau gynorthwywr, wybod dim...

Grisiau coed sy'n arwain o'r cyntedd i'r ail lawr. Mae yna landin ar dop y grisiau a drysau o
boptu. Fe aiff drws ar y chwith â ti i'r adran storio perlysiau, yr atig a'r groglofft yn rhan flaen y
tŷ. Mae rhes o risiau, sy'n serth iawn a pheryglus ac yn nodweddiadol o'r Iseldiroedd, yn arwain
o ffrynt y tŷ i ddrws arall sy'n agor i'r stryd. Mae'r drws ar y dde yn arwain i'r 'Rhandy Dirgel'
yng nghefn y tŷ. Fyddai neb byth yn dyfalu bod yna gymaint o stafelloedd y tu ôl i'r drws llwyd,
plaen. Un ris fach o flaen y drws, a dyna ti i mewn. Yn union o dy flaen, rhes serth o risiau. I'r
chwith, cyntedd cul yn agor i ystafell sy'n gweithredu fel ystafell fyw a llofft i'r teulu Frank. Y
drws nesaf, ystafell lai, llofft a stydi dwy foneddiges ifanc y teulu. Ar y dde i'r grisiau, ystafell
fechan ddi-ffenestr yn cynnwys y toiled a sinc ac yna ddrws arall i stafell Margot a fi.

Os ei di i fyny'r grisiau ac agor y drws ar y brig fe gei di syndod o weld ystafell mor fawr ac
mor olau mewn hen dŷ ar fin y canal fel hwn. Mae hi'n cynnwys stof (diolch i'r ffaith iddi fod
unwaith yn labordy i Mr Kugler) a sinc. Hon fydd y gegin a llofft Mr a Mrs van Daan, yn ogystal
â bod yn ystafell fyw, ystafell fwyta a stydi i ni i gyd. Yr ystafell fechan oddi ar y coridor fydd
llofft Peter van Daan. Mae yma atig a chroglofft fel yn ffrynt y tŷ. A dyna ti. Rydw i rŵan wedi
dy gyflwyno di i'r cyfan o'n rhandy hyfryd ni.

datgelu - disclose	*cyntedd - foyer*
fesul tipyn - bit by bit	*perlysiau - herbs*
cytundeb - agreement	*nodweddiadol - characteristic*
gweithredu - implement	*rhandy - secret apartment*
dygymod ag - to cope with	*boneddiges - lady*
dieithriaid - strangers	*brig - top*
hysbysu - notified	*yn ogystal â - as well as*
cynorthwywr - assistant	*oddi ar - off the*

Gwybodaeth

Daw'r darn hwn o *Dyddiadur Anne Frank*, a addaswyd i'r Gymraeg gan Eigra Lewis
Roberts. Cadwodd Anne Frank ddyddiadur o Fehefin 12 1942 hyd at Awst 1944,
yn ystod yr Ail Ryfel Byd pan oedd yn cuddio rhag yr Almaenwyr. Ar ôl iddi gael
ei harestio ganddyn nhw daeth dwy ysgrifenyddes oedd yn gweithio yn yr adeilad
o hyd i'r dyddiaduron a'u rhoi i'w thad.

Tasgau

Bydd y rhan fwyaf o ddysgwyr yn gyfarwydd â hanes Anne Frank a'i dyddiaduron. Dyma gyfle i'w cyflwyno i'r fersiwn Cymraeg, sydd yn seiliedig ar y fersiwn na chafodd ei olygu gan Otto Frank, ei thad. Awgrymir:

- Cael trafodaeth gyffredinol yn y dosbarth am hanes Anne a nodi'r pwyntiau ar y bwrdd gwyn. Gellir trafod ymweliadau aelodau'r dosbarth â'i chuddfan os yw hynny'n berthnasol.

- Gwrando ar y darn a dilyn y sgript. Nodi pwyntiau ychwanegol.

- Dosbarthu'r testun i barau a gofyn iddyn nhw greu llun syml o'r adeilad, ar sail eu darlleniad o'r ail a'r trydydd paragraff.

- Gofyn i'r aelodau ystyried, mewn parau, mai merch dair ar ddeg oed a ysgrifennodd y dyddiadur a cheisio rhoi portread ohoni ar sail y darn a'r hyn a ddywedwyd gan aelodau eraill y dosbarth.

Pwyntiau Iaith

Mae llawer o eirfa'n ymwneud ag adeiladau'n codi yn y darn, a gall y rhain fod yn anodd. Awgrymir dechrau drwy roi nifer ar y bwrdd gwyn, e.e. cyntedd, llofft, grisiau, to llechi, ac ati. Yna, awgrymir dosbarthu taflenni gwerthwyr tai'n disgrifio tai gwahanol (mae digonedd ar y rhyngrwyd). Gellir gofyn i bob un lunio disgrifiad Cymraeg tebyg i'r rhain o'i dŷ ei hun, gan ddefnyddio'r taflenni fel sbardunau.

Sgwrsio Pellach

Oes perthnasau ganddyn nhw sydd wedi bod mewn rhyfel neu sy'n aelodau o'r fyddin heddiw?

Ydyn nhw'n cofio ffilmiau neu lyfrau am ryfel ac effeithiau rhyfela?

Ydyn nhw'n cadw dyddiaduron?

Ysgrifennu

Ysgrifennu dyddiadur dychmygol am rywbeth a ddigwyddodd iddynt pan oedden nhw'n blant neu yn eu harddegau. Gellir gwneud y darn fel gwaith cartref gan ofalu peidio â'i ddangos i aelodau eraill y dosbarth. Ar ôl i'r tiwtor ei farcio, gellir teipio'r darn a dod ag ef i'r dosbarth. Gall y tiwtor gymysgu'r copïau a'u dosbarthu i aelodau'r dosbarth. Bydd yr aelodau yn darllen y darnau yn uchel. Bydd aelodau'r dosbarth yn dyfalu pwy ysgrifennodd y darnau ac yn rhoi rhesymau dros eu dewis.

22. Darnau allan o'r stori **Bleind Dêt**, o'r gyfrol **Darnau** gan Dylan Iorwerth

Yn rhyfedd iawn roedd hi'n fwy gofalus nag arfer wrth baratoi. Awr a mwy cyn bod wirioneddol raid, roedd hi wedi eistedd wrth y drych yng nghornel ei hystafell wely i weithio ar ei gwallt a'i cholur. A doedd dim pwynt gwadu ei bod hi'n nerfus. Roedd yna lawer o bobl wedi trio disgrifio'r teimlad - pili pala, cwlwm yn y perfedd - ond doedd neb yn gallu dal y cyfuniad o bwysau a chryndod yn nwfn y stumog. Y gamp, fel arfer, oedd taro'r balans iawn rhwng diniweidrwydd a phrofiad ond fod hynny, y tro yma, yn fwy anodd nag arfer. Bron nad oedd hi'n teimlo fel rhoi'r gorau i'r holl beth.

Codi ei gwallt wnaeth hi yn y diwedd, a'i gadw yn ei le gyda'r clip enamel lliwgar o Foroco. Roedd hynny'n rhoi cyfle iddi wisgo'r cylchoedd arian yn glustdlysau; fel arfer, roedd hi'n teimlo eu bod nhw'n rhy fawr, a thrwsgl hyd yn oed, ond heno roedd angen bod yn drawiadol a hyderus. Neu, o leiaf, rhoi argraff o hynny... Wyddai hi ddim sut fath o beth y byddai yntau'n ei hoffi. Mi wenodd arni hi ei hun yn y drych am fod mor wirion.

gwadu - to deny	*rhoi'r gorau - to give up*
perfedd - guts	*trawiadol - striking*
diniweidrwydd - innocence	*trwsgl - clumsy*

Disgwyl dynes fregus oedd o. Un oedd yn awyddus am ddyn. Ar ôl cyfnod heb yr un, efallai. Am argraff felly roedd o wedi chwilio wrth ddarllen yn fanwl trwy'r cynigion. Fel byseddu trwy gatalog Argos. Doedd y disgrifiad ohono'i hun ddim yn hollol gelwyddog. Gorliwio rhinweddau, o bosib, ond dyna fyddech chi'n ei ddisgwyl wrth drefnu bleind dêt - rhoi'r pethau gorau yn y ffenest. Y pethau oedd yn cael eu hepgor oedd fwyaf allweddol. Fyddech chi ddim yn cyfaddef eich bod yn alcoholig, neu wedi gadael eich gwraig gyntaf ar ôl ei churo, neu eich bod newydd ddod allan o'r carchar. Gêm oedd hi wedi'r cyfan, a phawb yn deall y rheolau. Doedd dim angen teimlo'n euog, felly. Roedd unrhyw un oedd yn chwilio am gariad trwy asiantaeth a hysbyseb papur newydd yn gwybod y sgôr, neu'n rhy ddespret i boeni. Roedd rhaid iddo yntau ddarllen rhwng y llinellau wrth ddewis. Trio teimlo'r awydd y tu ôl i'r geiriau a thrio gweld arlliw o unigrwydd yn y llygaid yn y llun. Dim ond gobeithio ei bod hi wedi anfon llun go iawn. Meg oedd ei henw hi. Roedd wedi gwneud yn hollol siŵr ei fod yn cofio'r enw. Jyst dros ei ddeg ar hugain. Digon smart ond heb fod yn fodel, chwaith. Mi fyddai hynny'n ormod i'w ddisgwyl.

bregus - vulnerable	*rhinwedd/au - virtue/s*
cynigion - offers	*hepgor - omit*
gorliwio - exaggerate	*arlliw - trace*

Gwybodaeth
Daw'r darnau hyn o'r gyfrol *Darnau* gan Dylan Iorwerth. Dyma'r llyfr a enillodd y Fedal Ryddiaith *(Prose Medal)* yn yr Eisteddfod Genedlaethol yn 2005. Mae Dylan Iorwerth yn Olygydd-Gyfarwyddwr cylchgrawn *Golwg*.

Tasgau

Yn y darn hwn mae'r dyn a'r ferch yn paratoi am ddêt. Gobeithir y bydd y darnau hyn yn symbylu'r dysgwyr i ddarllen y stori hon i gyd yn y pen draw. Awgrymir:

- Cychwyn trwy wrando ar y darnau. Gofyn i bawb geisio cofio popeth ynghylch y dyfyniadau sy'n dwyn atgofion iddyn nhw, a chrynhoi rhai o'r pwyntiau hyn ar y bwrdd gwyn.

- Ail-greu testun. Ar ôl gwrando ar y darnau a'u darllen nifer o weithiau, awgrymir gofyn i'r dosbarth guddio'r darnau. Yna, rhoi nifer o eiriau sbardun iddyn nhw o un o'r darnau ar y bwrdd gwyn, a gofyn iddyn nhw ail-lunio'r darn. Tasg lafar yw hon ac ar ôl gorffen, gellir ailedrych ar y testun gwreiddiol i weld pa mor agos oedden nhw. Dyma enghreifftiau o'r geiriau allweddol o'r darn cyntaf: gofalus, paratoi, drych, colur, pili pala, diniweidrwydd, gwallt, enamel, clust-dlysau, trwsgl, mi wenodd.

- Gellir ailedrych ar y darnau a thrafod a fyddai'r ddau gymeriad yn dod ymlaen yn dda ai peidio.

Pwyntiau Iaith
Awgrymir defnyddio'r testun eto a gadael bylchau. Rhaid cuddio'r darnau gwreiddiol a'u cyfannu, ar sail yr hyn maen nhw'n ei gofio. Gellir hepgor mwy a mwy o eiriau gyda dosbarth da, sydd wedi amsugno'r darnau o'r gweithgareddau blaenorol.

Sgwrsio Pellach
Sut maen nhw'n paratoi i fynd allan?
Ydyn nhw'n cofio mynd ar ddêt am y tro cyntaf?
Ydyn nhw'n cofio tro trwstan (*awkward incident*) wrth drefnu dêt erioed?

Darllen Pellach
Yn y stori *Bleind Dêt* mae rhywbeth annisgwyl yn digwydd. Mae hi yn y gyfrol *Darnau* gan Dylan Iorwerth. Gall y dosbarth ddarllen y stori i gyd, a'i thrafod.

Ysgrifennu
Gellir annog y dosbarth i ysgrifennu am brofiad rhyfedd neu am dro trwstan a ddigwyddodd iddyn nhw.

23.　Banc Sylwadau gan Aled Lewis Evans

Dewch i gyfarfod â'r peiriannau newydd,
dim isio amlenni,
dim ond cyffwrdd â'r sgrin,
anweswn y sgrin.
Yn lle gwên person gynt,
gogleisiwn orchmynion y sgrin.

A rŵan mae ciwiau pigog
nid at bobl ond at beiriannau,
a'r rheini'n torri.
'Dan ni'n aros am beiriant arall,' medd staff streslyd.
O'r cefnau yn rhywle daw fflyd â'u ffeiliau am beiriannau
gan straffaglu o'u cwmpas
heb fedru trin na pherson a pheiriant
i gynnig cwnsela am drin peiriannau nad ydyn nhw'n gweithio.
Gwenant yn ddel yn enw 'Gwella Gwasanaeth.'

Mae gan beiriannau, wedi'r cyfan, hawl i dorri
mewn arbrawf o'r fath efo'r banciau steil newydd,
ond fiw i bobl dorri!

Heibio i'r peiriannau a'r ddelwedd slic,
ym mhen draw'r ganolfan newydd,
er hwylustod,
os ydych chi wirioneddol ar ben eich tennyn,
fe eistedda
person o gig a gwaed,
â golwg ryfedd, anghysurus ar ei wep
o weld person arall yn cyrraedd am sgwrs.

Ceisia argyhoeddi'r cwsmer
sydd am ganslo'i forgais deugain mlynedd bod ymwared.
Efallai bod yn well ganddo siarad wyneb-yn-wyneb
efo pobl i lawr y lôn,
ond cyn iddo fod yn fyrbwyll, gofynnir iddo
aros mewn ciw arall, a chodi'r ffôn
ar y dyn bach clên sydd ar ben y lein yn India
i drafod unrhyw broblemau allai godi.

peiriant/peiriannau - machine/s
amlen/ni - envelope/s

anwesu - to fondle, cherish

goglais - to tickle, gorchmynion - commands

pigog - prickly, bad tempered

fflyd - llawer o bobl
straffaglu - ffwdanu, ffysian

cwnsela - counselling
gwella gwasanaeth - improving service

arbrawf - experiment
fiw i - but people must not

delwedd - image

hwylustod - convenience
pen eich tennyn - end of your tether

gwep - grimace

argyhoeddi - to convince
ymwared - deliverance

byrbwyll - rash, impulsive

clên - hoffus

Gwybodaeth
Daw'r gerdd hon o gyfrol Aled Lewis
Evans, *Dim Angen Creu Teledu Yma*.
Mae'n ysgrifennu yn nhafodiaith
gogledd Cymru ac yn cael ei ysbrydoli
fel bardd gan ardal y gogledd-ddwyrain
lle mae'n byw ac yn gweithio.

Tasgau

Mae'r gerdd hon yn trafod profiadau cyfoes sy'n gyfarwydd i lawer ohonom. Defnyddir llawer o eiriau ac ymadroddion gogleddol ynddi. Awgrymir:

- Cyflwyno geiriau tafodieithol anghyfarwydd i'r dosbarth cyn chwarae'r CD, yn enwedig i ddosbarthiadau mewn ardaloedd deheuol. e.e. geiriau fel *isio, rŵan, fflyd, clên, efo, straffaglu, ond fiw i...*

- Chwarae'r gerdd ar y CD ddwywaith gan oedi ar ôl pob pennill yr ail waith er mwyn sicrhau eu bod yn ei deall.

- Rhannu'r dosbarth yn barau a gofyn iddyn nhw greu deialog yn seiliedig ar sefyllfa pennill olaf y gerdd lle mae cwsmer eisiau canslo'i forgais deugain mlynedd.

- Rhoi cyfle i'r dosbarth cyfan wrando ar rai o'r deialogau uchod.

Pwyntiau Iaith

Gan fod y gerdd yn ymwneud â chyfleustra diwyneb y byd modern, dyma gyfle i drafod termau technegol yn Gymraeg. Mae rhai geiriau wedi hen ymsefydlu, e.e. cyfrifiadur, gwefan, ond ydy'r dosbarth yn gallu dyfalu beth yw ystyr y termau isod? Ydy'r termau Cymraeg yn well neu'n waeth na'r rhai Saesneg?

1.	bysellfwrdd	[keyboard]	6.	gwirydd	[checker]
2.	cof bach	[memory stick]	7.	rhyngwyneb	[interface]
3.	newidyn	[variable]	8.	unioni	[justify]
4.	cyrchwr	[cursor]	9.	mewnbwn/allbwn	[input/output]
5.	hafalnod	[= equal sign]	10.	meddalwedd	[software]

Gellir gofyn i'r dosbarth am unrhyw dermau rhyfedd y maen nhw wedi dod ar eu traws. Mae'n werth eu cyfeirio at *Y Termiadur* a gyhoeddwyd gan Awdurdod Cymwysterau, Cwricwlwm ac Asesu Cymru.

Sgwrsio Pellach

Ydy hi'n anodd delio â chwmnïau cyhoeddus dros y ffôn neu'r cyfrifiadur? Ydy cyfrifiaduron yn fwy o felltith (*curse*) nag o fendith (*blessing*)?

Ysgrifennu

Ysgrifennu llythyr at bennaeth cwmni neu wasanaeth yn cwyno am brofiad anffodus a gafwyd.

24. Darn o **Martha, Jac a Sianco** gan Caryl Lewis

"Dewch nawr te, myn uffarn i, ne bydd hi 'di goleuo cyn i ni gyrradd."

"F...f....fi ff...ff...ffeili gweld..."

"Dewch nôl â'r gole 'na fan hyn, Jac, er mwyn Duw, ne byddwn ni 'di torri'n coese'n tri."

Roedd Jac yn mynd yn ei gyfer a golau'r fflachlamp yn bownsio o glawdd i glawdd wrth iddo hercian lan y lôn.

"Fe ddalwn ni'r diawled wrthi nawr. Ma rhywbeth od yn mynd mla'n 'ma a dwi'n gweud tho chi, Duw â'u helpo nhw pan ga i afael ynddyn nhw."

Gwyliodd Martha gefn Jac yn mynd o'i blaen yn y tywyllwch wedi ei amlinellu yng ngolau'r tortsh. Roedd hi'n dywyll bitsh.

"Jac achan! Dos dim prawf bod neb yn neud dim iddi. Falle bod rhyw lo yn dod ac yn 'i sugno hi yn y nos".

"Pwy lo sy'n dod mewn, fenyw? Rhowch drad yn tir, wir, a peidwch bod mor dwp. Y rhacsyn na drws nesa sy wrthi ynta... gadel gate ar agor a rhoi harne yn y rhesi gwair amser c'nea. Ne'r Wil na ochr arall i Ca' Marged. Tato o'r un rhych ŷn nhw i gyd. Synnen i fochyn 'u bod nhw'n chwerthin ar 'yn penne ni nawr."

Clywodd Martha Sianco'n gwenwyno y tu ôl iddi.

"Dere mlan nawr te, Sianco bach, dala lan wir."

Cyrhaeddodd Jac a Martha ben y lôn dywyll a oedd yn rhedeg gyda'r clôs ac yn hollti fferm Graig-ddu yn dair: y Banc, Hendre a'r Macyn Poced. Pwysodd y ddau ar y giât er mwyn aros am Sianco a oedd yn dal i straffaglu ei ffordd drwy'r stecs a'r tywyllwch. Cydiai Jac mewn pocer hir yn un llaw - roedd yn mynd i'w ddefnyddio ar gopa unrhyw un y deuai ar eu traws. Wrth i'r ddau edrych i mewn i'r tywyllwch sylwodd Martha fod y fuwch yn y cae wedi codi ar ei thraed. O'r diwedd cyrhaeddodd Sianco â'i gap gwyrdd gwlân yn dynn am ei ben, ei derier yn edrych mas o dan ei siwmper gyda'i lygaid bach duon wedi'u serio ar y fuwch yn barod.

"Reit te, yn dawel bach nawr, ewn ni i gwato yn y claw'. Os daw rhywun ar gyfyl y lle 'ma wedyn, fe sbadda i fe!"

ffaelu - methu	*tato o'r un rhych* - *all the same*
yn ei gyfer - yn gyflym	*gwenwyno* - cwyno
hercian - *limping*	*clos* - buarth, *farmyard*
diawled - *devils*	*macyn* - hances
amlinellu - *outlined*	*cwato* - cuddio
trad yn tir - cyflymu	*sbaddu* - *to castrate*
rhacsyn - dyn drwg	
c'nea - cynhaeaf	

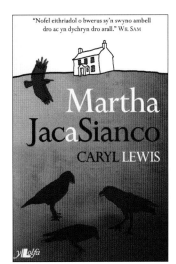

Gwybodaeth
Dechrau'r nofel *Martha, Jac a Sianco* (2004) gan Caryl Lewis. Enillodd y nofel hon gystadleuaeth Llyfr y Flwyddyn a chafodd ei haddasu yn ffilm yn 2008. Hanes dau frawd a chwaer sy'n byw gyda'i gilydd ar fferm yng nghefn gwlad Ceredigion a geir ynddi. Daw Caryl Lewis, y nofelydd ifanc, o Geredigion hefyd, ac mae hi wedi cyhoeddi nifer o lyfrau eraill.

Tasgau

Mae'r nofel hon yn llawn tafodiaith. Awgrymir:

- Chwarae'r CD yn syth neu gyflwyno geirfa yn gyntaf, yn ôl gallu a lleoliad daearyddol y grŵp.

- Yn union ar ôl y gwrandawiad gellir edrych ar y sgript a'r geiriau cyn gwrando ar y CD unwaith eto.

- Er mwyn rhoi profiad pellach o'r dafodiaith gellir rhannu'r dosbarth yn barau neu drioedd a cheisio darllen ac ynganu darnau o'r deialogau.

- Rhannu'r dosbarth yn grwpiau bach unwaith eto a gofyn iddyn nhw drafod a disgrifio'r tri chymeriad.

- Adrodd yn ôl i'r dosbarth cyfan a gwrando ar y darn unwaith eto.

Pwyntiau Iaith

- Rhannu'r dosbarth yn barau a gofyn iddyn nhw lunio tair colofn. Yn y golofn gyntaf, byddant yn nodi 5 enghraifft o dafodiaith o'r tesun. Yn yr ail golofn, byddant yn trosi'r geiriau / ymadroddion tafodieithol i iaith safonol. Yn y drydedd golofn, byddant yn rhoi ffurf ogleddol y geiriau / ymadroddion. Dyma enghreifftiau posib:

Ceredigion	'Safonol'	Gogleddol
gole		
coese		
lan		
achan		
Synnen i fochyn		
cwato		
rhacsyn		

Sgwrsio Pellach

Oes pobl hen ffasiwn, fel cymeriadau'r nofel hon, y mae'r dysgwyr yn eu nabod?

Gellir gwylio darn cyntaf y ffilm sy'n seiliedig ar y nofel hon. Enillodd y ffilm hon lawer o wobrau. Ond dylid eu hannog i ddarllen y nofel cyn dangos y ffilm i gyd. Ydyn nhw'n mwynhau'r llyfr yn fwy na'r ffilm?

Ysgrifennu

Gofyn iddyn nhw ysgrifennu darn o ddeialog rhwng dau gymeriad o gefn gwlad, gan ddefnyddio tafodiaith leol.

25. Darn allan **Cymru Fydd** gan Saunders Lewis

ACT II - *yr un noson, tua 10.15*

DEWI: Mi ddoist heb drwbwl?
BET: Dim trwbwl yn y byd.
DEWI: Dros y caeau?
BET: Mi ddois ar hyd y ffordd fawr drwy'r pentre ac wedyn ar hyd y lôn yma.
DEWI: Welaist ti ddim plismyn?
BET: Mae'r plismyn siŵr o fod yn gwylio'r caeau amdanat. Roedd y pentre a'r lôn yn rhydd. Heblaw hynny mi all merch y ficer alw i weld gwraig y gweinidog am ddeg o'r gloch, debyg gen i.
DEWI: Dyro dy gôt i mi. *(Mae hithau'n tynnu ei chot a'r ffunen am ei phen ac yn ysgwyd ei gwallt yn rhydd. Mae hi'n ferch hardd tua'r ugain oed. Mae Dewi yn rhoi ei dillad hi ar y gadair.)*
BET: Roedd dy hanes di yn y newyddion ar y teledu heno.
DEWI: Be' ddwedson nhw?
BET: Iti ei gloywi hi yn y niwl a bwrw rhyw drafaeliwr yn ei ben a mynd â'i gar o.
DEWI: Ac wedyn?
BET: Rhoi rhif y car a gofyn am unrhyw wybodaeth.
DEWI: Wyt ti'n fy ffieiddio i?
BET: Ti ddaru fy ffonio i.
DEWI: Mentro.
BET: A dyma fi.
DEWI: Mae fy mywyd i yn dy law di.
BET: O'r gorau. Dyro gusan i mi. *(Cofleidio a chusanu)...* O Dewi!
DEWI: Sigarét?
BET: Diolch. *(Mae ef yn tanio a'r ddau yn smocio)*
DEWI: Does gen i ddim diod yma. Tŷ gweinidog.
BET: Does gen innau ddim acw. Tŷ ficer. *(Mae'r ddau yn chwerthin..saib)*
DEWI: Wel?
BET: Wn i ddim sut mae dechrau, Dewi.
DEWI: Na finnau.
BET: Mae dy weld di... fel deffro o hunllef. Ie, hunllef.
DEWI: Fuost ti'n poeni?
BET: Paid â dechrau fel yna.
DEWI: Y peth gorau ydi cychwyn fel y bydd pobl mewn sosial. On'd ydy hi'n noson gas? Ddaru ti 'lychu wrth ddŵad?
BET: Naddo diolch yn fawr, syr. Doedd dim glaw. 'Lychais i ddim.
DEWI: A sut mae'r ficer y dyddiau yma? Ydy o'n cael iechyd?
BET: Rhyw fymryn o beswch reit hwylus. Newydd fynd i'w wely. Gan amlaf tua'r un ar ddeg y bydd o'n clwydo.
DEWI: Rwyt ti'n para i gadw tŷ iddo fo?
BET: Does gen i ddim dewis a Nain wedi marw.

debyg gen i - it seems to me
ffunen - hances/sgarff
gloywi hi - dianc/rhedeg
ffieiddio - casáu
ddaru - wnaeth
cofleidio - to caress
saib - pause
hunllef - nightmare
lychu - gwlychu
sosial - social event
clwydo - mynd i'r gwely

Gwybodaeth
Roedd Saunders Lewis yn un o ddramodwyr Cymraeg mwyaf enwog yr ugeinfed ganrif. Ganwyd ef yn Lerpwl ac yn fab i weinidog Methodist. Perfformiwyd *Cymru Fydd* gyntaf yn 1967. Mae Dewi, sydd hefyd yn fab y Mans, wedi troi yn droseddwr ac wedi cael ei garcharu. Cyn yr olygfa hon mae Dewi wedi dianc o'r carchar. Mae e'n cuddio yn nhŷ ei rieni ac mae ei gariad, Bet, wedi dod i'w weld. Dyma mae Saunders Lewis yn ei ddweud am y ddrama: 'Drama sy'n ymwneud â gwleidyddiaeth a chrefydd yw hi... Dweud rhywbeth am y dewis sy'n wynebu Cymru heddiw yw mater y ddrama... a hynny ar lun stori.'

Tasgau

Mae'r ddeialog ar ddechrau'r ail act yn llifo'n hawdd ac wedi cael ei hysgrifennu mewn tafodiaith ogleddol. Awgrymir:

- Chwarae'r ddeialog ar y CD cyn rhoi cefndir y ddrama a'r awdur, a gofyn i'r aelodau nodi popeth maen nhw wedi'i ddeall. Beth sydd wedi digwydd i'r cymeriadau - Dewi a Bet - a beth yw'r cysylltiad rhyngddyn nhw? Dylid nodi'r pwyntiau ar y bwrdd gwyn.

- Rhoi'r cefndir iddynt cyn chwarae'r CD yr ail waith gan nodi rhai pwyntiau ychwanegol ar y bwrdd gwyn ar ôl yr ail wrandawiad.

- Ar ôl y darlleniad mewn parau, gellir uno dau bâr i ffurfio grŵp o bedwar gan ofyn i'r parau 'gyfarwyddo' darlleniadau ei gilydd. Gellid eu hannog i wella ambell ynganiad, cyflymder y darn, newid goslef y lleisiau wrth esgus eu bod yn barchus mewn 'sosial'.

Pwyntiau Iaith

Mae'r ffurf 'ddaru' yn codi'n aml, a gall fod yn ddieithr, gan ei bod yn fwy cyffredin yn y gogledd ddwyrain. Gellir esbonio ei bod yn ffordd arall o fynegi'r gorffennol cwmpasog,

e.e. Ddaru mi fynd   - Mi wnes i fynd   - Es i

Awgrymir gofyn i'r dosbarth newid y ffurfiau isod, sy'n cynnwys 'ddaru', gan ddefnyddio 'gwneud' ac yna'r gorffennol cryno.

1. Ddaru ni weld
2. Ddaru hi fwynhau
3. Ddaru'r plant wlychu
4. Ddaru chdi ffonio adre?
5. Ti ddaru brynu'r car?
6. Ddaru mi mo'i weld o
7. John ddaru ffonio ddoe?
8. Beth ddaru chi 'neud?

Sgwrsio Pellach

Mae Saunders Lewis yn dweud ei bod yn ddrama am y dewis sy'n wynebu Cymru ym 1967. Ceir tyndra a gwrthdaro ynddi rhwng yr hen werthoedd e.e. crefydd y tad a'r mab digrefydd. Gellir gofyn y cwestiynau isod:

Oes tyndra a gwrthdaro yng Nghymru heddiw, ym marn y dysgwyr?
Beth yw'r dewisiadau sy'n wynebu pobl Cymru heddiw?

Ysgrifennu

Gellir annog y mwyaf mentrus yn y dosbarth i ysgrifennu deialog rhwng dau gymeriad sy'n dangos gwrthdaro cyfoes.

26. Detholiad o **Ciwcymbars Wolverhampton** gan Ifor ap Glyn

Gwnes ddarganfyddiad brawychus
a'm gadawodd yn gwbl syn;
mae ciwcymbars Wolverhampton
yn Gymreiciach na'r bobl ffor' hyn.

*darganfyddiad brawychus -
frightening discovery*

Cymreiciach - yn fwy o Gymry

Darllenais i'r peth yn y papur,
cynhyrfais yn lân reit drwydda'.
Roedd y peth yno'n glir, mewn du a gwyn
a dyw'r *Sun* ddim am ddeud c'lwydda.

c'lwydda - celwyddau

Rhyw fodio'n ddiniwed yr oeddwn
rhwng pej thri a thudalen y bets
pan ddarllenais fod ein cyrff ni
'fath 'nunion â cemistri sets!

bodio - to thumb

'fath 'nunion - yr un peth

O'n i'n meddwl mai esgyrn a pherfedd
fu gen i tu mewn erioed,
nid rhyw *calcium, potassium,*
carbon a dŵr - a haearn hyd yn oed.

esgyrn - bones
perfedd - guts, entrails

haearn - iron

Ie, rhywbeth fel dur ydi cariad pur
ond mae haearn go iawn gin bob dyn,
ac mae haearn ym mynwes pob dynes
a silicon ym mrest ambell un.
(Ond awn ni ddim ar ôl hynny rŵan.)

dur - steel
gin - gan
mynwes - bosom

Er bod gennym dipyn o haearn
'dan ni 70 y cant yn ddŵr!
(Pam 'di'r dŵr ddim yn rhydu'r haearn?
Dyw'r gwyddonwyr ddim yn siŵr.)

rhydu - to rust
gwyddonwyr - scientists

Ie, mae 70 y cant o bob un yn ddŵr.
Wel, dyna i chi ffaith!
Galwyni o Dryweryn wyf
yn slochian ar fy nhaith.

galwyni - gallons
slochian - dŵr yn cadw sŵn

Nawr, dyw'r bobol yn Bilston a Handsworth
ddim yn swnio fel Cymry, bid siŵr,
ond maen nhw'n yfed y dŵr o Dryweryn
ac maen nhw 70 y cant yn ddŵr!

bid siŵr - mae'n sicr

Cymry pibell os nad Cymry pybyr
ydi'r rhain; mae'r cyfrifiad yn rong:
cans Cymry o waed coch cyfa'
yw pob Leroy, pob Singh a phob Wong.

pybyr - staunch, enthusiastic
cyfrifiad - census
cyfa - cyfan

Achos wedyn y daeth y dadrithiad.
Roedd y papur hefyd yn crybwyll
be sy mewn llysiau a phethau byw eraill -
fel y ciwcymbar bondigrybwyll!

dadrithiad - disillusionment
crybwyll - yn sôn

*bondigrybwyll - hardly
mentionable*

Er bod lot o ddŵr ynom ninnau
mae gan giwcymbars 90 y cant!
Mae ciwcymbars Wolverhampton
yn Gymreiciach na ninnau a'n plant.

Gwybodaeth
Daw'r gerdd hon o gyfrol Ifor ap Glyn, *Holl Garthion Pen Cymro Ynghyd*.
Mae'n enedigol o Lundain ac yn fab i deulu Cymraeg. Ef yw'r unig fardd
i ennill coron yr Eisteddfod Genedlaethol am lunio cerddi am ddysgwyr.
Mae'n gyfarwyddwr a chyflwynydd rhaglenni teledu Cymraeg ar S4C.

Tasgau

Mae'n bwysig bod y dysgwyr yn mwynhau'r perfformiad o'r gerdd ddoniol hon.

Awgrymir:

- Er mwyn sicrhau eu bod yn mwynhau'r perfformiad yn syth, cyflwyno'r eirfa anoddaf a'r ffurfiau tafodieithol i'r dysgwyr ar gardiau fflach cyn gwrando ar y gerdd, e.e. darganfyddiad, brawychus, bodio, diniwed, perfedd, esgyrn, dur, haearn, crybwyll, bondigrybwyll, Cymreiciach. Gellir egluro'r ffurfiau gogleddol e.e. ffor' hyn, c'lwydda, drwydda, rŵan, 'fath 'nunion - os oes angen.

- Gwrando a mwynhau'r perfformiad ohoni. Adolygu'r eirfa a'r anawsterau.

- Gwrando arni yn syth eto ar ôl egluro'r anawsterau.

- Trafod, mewn parau, pa bethau sy'n eu goglais/neu ddim yn eu goglais nhw. Dyfynnu llinellau doniol ac adrodd yn ôl i'r grŵp mawr. Ydyn nhw'n gallu esbonio'r jôc sydd wrth wraidd y gerdd yn eu geiriau eu hunain?

Pwyntiau Iaith
Awgrymir cymryd y gair 'Cymreiciach' fel man cychwyn. Ydy'r dysgwyr yn gallu creu ffurfiau cymharol tebyg, ac yna frawddegau, ar sail y sbardunau hyn? A oes patrwm i'w weld?

1. Seisnig
2. cyfoethog
3. diniwed
4. caled
5. gwlyb
6. ffyrnig
7. teg
8. llydan

Sgwrsio Pellach
Gellir eu hannog i siarad am bethau doniol a ddigwyddodd iddyn nhw neu i'w cydnabod yn ddiweddar. Gall fod yn ddigwyddiad yn y pentre neu'r ardal, neu stori a oedd yn y papur newydd hyd yn oed.

Ysgrifennu
Pa raglenni teledu neu radio, neu lyfrau sy'n gwneud iddyn nhw chwerthin? Gellir gofyn iddyn nhw lunio adolygiad byr yn esbonio pam mae'r rhaglen neu'r llyfr yn ddoniol.

27. Llwybr Llygoden allan o **Pentigily** gan Hefin Wyn

A fuoch chi erioed ar hyd Llwybr Llygoden? Naddo, ddim erioed? Damed mwy nag y buoch chi erioed efallai yn 'Alltcafan' yng nghwmni dychymyg y bardd. Wel fuoch chi ym mhentref Llandudoch 'te? Mae cropian ar hyd y Llwybr Llygoden yn her i'r fegin... os am gyrraedd y copa heb gymryd hoe.

Tebyg eich bod wedi synhwyro nad yw Llwybr Llygoden gyda'r hawsaf o lwybrau i'w ddringo. Prin y gellir ei goncro trwy gerdded ling-di-long gan oedi i fwrw golwg ar yr aber obry neu i syllu'n freuddwydiol i gyfeiriad Ynys Aberteifi.

Mae Llandudoch, neu Lland'och i'r cyfarwydd, yn wynebu tref Aberteifi ar draws yr afon a dyma'r pentref sydd yn eich croesawu i Sir Benfro wrth deithio ar hyd yr arfordir o gyfeiriad y Gogledd. Dyma'r adwy i'r sir sy'n llifeirio o hud a lledrith o ran ei thirwedd a'i phobol. Beth am ymuno â mi ar daith ar hyd arfordir y sir pentigily gan gychwyn ym mogel pentre Lland'och ar gopa Llwybr Llygoden? Dewch, wir, ar eich union.

Yn ôl Cyfrifiad 2001 dim ond 51 y cant o drigolion y pentref sydd bellach yn medru'r Gymraeg. Doedd dim amau mai pentref Cymraeg oedd Lland'och ym 1971 pan gofrestrwyd 77 y cant o drigolion yn medru'r Gymraeg ond ni ellir defnyddio'r disgrifiad hwnnw gyda'r un sicrwydd bellach. Er yr ymdrechion ymwybodol a wneir i gynnal a defnyddio'r Gymraeg yn gyhoeddus, ni ellir osgoi'r casgliad bod ei dyfodol, heb os, ar groesffordd yn sicr o ran parhau fel iaith y gymuned...

O gopa Llwybr Llygoden... does dim eisiau llawer o ddychymyg i gredu ein bod yn wynebu naill ai Sorrento neu Amalfi yn yr Eidal. Mae rhesi o dai ar hyd y llechwedd yn ddigon o ryfeddod ar fore clir. Hawdd credu bod rhywun rywbryd wedi cymryd hansh sylweddol o'r dirwedd fel petai'n cnoi afal. O edrych ar yr afon ddioglyd gellid dychmygu am eiliad ein bod yn syllu ar un o ddarluniau nodedig Richard Wilson. Wedi'r cyfan, gwyddom y bu'r Cymro yn y cyffiniau am iddo dynnu llun o Gilgerran a'i gastell sydd dim ond ychydig filltiroedd i fyny'r afon.

her i'r fegin - *challenge to the lungs*
hoe - seibiant
copa - *summit*
ling-di-long - cerdded yn araf a hamddenol
adwy - *gap*
obry - lawr yn y gwaelod
llifeirio o hud a lledrith - *flowing with magic and fantasy*
pentigily - bob cam, i gyd (*gair Sir Benfro*)
ym mogel (bogail) - *navel*
ymwybodol - *conscious/aware*
digon o ryfeddod - digon o syndod
cymryd hansh - *to take a bite*

Gwybodaeth
Dyma ddetholiad o bennod gyntaf llyfr Hefin Wyn am ei daith gerdded ar hyd llwybr arfordir Sir Benfro. Teitl y llyfr yw *Pentigily* (Gwasg y Lolfa 2008). Mewn unrhyw lyfr taith ceir cymysgedd o ysgrifennu disgrifiadol, dychymyg a ffeithiau.

Tasgau

Mae llyfrau taith yn boblogaidd iawn a cheir blas llenyddol yn y darn hwn, a blas ar dafodiaith Sir Benfro hefyd.

Awgrymir:

- Cyn gwrando ar y darn ar y CD, sôn am y cyfeiriadau a geir yn y darn at gerdd T.Llew Jones, *Cwm Alltcafan,* a lluniau'r arlunydd tirluniau Richard Wilson, ac os oes modd, dod â chopïau i'r dosbarth.

- Gwrando ar y CD yn gyntaf a gofyn i'r grŵp beth ddeallon nhw yn y darn. Gwrando eto, gan nodi'r eirfa anodd ar y bwrdd gwyn.

- Gofyn iddyn nhw nodi disgrifiadau'r awdur yn y darn. Ydyn nhw'n gallu dychmygu'r olygfa?
  Gellir awgrymu eu bod nhw'n disgrifio'r olygfa yn eu geiriau eu hunain.

Pwyntiau Iaith

Ceir nifer o idiomau diddorol yn y darn hwn. Dyma nifer o idiomau (mae rhai yn codi yn y darn ei hun) i'w rhoi ar y bwrdd gwyn. Yna, gellir gofyn i'r dysgwyr greu brawddegau gan ddefnyddio'r idiomau hyn:

1. mynd ling-di-long
2. cropian cyn cerdded
3. hud a lledrith
4. does dim dwywaith amdani
5. digon o ryfeddod
6. mynd yn ara' deg
7. bwrw'r Sul
8. igam ogam

Ydyn nhw'n gwybod am idiomau Cymraeg eraill?

Sgwrsio Pellach

Ceir un paragraff mwy ffeithiol yn y darn sy'n sôn am y Gymraeg ym mhentref Llandudoch. Gellir ailddarllen y paragraff a thrafod ei gynnwys.

Ydyn nhw'n synnu bod nifer y Cymry Cymraeg wedi syrthio o 70 y cant i 50 y cant mewn 30 mlynedd?

Ydyn nhw gallu cynnig rhesymau dros y dirywiad hwn?

Oes ateb i'r broblem?

Ydyn nhw'n gwybod am ardaloedd yng Nghymru lle mae nifer y siaradwyr wedi cynyddu?

Ysgrifennu

Annog y dysgwyr i lunio disgrifiad o'u hoff daith gerdded a gofyn iddyn nhw gymysgu darnau disgrifiadol ag ambell i ddarn ffeithiol, fel awdur y darn hwn.

28.   Darn o **Dirgel Ddyn** gan Mihangel Morgan

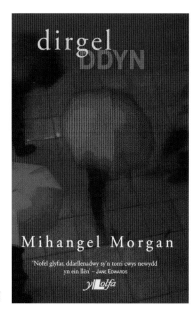

... Fe lwyddais i gael tipyn o waith yn y ddinas y flwyddyn
honno yn dysgu llenyddiaeth Gymraeg i oedolion, fel y
dywedais. Er gwaethaf fy ngradd ddilewyrch - ym marn
y cyflogwyr, - er gwaethaf f'awdlau aflwyddiannus - ym
marn y beirniaid, fe gyflwynwyd llenyddiaeth Cymru
i'm gofal i'w throsglwyddo i'm disgyblion a disgyblion
fy nisgyblion neu i'w plant ac i blant eu plant. Ac, wrth
gwrs, roedd llenyddiaeth fy mamiaith yn fy nghynnal;
y fath deimlad braf.

Ond pan ddihunais y bore hwnnw ac edrych ar y stafell o
un cwr i'r llall, gwelais nad oedd y gwaith, er mor glodwiw
ac anrhydeddus ydoedd, yn ddigon i gynnal hunan-barch.
Doedd cyflwr fy myw ddim wedi gwella llawer ers imi fod
ar y dôl. Roeddwn i'n dal i fyw yn yr un stafell fechan, yng
ngŵydd yr un llenni llwydion, yr un dillad gwely melyn,
yr un budreddi, yr un drewdod. Ac, ar ben y cyfan, roedd gen i ofidiau newydd: y baich o
sicrhau bod digon o bobl yn ymuno â'r dosbarthiadau, y gofid o orfod paratoi gwaith ar eu
cyfer. Doedd gen i mo'r gofidiau hynny ar y dôl, dim ond y budreddi a'r diffyg hunan-barch.

Roedd hi'n ddydd Mawrth eisoes a dosbarth i baratoi ar ei gyfer y noson honno. Trydydd
dosbarth y tymor newydd hefyd. Y rheol y pryd hynny oedd bod rhaid cael deg aelod
cofrestredig o leiaf wedi tanysgrifio i ddilyn y cwrs erbyn y drydedd wythnos; fel arall,
byddai'n rhaid cau'r dosbarth. Roeddwn i'n dibynnu ar yr arian yr oeddwn i'n eu cael
am y dosbarth hwnnw, felly doeddwn i ddim yn awyddus i'w weld yn dirwyn i ben.
Felly, penderfynais y cymerwn un o'r cardiau ymaelodi a'i lenwi. Roedd yna bentwr
ohonyn nhw ar y llawr ymhlith fy nodiadau. Heb godi o'r gwely, estynnais am un ac am
ysgrifbin ac yna dechrau ar y dasg o'i lenwi. Bu'n rhaid imi ddyfeisio cymeriad. Ni allwn
feddwl am enw - does gen i ddim dychymyg, dyna pam y byddwn i'n barddoni mewn
cynghanedd yn hytrach nag ysgrifennu rhyddiaith - felly, penderfynais ar yr enw Ann
Griffiths gan fy mod yn bwriadu cynnal dosbarth ar yr emynyddes y tymor hwnnw. Dyfeisiais
gyfeiriad ffug. Yna rhoddais y fenyw rithiol hon yn adran yr henoed. Fy mwriad oedd mynd
â'r cerdyn a'r arian i'r swyddfa y noson honno. Fe lyncid y celwydd ac fe achubid y dosbarth
o ganlyniad. Roedd yr ystryw yn un a dalai, felly - ddim ar ei chanfed, hwyrach, ond fe dalai.

dilewyrch - lacklustre
clodwiw - praiseworthy
yng ngŵydd - in the presence of...
emynydd - hymn-writer
ystryw - ruse

Gwybodaeth
Daw'r darn hwn o ddechrau'r nofel *Dirgel Ddyn* gan Mihangel Morgan. Cafodd y
nofel ei hysgrifennu yn y person cyntaf am helyntion tiwtor dosbarth nos. Cafodd
ei disgrifio fel nofel ddinesig, gyda'i 'blas cyfoes Ewropeaidd a'r panorama o ffilmiau
sy'n gefndir lliwgar iddi.' Daw Mihangel Morgan o Aberdâr yn wreiddiol. Dysgodd y
Gymraeg fel ail iaith ac erbyn hyn mae'n ddarlithydd yn y Gymraeg ym Mhrifysgol
Aberystwyth. Mae'n adrodd ei straeon mewn dull dychanol, doniol, ôl-fodern.

Tasgau

Daw'r darn hwn o ddechrau'r nofel, gan obeithio y bydd hynny yn symbylu'r myfyrwyr i'w darllen i gyd. Awgrymir:

- Chwarae'r darn ar y CD. Dylai'r elfen storïol yn y bennod hon ddenu'r dysgwyr i wrando heb orfod egluro llawer o'r eirfa ymlaen llaw.

- Annog y dosbarth i gydweithio â phartneriaid a cheisio cofio cymaint o ffeithiau am y siaradwr ag sy'n bosibl. Yna, gofyn iddynt newid partner a dechrau adrodd y stori ar sail eu nodiadau.

- I roi ychydig o amrywiaeth, gellir gofyn i bawb lunio cwestiynau darllen a deall ar ddarn o bapur, mewn parau. Yna, cyfnewid papurau â phâr arall ac ateb y cwestiynau hynny.

- Trafod fel dosbarth: Ydyn nhw eisiau darllen mwy? Pam? Pam ddim?

Pwyntiau Iaith

Mae nifer o enghreifftiau o ragenw mewnol yn codi yn y darn, e.e. *i'm, o'm, â'm*. Mae'r rhain yn codi mewn Cymraeg ffurfiol neu lenyddol gan amlaf. Maen nhw'n codi ar ôl: *a (and), â (as/with), gyda, tua, efo, na, i, o, mo (ddim o...)*. Dyma ymarferion lle bydd rhaid i'r dosbarth gywasgu'r rhagenw. Cofier bod y treiglad yn wahanol yn y person cyntaf - does dim treiglad meddal ar ôl *'m*, ond ceir *h* o flaen llafariad.

1.	Dw i'n mynd i + fy ngwaith am wyth o'r gloch.	[i'm gwaith]
2.	Dw i wedi chwarae mwy o rygbi na + fy mrawd.	[na'm brawd]
3.	Dw i'n teithio o + fy nghartref bob dydd.	[o'm cartref]
4.	Dw i a + fy nhad yn canu yn yr un côr.	[a'm tad]
5.	Dw i mor gyfoethog â + fy athro	[â'm hathro]
6.	Dw i ddim yn cofio fy mam-gu, na + fy nhad-cu.	[na'm tad-cu]
7.	Dw i'n deall i + fy ewythr gysylltu â + dy frawd.	[i'm hewythr, â'th frawd]
8.	Dw i'n mynd i + eu gweld nhw a + fy mhennaeth.	[i'w gweld, a'm pennaeth]

Ar lafar, gellir trafod yr un brawddegau yn y trydydd person, gan ddechrau pob un â 'Mae John...' ac yna 'Mae Mair...' Os bydd pawb yn ymdopi'n hawdd, gellir ymarfer yr ail berson unigol, gan ddechrau pob un â 'Rwyt ti...', e.e. Rwyt ti'n mynd i'th waith...

Sgwrsio Pellach

Ydy'r grŵp wedi cael trafferthion tebyg wrth ddod i gyrsiau Cymraeg neu gyrsiau llenyddiaeth?
Ydy'r tiwtor yn y darn yn debyg i diwtoriaid y maen nhw'n eu nabod?

Ysgrifennu

Gofyn i bawb ysgrifennu am eu profiad yn ymuno â dosbarth Cymraeg (neu unrhyw ddosbarth) fel oedolyn am y tro cyntaf.

29. Cerddi allan o **Dauwynebog** gan Ceri Wyn Jones

Y Cei yn Aberteifi

Fel glaw hallt, fel awel glyd, fel hiraeth,	*awel glyd - cosy breeze*
fel y wawr a'r machlud,	
mae ffarwél a dychwelyd	*dychwelyd - returning*
yn yr afon hon ynghyd.	*ynghyd - gyda'i gilydd*

Cywydd: Yr Aber

Pan ddaw mor ddistaw o ddu	
gŵn Annwn i gynhennu,	*Annwn - Underworld*
mae man a wnaiff wahaniaeth	*cynhennu - to quarrel*
- af am dro i'r fam o draeth.	
Mae o hyd ei storom wâr	*gwâr - civilised*
yn wallgof o gyfeillgar,	*gwallgof - insane*
a cheseirio'i chysuron	*ceseirio - hailstoning*
at fy mêr wna'r aber hon.	*mêr - marrow*
Ie, at y traeth af bob tro -	
fe wn y caf i yno	
dawelwch yn y dilyw,	*dilyw - deluge*
puraf oll po arwaf yw.	*po arwaf - the rougher (it is)*

Gwybodaeth

Daw'r darnau o'r gyfrol *Dauwynebog*, 2007. Enillodd Ceri Wyn Jones y
gadair yn yr Eisteddfod Genedlaethol yn y Bala yn 1997 am ysgrifennu awdl.
Fel y mae'r teitl yn awgrymu mae gwaith y bardd yn llawn deuoliaethau
(dualities). Gallwch weld yr englyn wedi ei gerfio ar y cei yn Aberteifi.

Tasgau

Dyma gyfle i'r myfyrwyr ymglywed â rhythmau'r gynghanedd a dysgu rhyw gymaint am fesurau fel yr englyn a'r cywydd. Awgrymir y dylai'r tiwtor:

- Eu hannog i wrando ar y darnau hyn yn cael eu hadrodd ar y CD ddwywaith cyn dechrau eu deall a'u trafod, gan fod gwrando ar farddoniaeth gynganeddol yn hollbwysig. Gellir nodi'n syml bod cynghanedd yn y llinellau a'u hannog i wrando ar eco'r cytseiniaid ymhob llinell.

- Annog y dosbarth i ddarllen yr englyn a'r cywydd mewn parau. Un aelod i ddarllen a'r llall i wrando bob yn ail.

- Fel dosbarth gofyn i rai ohonynt adrodd eu hoff linellau o safbwynt eu sain a'u hystyron.

- Er mwyn eu hannog i glywed y gynghanedd, gellir rhoi'r llinellau canlynol ar y bwrdd gwyn, **heb eu rhannu**, e.e. 'Fel glaw hallt fel awel glyd'. Wedyn gofyn i'r dysgwyr eu hadrodd yn eu pennau yn dawel yn gyntaf a gwrando ar eu sŵn. Yna, rhannu'r dosbarth yn ddau a gofyn i un hanner ddechrau dweud y llinell yn uchel a stopio pan fyddan nhw wedi cyrraedd canol y llinell, gan adael hanner arall y dosbarth i gario ymlaen.

hanner y dosbarth	yr hanner arall
Fel glaw hallt	fel awel glyd
yn wallgof	o gyfeillgar
a cheseirio'i	chysuron
af am dro i'r	fam o draeth

Gallwch ofyn iddyn nhw nodi'r cytseiniaid o dan y llinellau uchod er mwyn iddyn nhw weld y patrwm hefyd. Does dim angen i chi wybod am y gwahanol gynganeddion a manylu. Clywed yr eco sy'n bwysig.

- Gofyn i'r aelodau geisio crynhoi cynnwys yr englyn i frawddeg neu ddwy.

- Rhannu'r dosbarth yn barau a gofyn iddyn nhw wneud yr un peth gyda'r cywydd. Wedyn gellir cymharu eu disgrifiadau.

Pwyntiau Iaith
Mae'r cerddi'n llawn deuoliaethau a chyferbyniadau e.e. 'storom wâr'. Gellir rhoi tasg i'r grŵp feddwl am gyfuniadau annisgwyl fel hyn eu hunain. Awgrymir dechrau drwy roi enghreifftiau, e.e. Mae'r cerflun yn aflonydd... (er nad yw'r cerflun yn symud, mae'n gallu aflonyddu'r rhai sy'n edrych arno o bosib); Roedd y tawelwch yn swnllyd iawn... (roedd saib yn y sgwrs, ond y seibiau hynny'n llawn ystyr i'r siaradwyr). Bydd angen tipyn o ddychymyg i wneud hyn!

Sgwrsio Pellach
Gellir defnyddio'r cerddi fel sbardun i rannu profiadau ac atgofion, e.e. Ydyn nhw wedi bod yn Aberteifi erioed? Oes storm neu dywydd garw sy'n aros yn eu cof?

30.   Tŷ'r Ysgol gan T.H. Parry-Williams

Mae'r cyrn yn mygu er pob awel groes,   *awel groes - cross breeze*
A rhywun yno weithiau'n sgubo'r llawr   *sgubo - sweeping*
Ac agor y ffenestri, er nad oes
Neb yno'n byw ar ôl y chwalfa fawr;   *chwalfa - dispersal*
Dim ond am fis o wyliau, mwy neu lai,   *mwy neu lai - more or less*
Yn Awst, er mwyn cael seibiant bach o'r dre
A throi o gwmpas dipyn, nes bod rhai
Yn synnu'n gweld yn symud hyd y lle;
A phawb yn holi beth sy'n peri o hyd   *peri - achosi*
I ni, sydd wedi colli tad a mam,
Gadw'r hen le, a ninnau hyd y byd,   *hyd y byd - o gwmpas y byd*
Ond felly y mae hi ac ni wn paham,
Onid rhag ofn i'r ddau sydd yn y gro,   *onid - is it not, gro - gravel, grave*
Synhwyro rywsut fod y drws ynghlo.   *ynghlo - ar glo*

Gwybodaeth

Daw'r soned Shakespearaidd hon o'r gyfrol *Detholiad o Gerddi* gan
T.H. Parry-Williams (1887-1975), un o feirdd a llenorion Cymraeg
mwyaf yr ugeinfed ganrif. Cafodd ei fagu ym mhentref Rhyd-ddu
yn Sir Gaernarfon, yn fab i'r ysgolfeistr lleol. Enillodd y gadair a'r
goron yn yr Eisteddfod Genedlaethol ddwywaith. Ysgrifennodd
y soned hon yn 1931 ar ôl marwolaeth ei rieni.

Tasgau

Mae'r eirfa a phatrymau'r brawddegau yn y gerdd yn eithaf syml er ei bod wedi cael ei hysgrifennu yn agos i 80 mlynedd yn ôl.

- Gellir annog y dosbarth i wrando ar hon yn syth ar ôl cyflwyno cefndir y bardd i'r grŵp. Awgrymir gofyn i'r dosbarth beth mae'r bardd yn ei feddwl, a nodi'r syniadau ar ffurf pwyntiau ar y bwrdd gwyn.

- Mae'n bosib dweud ychydig am batrwm y soned Shakespearaidd, e.e. nodi bod ynddi 14 llinell a rennir yn wythawd a chwechawd, a bod 10 sillaf ymhob llinell. Gellir sôn am batrwm yr odlau fel hyn hefyd: groes (a) llawr (b) oes (a) fawr (b)... a gofyn iddyn nhw gwblhau'r patrwm.

- Dylid tynnu eu sylw at eiriau anodd ac ailchwarae'r cryno-ddisg. Gellir tynnu sylw at rai ffurfiau mwy llenyddol, e.e. peri, paham, onid.

- Gellir eu rhannu yn barau a'u hannog i lunio stori'r soned ar y cyd, gan ofyn i rai parau adrodd yn ôl i'r dosbarth cyfan trwy roi brawddeg neu ddwy bob yn ail. Dylid eu hannog i wneud hynny heb unrhyw nodiadau na sgript.

Pwyntiau Iaith

Gellir tynnu sylw'r dosbarth at y ffaith bod y soned hon yn un frawddeg hir, gymhleth. Gellir gofyn i'r grŵp ailysgrifennu'r soned, ond ei rhannu'n frawddegau byrion. Ydy hynny'n gwneud gwahaniaeth i effaith y gerdd, o'i darllen yn uchel?

Mae hyn yn gyfle i annog dysgwyr i lunio brawddegau hirach, sy'n cynnwys mwy nag un cymal. Gwneir hynny drwy gysyllteiriau. Awgrymir rhannu pawb yn barau a gofyn iddyn nhw lunio brawddeg sy'n cynnwys sawl cymal, gan ddechrau ag:

Er bod y gwynt yn chwythu o'r de roedd hi'n oer iawn...

Sgwrsio Pellach

Ar ddiwedd y soned mae'r bardd yn awgrymu y byddai ei dad a'i fam yn: 'synhwyro... bod y drws ynghlo.' Gellir gofyn i'r grŵp drafod beth mae'r bardd yn ei olygu trwy ddweud hyn. Ydyn nhw'n credu bod y meirwon yn medru synhwyro? Ydyn nhw'n credu mewn ysbrydion?

Ysgrifennu

Gofyn i'r aelodau ysgrifennu am dŷ neu adeilad sy'n golygu llawer iddynt gan nodi'r rhesymau. Gall fod yn dŷ, capel, ysgol, castell neu'n adeilad a welson nhw ar wyliau yng Nghymru neu unrhyw wlad arall.

Subjects

TO PAINT

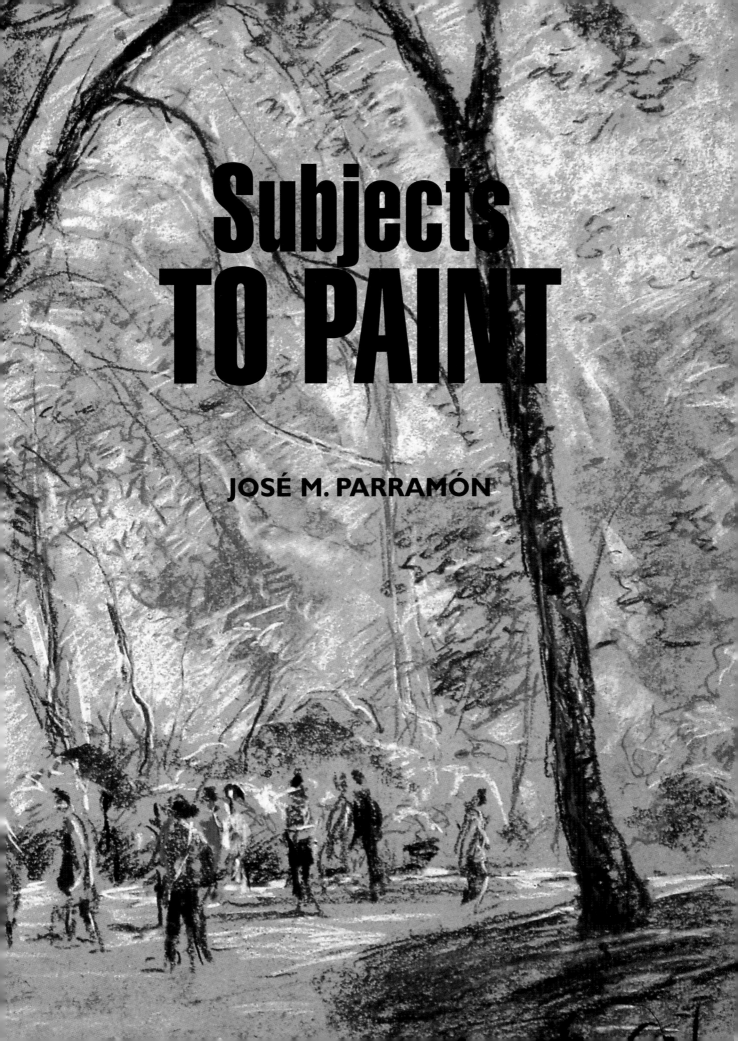

Subjects
TO PAINT

JOSÉ M. PARRAMÓN

Overall manager: José M. Parramón Vilasaló
Texts: José M. Parramón and Gabriel Martin
Editing, layout and design: Lema Publications, S.L.
Cover: Lema Publications, S.L.
Editorial manager: José M. Parramón Homs

Photography and photosetting: Novasis, S.A.L.

First edition: february 2001
© José M. Parramón Vilasaló
© Exclusive publishing rights: Lema Publications, S.L.
Published and distributed by Lema Publications, S.L.
Gran Via de les Corts Catalanes, 8-10, 1st 5th A
08902 L'Hospitalet de Llobregat (Barcelona)

ISBN 84-8463-101-X
Printed in Spain

4

Index

1

Fig.1. "Interior" by Maria Vayreda (private collection). Interiors are a very interesting subject which are ideal for capturing the transitory effects of light and for showing figures within a certain context.

Fig. 2. "Near Olot" by Josep Berga (Museo Comarcal de la Garrotxa). Rural landscapes are of great interest as they tend to combine natural landscape with architectural constructions.

3

Whilst many artists approach painting with excessively preconceived ideas about what comprises an appropriate subject for painting, others are indecisive when it comes to asking themselves "What shall I paint?". The answer to this question is – anything within reach. In fact, there is no such thing as an appropriate or inappropriate subject, as any artist is capable of finding something in a subject which is extraordinarily meaningful to him/her, and it is this ability that makes everyone a special kind of artist. In the past, such was not the case. Academic institutions made a clear distinction between what were considered noble subjects, worthy of a great artist (such as architectural drawings, the human figure and portraits) and those for more

2

lowly artists (floral compositions, landscapes and still lives). With the emergence of Impressionism, artists were freed from the excessively strict impositions of the academy and discovered that reality provides an infinite number of pictorial possibilities; subjects are to be found everywhere. Even so, if you look through a book of impressionist and post-impressionist works, you will immediately see that certain preferences of subject matter tend to repeat themselves.

As well as knowing how to see, we must also know how to translate what we see and feel onto a support. All artists need to develop their skills, learn new techniques and use them in drawings of the widest possible range of subjects. That is why this book

Fig. 3. "The lady of the anemone" by Armand Point (private collection in Paris). Portrait may be one of the most difficult subjects to paint as besides correctly represent forms, volume and colour, a good portrait must look like the real model, thus requiring a high level of drawing skills.

emphasises experimenting with different mediums and techniques to show you how even in a single drawing, introducing a further medium can completely transform not only the subject, but also the artist's perception of it.

Even today, people with academic prejudices are to be found who claim that the figure is far superior to landscape as a subject, that urban landscapes are far superior to natural ones, and who consider still-life works to be for learners. These errors tend to be accompanied by demanding knowledge of cer-

Introduction

subjects to show you how to compose, harmonise and interpret landscapes, seascapes, cityscapes, still-lives, interiors and figures. Whilst it is fascinating to read about different techniques, their true potential can only be discovered through personal experience with each particular subject.

Gabriel Martín Roig
(Art critic).

Fig. 4. "The gypsy muse" by Julio Romero de Torres (Julio Romero de Torres Museum in Cordoba). The nude figure is one of the most academic, and hence most extensively practised subjects in art schools. It is an interesting exercise for putting our notions of proportions and human anatomy in practice.

tain technical disciplines such as anatomy for figure painting and perspective for urban work. I would ask the readers of this book to forget such preconceived ideas, and find out for themselves that any subject is potentially extremely rich. Following the example of the impressionists, today's artists can select the widest range of subjects from the infinite range of possibilities available to us in our environment and nature. In this book we shall cover the basic considerations to be born in mind before projecting your vision of a subject onto paper. We will examine the basic factors to be taken into consideration in choosing a subject (choosing a subject for drawing should not be a random process): how to educate the hand, how to recognise a subject in order to select good subjects to paint. The range of paintings shown in this book, selected to illustrate a wide variety of subjects and styles, show how each artist adapts to numerous technical options in the process of interpreting his/her own ideas. The paintings are explained in text and images, and are arranged into different

Fig. 5. "Flowers" by Emil Nolde (Sprengel Museum in Hanover). Floral compositions enable one to use bright colours more uninhibitedly and are an excellent way to practice different pictorial effects and sharp contrasts in colour.

Fig. 6. "Still-life" by Paul Cézanne (Orsay Museum in Paris). Besides being one of the simplest subjects, still-life painting has many advantages for painting enthusiasts: you can create your own model using objects at hand, you can control the action of light on the objects and you can rearrange it until a desirable composition is obtained.

1

Fig. 1. "Pampliega Landscape" by Juan de Echevarría (Museum of Fine Arts, Bilbao). Not only must a subject be found, it must be infused with factors that make it interesting to the eye of the beholder: the viewpoint, harmonising of colours, contrasts between greens and browns and rich, generous brushstroke treatment.

BASIC FACTORS FOR SELECTING A SUBJECT

Everybody is capable of finding something about any subject which says something special for them, and it is t his ability that makes everyone a unique kind of artist. Nevertheless, not only must the subject be found, it must be presented to observers interestingly in order to avoid the danger of making an excessively broad or random choice with the result of a boring composition and disconnected placement of the elements within it. There are various factors which must be taken into consideration if you wish to select a visually stimulating subject, including analytical observation, contemplation of the great masters, the study of other works to analyse how the same subject has been treated by other artists, framing and the personal factor, or in other words the artist's interpretation.

Painting a Basket of Flowers

In this first exercise the artist Carlant will paint a flower basket in a simple and clear manner, allowing you to understand the way in which the flowers are structured and how the effects of light can be represented. This is a good exercise to begin this section, working with a very limited range of colors and without super-imposing too many of them.

Notice that the basket is in a well lit position, against a flat or gradated background just as shown in the model (fig. 1).

First of all, make a sketch by skimming over the surface of the paper with the point of a graphite stick without applying any pressure (fig. 2). Draw the outline in a way that frames all the basic shapes and gives the idea of a whole.

As you are making the strokes, constantly establish a connection between one area and another, constantly measuring and joining them with lines, or identifying the places where the flowers and leaves will be positioned by using circles or rough marks. Go over the outline putting more pressure on the graphite point. When the motifs are more complicated it becomes more comfortable to show the position of the elements with geometric shapes instead of directly tackling the subject. In this way you will always preserve the original outline as well as the relationship and proportions established between the different parts of the model.

Once the drawing's structural lines have been determined begin to apply

1

Fig. 1. This is the flower arrangement, still life, which you are going to paint. It has been decided to maintain the light directly above the subject to make the contrast between the dark and light aspects much clearer.

Fig. 2. The sketch is made by using a pencil. Your main concern has to be how to compose and distribute each one of the elements making up the subject.

2

3

Fig. 3. When the outline is finished begin extending the first washes in the background and in the basket.

Fig.4. Draw the flowers on the upper part with uniform washes which appear cut back. The harmonious range of grays bring these colors together with the rest of the subject.
Fig. 5. Continue working on the flower petals with uniform washes, without paying attention to the volume or the contrasts in shade.
Fig 6. Gradually the composition is beginning to fill up with small details. Notice the chromatic variety presented by the group of leaves to the left.

the paint: take a thick paintbrush and add the first wash with a diluted burnt umber earth color for the basket. With the same, but very diluted color tinge the background (fig. 3, previous page). Begin with the group of violet flowers, which should be done with uniform washes applied by a medium-sized round paintbrush. With Payne gray paint the small dark spaces between the flowers. With cadmium yellow paint the petals of the group of flowers in the center of the bunch, and with a little diluted carmine begin to fill in the flower in the right (fig. 4). Continue adding colors and painting more flowers. With a little vermillion and umber earth paint the petal corolla of the three central flowers, those with a brownish-gray color. With Payne gray mixed with emerald green, violet and cadmium green begin to paint the series of leaves. Now begin to work on the basket details, doing so by washing it over with a darker mixture than the earlier one. The aim being to reproduce its texture. As you can see, the washes applied by the artist are uniform and clean, having been treated delicately and with subtlety (fig. 5).

Painting follows its course: paint the basket handle and the center of the flowers, patiently continuing the job of painting the leaves. With emerald green and a drop of brown complete the group of leaves which have the most intense color, in the lower part of the bunch (fig. 6). Once finished painting the leaves the work has to be complemented with a small paintbrush. Draw lines for the stems in a broken and subtle way, with a little Sienna color. Mix in large washes with smaller paintbrushes, this giving the work a greater and richer textural quality. With the model now some-what advanced see how the central part shows the "empty horror" of the flowers which completely cover the white background spaces (fig. 7).

Despite having represented every one of the elements making up the bunch, the work is still a collection of areas with differently washed surfaces and few details. Continue then to decide on the main areas and then highlight them with respect to the tone of the painting, profiling the small shapes with more detail and superimposing washes with more intense colors on those done earlier. Give the basket the same treatment as the rest of the painting: add new washes of natural umber and burnt umber colors, although doing so in a simplified way (fig. 8). Last, adjust the shades to achieve a natural contrast. Use different types of paintbrushes and intensify the tone to establish the relation-ships between the different parts of the plant. As you can see, the circular centers of the flowers have also been retouched and profiled more realis-tically.

The finished painting is an example of how a motif can be dealt with by using a limited palette and by super-imposing a small quantity of materials. The method used involves the gradation of different areas through contrasting tones (fig. 9). The main difficulty of this work lies in the synthesis that you have to develop, meaning that you have to be capable of reducing the motif from the use of a few basic brushstrokes. It will be easier to simplify the object if you look at it through halfclosed eyes. When working on the motif you will be tempted to superimpose excessive details, lines, branches,

7

8

9

Fig. 7. The painting should continue being developed until it reaches this state. At this point each one of the elements in the painting are represented. However, the subject now appears to have little volume and also little contrast amongst the features.

Fig. 8. Take the localiced colors into consideration, defining each element in characteristic tones, giving them shape, drawing with accuracy, forming them by superimposing more intense color washes.

Fig. 9. Now the work appears to have more contrast and is more defined. The background has been darkened and the shadow of the subject has been projected by extending a diluted wash to the right.

stems, but getting closer to the model the compo- sition appears very defined, in fact I would say too defined. However, moving further away you will discover that the shapes and the tones merge, and in some cases even blend together. Maintaining this spirit means that instead of treating it as a photograph, you are simplifying the subject so that the essential features of the composition stand out. Try to keep the paint clear, with clean and well-defined

colors and don't mix colors unnecessarily to try and make the work more realistic; lighten the tones only when it is really necessary to do so. Some uneven paintbrushes can strengthen the appearance of the leaves on both sides of the compo-sition. However, see how the violet leaves on the upper part are still simple sketched shapes. Leave them like this indefinitely (fig. 10). Finishing off, intensify the background colors and slightly project the shadow of the bouquet.

Fig. 10. The finished work gives a result offering volume, light and shapes which are much more defining. The work, despite not giving detailed or photographic precision comes across with many artistic qualities including subtle changes in tone and an appearance which is visually satisfactory.

Painting a Park in an Impressionist Style

The artist Óscar Sanchís is going to paint the beautiful view of a park using the wet watercolor technique. This is a technique which is normally used for painting floral compositions. It basically consists of first dampening the area with water, doing so lightly, and as such controlling the limits of the area or shape that we are going to paint. The model is a view of a sunny urban park, with flower beds, in the historic center of Dublin.

Take a pencil and make a preparatory sketch with a careful estimate of the dimensions and proportions. It may seem difficult with the level of complexity of elements, including trees, buildings, benches, vegetation..., but it is exactly this number of elements, as well as their ordered distribution, which will help us to come up with a composition with a satisfactory result.

First of all, you should begin drawing, with a pencil, the line of buildings located in the background, given that in this case the architectural features are the ones which will present the greatest difficulties (fig. 1).

Begin the watercolor by painting the sky with a mixture of cobalt blue and yellow, applied from the upper edge of the paper until the row of trees and houses, in a way which gives a gradated tone (fig. 2). Note that in this first phase you must not only paint the sky, but the tops of the trees. With this last part the limits should be well controlled so that the green of the trees does not mix with the wash used for the sky. This type of control means that, on occasions, it is necessary to dry the wash with absorbent paper, this applying to cases where unwanted drops of paint drip or the color over-runs the predetermined space. The green used is a mixture of Payne gray, permanent green and burnt umber colors (fig. 3).

Take into consideration the fact that because the colors have been mixed on wet areas you will have to work quickly (fig. 4, on the next page).

Fig. 1. The spatial extent of this scene obliges us to make a planning sketch in pencil, drawing the series of profiles corresponding to trees, buildings, the edges of the lawns and flower beds.

Fig. 2. First of all, paint from the top down, gradating the sky and distant boundaries.
Fig. 3. The process continues with the sky wash drying out and the painting of those areas which correspond to the group of trees.

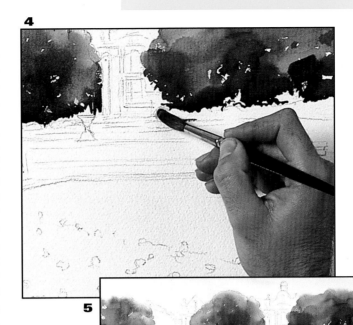

Next, paint in the colors of the lawn with a first wash; in the first attempt, cover the white of the paper to avoid false contrasts. Note what the condition of the painting is like, in figure 5, when this phase is finished.

Now comes the first of the elements. This concerns the flower beds, something which is simple enough. First of all, take a small paintbrush and using a pink color paint the flowers in the appropriate positions, but without any great detail, instead doing so in a semi-abstract way with strokes of color. After leaving the pink colored layer (corresponding to the flowers) to dry slightly, use the same brush to paint the surrounding vegetation with an olive green. Do this with a lot of care, without superimposing colors, endeavouring to go around the color of the flowers. It is advisable to leave small spaces so that the background paper shows through, the aim being to achieve a surface with a richer texture and more spontaneous result (fig. 6).

In a few seconds you will have the flower bed painted in. As you can see the plant which takes up the main position has been kept in white. Now paint this *alla prima* using the wet into wet technique (fig. 7). Paint the effects of light and shade on the plant. For this, work with three basic tones: a semi-transparent wash of green bluish-yellowish for the back leaves; a green-purplish one for the central part and blue with a little burnt umber color to highlight those parts where the contrast between light and shade is most obvious (fig. 8). Next, with the same greenish wash used for painting the lawn

Fig. 4. In this detail we can see the spontaneity and swiftness of work necessary, with colors being mixed on wet.

Fig. 5. Paint the lawn in this last part and its light effects with a paintbrush dipped in cadmium yellow.

Fig, 6. In this image observe how the artist has painted the flowers. First of all their position has been marked, this then followed by the extension of the green color, endeavouring to silhouette each one of the flowers.

Fig. 7. In a few seconds the first of the flower beds has been painted. If you look at it the green color is not uniform, but instead presents its own qualities and effects which are related to the technique of painting on wet.

below the line of distant trees, paint the grass covering the ground in the front and middle views of the painting. Do this with a uniform wash.

Begin the last phase of the painting by painting in the shape of the buildings positioned in the background and the people passing through the park. This is a laborious process which requires a lot of attention on your part because of the necessity to paint many small features on the building facades. This means that these areas must be worked on with a small paintbrush (fig. 9).

Go back to the foreground to continue painting flowers. The artist has decided to add more groups of flowers to both sides of the composition. Before painting, open up white areas on the earlier wash by rubbing the surface with a paintbrush soaked in water. Next mark the rose positions with bright and intense colors (to the right) and a group of anemones (to the left)- see fig. 10. Finally, with a small paintbrush give a second appraisal to the nearest group of flowers with the aim of showing the contrasts, to describe the definition and shape of the flowers better and also to add new groups of flowers, such as the collection of purplish flowers emerging from the plant in the center (fig. 11, next page). Also work on the middle section of the painting adding new flower beds which, given the distance, have to be dealt with from the viewpoint of using small strokes, coming together as a group of superimposed points.

8

9

Fig. 8. With a wide brush paint the middle section by extending a uniform wash over the area.
Fig. 9. The street furniture and people passing through the park should be painted with a small brush and the shapes worked on as much as possible.

Fig. 10. Go back to the foreground and form new flower groups by adding new color. Before applying these colors it is necessary to remove some of the earlier paint.

10

TIPS

-When painting the sky do it with the paper reversed, in other words, upside down, so that the wash will run down with the sky left darker in the upper part.
-The professional watercolor artist will also turn to opening up white parts of the painting by using his nail or the end of the paintbrush, doing so on a surface which is still wet to produce a texture effect or the impression of growth (to represent the vegetation).

11

Almost certainly you have tried to give great detail to the figures which appear in the park. Do not overly complicate this because it is not necessary. Notice that in the work painted by Oscar Sanchís there are no facial features to identify any of the characters, because it is not necessary in a painting like this. Possibly, when you are working naturally you will have problems painting groups of figures incorporated in urban scenes, but this is generally the case. As such when doing an outdoor painting like this, which requires a certain amount of speed, deal with it by avoiding the details and paying attention to the interpretation of the model: paint in synthesis.

Apply this same principle to the vegetation. As you can see it is also not necessary to express the flowers and the foliage of the trees in a realistic manner when these are to be found in such a distant view. Manage to bring them across in an impressionist style, this meaning that they should be painted with only a few strokes, doing just what is necessary. At the same time look at the model through halfclosed eyes. In contrast, it is appropriate to take some care over the flowers in the foreground; first painting them in synthesis filling out the painting in a style which borders on the abstract, in a way which manages to reproduce the texture of the elements being represented. This then gives content which is more intense, working with volumes and contrasts. All in all, this makes the shape more recognizable, in ways which can allow the type of flowers being dealt with to be identified.

Fig. 11. And this is the final result. Apart from those watercolor effects coming from the application on wet note the variety of brush strokes and textures offered by this work from the first details in the foreground to those further away in the background.

Painting a Still Life with the Dry Brush Technique

Now paint a still life, a good theme for a beginner to start practicing the painting on dry technique, since the objects that will be used as models are usually familiar objects that can be found on hand, and for this reason their basic structure is well known to the artist. Óscar Sanchís is the artist chosen to carry out the following exercise, which he will do using the dry brush technique. I advise you to practice the exercise following these instructions.

Before you begin, lets look at the model, a simple still life composed of a jug, a ceramic bowl with some fruit, a few objects with different textures, the tones of which contrast with the red background (fig. 1).

The paper chosen by the artist has a granular texture and it's ochre in color. This textured paper will enhance the effect of the brushstrokes applied with the dry brush technique, while the colored background will give the painting as a whole a certain sense of harmony. Start by drawing a simple sketch of the model onto the cardboard with a hog bristle brush and a little cobalt blue and violet. It is only necessary to indicate with a minimum amount of precision the sizes and shapes of the objects and their relation to each other (fig. 2).

The second stage of the painting consists in painting, or rather, outlining the red of the background with a wide brush, leaving the ochre of the paper visible. To do this, mix some cadmium red and pale pink (fig. 3).

We have begun with the background, because it is the largest individual area, but once you've given it a general exposure, move on quickly to the remaining areas of the painting

From now on you should work with a big, flat brush with hard bristles. Using a little orange and cadmium yellow paint the group of fruits, and with terra sienna mark the shaded areas of the jug and the fruit in the foreground (fig. 4). In this first stage, it is important to try to relate the tones and the colors as closely as possible, although they will change as the painting progresses.

Use big brushes so that the surface has

Fig. 1. When you prepare the composition of a still life painting for a beginner, it is important to keep it simple and not include too many colors, textures or complex shapes.

Fig. 2. Paint the outlines of the objects with a sable brush and neutral colors. In this case the artist used bluish hues.

Fig. 3. Once the drawing has been established, the first touches of paint are applied with a wide brush.

4

a feeling of freedom. In this way you will also avoid stubbornly wanting to prematurely paint small details. Use ultramarine violet to paint the darker areas of the background, and with a little cadmium green, paint the single apple in the foreground (fig. 5).

Now paint the ceramic bowl with short thick juxtaposed strokes of ultramarine blue (for the darker parts) and cobalt blue and a little white (for the lighter ones). Build up the painting as a whole. By this I mean that if you are painting part of the bowl or a reflection on the fruit, look, compare and make a decision about the tone and the color of the adjacent area, which might be a different fruit, the jug or the background. In this way you will build up the entire painting little by little without having to paint the objects separately (fig. 6).

The texture of the jug is finished off carefully with a fan brush and successive applications of color. Since acrylic dries so rapidly, the layers of paint can be laid on without waiting.

Take the wide brush again and intensify the red background with a medium shade of cadmium red and a little raw umber leaving the left side of the composition darker (fig. 7). The dry brush technique can be limited to just one area of the painting. However, in this case the artist wants the texture of the

5

6

Fig. 4. The paint is applied on the paper using the dry brush technique, that is, dipping the brush in paint that has hardly been diluted in water.

Fig. 5. Although the painting is being built up with touches of color, the artist must pay careful attention to the tonal relations.

Fig. 6. Here is the first chromatic appraisal of the composition. From this stage on, we will work with a medium-size brush in order to give more detail to the shapes and create more precise effects.

surface to be uniform and therefore, uses this technique for the background, the foreground and the fruits. You should do the same (fig. 8).

In order to carry out the last stage, before you finish it is worth observing the shapes and the small chromatic changes within each object more closely, paying special attention to the reflection of the colors on the surrounding colors. Use thick impasto strokes on the fruit in the bowl, to make their surfaces seem to reflect the light, while reinforcing the dark areas with an intense blue. See, for example, the background on the left side of the painting, that has been made darker to intensify the play between light and shade in the painting (fig. 9).

A simple still life like this one is an excellent way for the painter beginning to work with acrylics to get to know and experiment with this medium and practice the dry brush technique. It is also a very useful theme for suggesting textures, in addition to allowing the artist to obtain subtle but vivid interactions between colors. By

Fig. 7. The chromatic variations of the jug have been achieved by concentrating and superimposing brown and blue brushstrokes.

Fig. 8. Different colors and brushstrokes are used in different areas of the painting. Variations between diluted and concentrated paint are used to achieve a greater contrast.

Fig. 9. Creamy, concentrated paint is used for the reflections on the fruit in the bowl.

10

Fig. 10. The painting is nearly finished, but the bottom part of the composition has too much power. For this reason, the artist has decided to apply additional pink glazes to soften and unify the colors in the foreground.

working inside, you won't have any of the typical problems encountered when working out-of-doors, such as changes in light or the too rapid drying of paints. Surely you became worried when you saw that, as you continued painting, the initial part of the drawing was lost or distorted by the paint. This is not a reason to worry, it is normal in a work like this one. All it means is that when you approach the final part of the process, you will need to reestablish the drawing in those areas where you consider it necessary.

We don't need to worry about the fact that the colors are laid over each other, either. Nor, as has been stated on sev-

eral occasions, should each object be painted separately. But we should avoid adding the light effects before it's time, for they should be saved until the end. Otherwise, the touches of light could give the sensation of being part of the surface of the painting instead of something inherent to the objects. In other words, it could appear that they have no relation to the painting as a whole. You should try to see the touches of light as gaps that are clear of color, instead of considering them white reflections. Keep in mind that in order to carry out this painting the artist has not used one bit of white (fig. 10).

TIPS

—Each time that you clean the brushes with water you should rub them dry with your fingers or with a piece of absorbent paper. Otherwise, the effect of the dry brush technique will be spoiled.

—Do not load the brush with too much paint for each stroke. If you do, the effect you will get will be that of impasto. The bristles of the brush should rub against the surface of the paper softly and leave paint only on the crest of the grain of the paper, not cover it all with a thick layer of paint.

—However, the dry brush technique will make it necessary for you to dab the brush in paint more often and also to use more paint, since this technique hardly uses any water to dilute the paint.

Painting a Still Life with Dry, Merged Strokes

We are going to start to paint a still life using the dry brush technique. As its name suggests, this technique involves the use of barely diluted paint, whereby color is applied to the grainy roughness of the support. The best kinds of strokes for the task are flat, because they produce the widest and most vigorous marks. This exercise is going to follow the steps of an artist called Carlant. Take a sheet of card, canvas or primed board and do as the artist does. The model is a simple still life of fruit, silver cups and ceramic objects, all with different colors and textures (fig. 1)

Before starting, the artist has decided on the composition of the elements that he is going to paint. Play around with the layout of your still lives before deciding on the most attractive arrangement. You might place them intuitively, but as you observe your arrangement, you should think about Plato's basic rule of "finding unity within variety". An excess of variety can generate a sensation of dispersion, whereas a lack of it can look too forced and monotonous.

Once you have decided on the layout of the elements, start drawing the model, synthesizing the forms and molding the main details (fig. 2). Notice how the artist has depicted the folds of the cloth with a few simple lines. You should do the same.

The first thing to worry about is the construction of the forms with colored strokes that can then progressively be made to resemble the model more. Paint the jug with a mixture of burnt umber and gray. For the apples in the bowl, use carmine, and for the rest of the fruit, dark cadmium yellow with a little ochre. This same ochre should be added to the fruit bowl (fig. 3). Notice that when he paints these initial colors, the artist is already starting to add volume and shadow to the objects. Start painting the background to draw the image together as a whole. This is painted with gray gradations that lead from violet tones to browner ones (fig. 4). Notice that the softer folds have been painted as tenuous gradations of color, while the darker ones are painted with more intense, burnt umber lines.

The artist continues working on the background and the volume and texture of each element. Do the same. Notice how the artist manages to represent the qualities of the materials with strokes and color – the roughness of the ceramic jug, the flat, shiny surface of the glasses and the sinuous waves of the cloth (fig. 5). Once the first phase is complete, the artist steps back to see how everything works in unison,

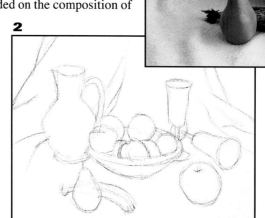

Fig. 1. The model is quite straightforward. It is a simple still life made up of different materials and qualities.

Fig. 2. The composition of a still life is very important. The preparatory sketch is fundamental in representing the model correctly, and will affect the overall appearance of the piece.

Fig. 3. The artist does not work in monochrome. From the very start, he is interested in putting volume into the objects.

Fig. 4. After the first few applications of color, the artist works on the background in a synthetic way.

5

Fig. 5. The first lights are incorporated to highlight each form.

Fig. 6. The dry brush technique allows for superimposed textures, merging and attractive chromatic variations.

Fig. 7. At this stage, the details of the painting are much more evident.

making sure that he has managed to integrate the background and the objects with the right projections of light, shadow and color. Now it is time to accentuate the contrasts and define the forms a little more, working on each object separately, adding color, touching up outlines and projecting shadows (fig. 6).

As the piece progresses, you can see how rich textures can be when we merge colors with the dry brush technique. There is a very definite chromatic harmony and several blurred, sinuous outlines (fig. 7). The artist goes back to the cloth, now with a bigger brush to apply pinker colors and light ochres to suggest the patterns of light more clearly.

To finish, the artist takes a small brush and using short, pasty strokes he accentuates contrasts, the quality of the materials and the reflections and sparkles of light. The painting is now finished (fig. 8).

6

7

Fig. 8. The final result is much closer to a realist interpretation of the subject.

8

Portrait of a Boy with Dry Pastels

We are going to paint a portrait, one of the most recurrent themes in pastel painting. To produce this step by step exercise, the artist Josep Antoni Domingo is going to use a combination of rich textures by employing superimposed lines that will be carefully manipulated to portray the forms and relationships between the colors, and to correctly highlight certain curves and angles of the features and character of the subject.

Here is the subject, the portrait of a young boy frozen in time. To achieve the complete portrait, it should include a large proportion of his shoulders and shirt (fig. 1).

Work on an intermediate colored paper, to make the most of the full range of pastels. Start by making a detailed sketch with a brown pencil and outline each of the boy's individual facial characteristics, indicating areas of shadow right from the beginning (fig. 2).

Work on the large areas of color by spreading intense, irregular lines. Leave the color of the paper to show through your lines. You should select warm, bright colors and use them in several directions to help convey the sensation of a lively, instantaneous image (fig. 3).

Start modelling the facial features by blending the lines you drew beforehand. To show form, use lines as much as much as you use tone, keeping the colors of the pastels clear and fresh. Do likewise with the tonal contrast between the lighter areas (cheeks, chin, ears and brow) and the dark areas of the face (eye sockets, fringe...). In those areas where the tones and colors seem too contrasted, blend the pastels with your fingers (fig. 4).

Trace over the contours of the hair and neck with white and sky blue to improve the sense of contrast and outline their volume and form. Draw the eyes and mouth. Be careful, because these two features should be drawn accurately, trying to make their form identical to the original. It is important that your picture resembles the person you are drawing (fig. 5, next page).

Continue by coloring the background with the edge of the pastel, blending the color and integrating the areas shaded in gray. Look at how the lines that describe the child's hair go in the appropriate direction (fig. 6, next page). Add ochre and grayish lines to the his hair.

1

2

3

Fig. 1. This is the subject: the face of a happy young boy bathed in a direct light that does not create much contrast and brightens up the colors of his skin and clothes.

Fig. 2. In these cases, a preparatory sketch is absolutely vital. The main aim to make it look like the subject.

Fig. 3. The first color should indicate the areas of light in the picture.

Fig. 4. If we look closer, we can see the first appraisal of the face. A few basic colors should be applied first, to which we can add tonal variations later.

Simplify the design on the boy's shirt, and try to highlight its shape, making sure that your lines go in the same direction as the folds. Add more colors and values to the shirt. Use violet in the dark areas and pink on the lighter ones. Keep using your fingers to merge and fade the colors whenever it might be necessary. Draw the design on the shirt in white and ultramarine blue.

Lightly blend the colors. Without pressing too hard, pass your hand over the colors of the shirt. Add black and intense green to the shirt design. Finish off the background by adding new dark values that contrast with the lighter parts of the boy's face, which will help to define the shape of his head. For example, darken the shadow behind his eyes with burnt umber and then use the same color to outline some of the contours of the fold in his arms and on the neck of his shirt (fig. 7).

Look how the finished product has a loose and sketchy feel to it. The portrait should not look too detailed, but should maintain the fresh colors and lively line drawings of pastels (fig. 8). This portrait brings together two basic conditions: that the drawing should look as much like the original person as possible, and that it should be a work of art in its own right.

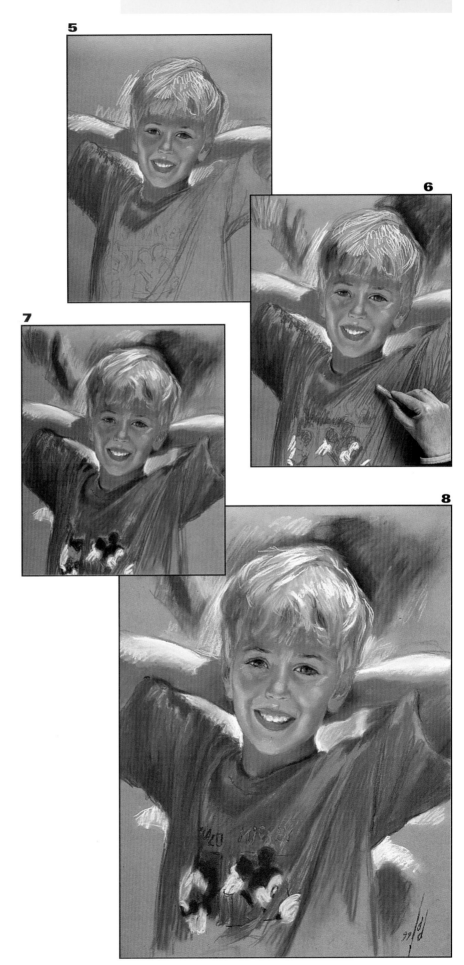

Fig. 5. The colors of the face have been spread by the artist's fingers, and intense lines have silhouetted the child's head, showing their shape and volume better.
Fig. 6. With the pastel stick slightly tilted, draw a series of parallel lines to show the folds in the boy's shirt.
Fig. 7. A little later, and effects of light and shadow have appeared on the boy's clothes.
Fig. 8. The finished work shows a face full of bright colors, with contrast between light and dark and a clever combination of heavy lines and smooth shades.

Painting Flowers with Colored Pastes

In this exercise, the artist Teresa Trol is going to show you how to use pasting techniques to represent a floral arrangement, possibly the most popular of all still life themes. As you know, pasting involves applying thick layers of scarcely diluted paint, so that the texture of the strokes is evident on the painting surface. Painting flowers demands a vigorous, colorist treatment. The pasting technique is highly appropriate for this kind of work because of the way it accentuates volume and creates results with a characteristic plasticity.

The artist starts by drawing the subject with charcoal. You will notice that the artist has opted for a frontal view, with hardly any of the background in sight (fig. 1). She has done this to make the most of the vivacious brightness of the flowers. A floral arrangement, no matter how simple it may be, requires careful layout and composition.

Start working in the same way as Teresa Trol, with accurate, synthetic lines, adjusting proportions and defining forms. Don't worry too much about the particular details of each flower (fig. 2).

Now you can start painting. Start applying a background of ochre diluted in thinners. Vary the proportion to make small degradations and so that the wash does not look too regular. Over this first mixture, when it is still wet, add a pinch of burnt sienna to highlight and silhouette the aura around the edges of the flowers. For the table, use a dark and very diluted green with a touch of ochre added to it (fig. 3).

Now the artist prepares the colors that she is going to use to paint the flowers. As you will have seen in the photograph, this is a warm color range. The artist prefers to work with just a few colors and use them to create the different tones.

So it should be enough to have just cadmium yellow, cadmium red and white on your palette, along with the colors you used for the background. You will be able to use these colors to get all of the rich shades that you are after. Teresa has started constructing the forms with areas of color and pen-cil lines (fig. 4).

She now makes short, energetic movements to superimpose colors and create volume. You should do the same. Notice how a few touches of white in some flowers help to accentuate shape. At the same time, the artist modifies the treatment of the background to increase the harmony of the piece as a whole.

To show the shadow of the flowers, which is caused by an intense frontal light, darken the left of the background with burnt umber and a touch of black. This will highlight the flowers even better and the picture will seem deeper. To put texture into the table, use freer, more relaxed strokes.

1

2

Fig. 1. This is the model that has been chosen for painting. One color usually dominates in floral arrangements. In this case, warm tones contrast on a neutral background.

Fig. 2. Before drawing, the artist observes and analyzes to decide which fit most highlights the characteristics of the subject matter.

3

Fig. 3. If you mix a few basic colors, you can create a wide variety of tones. By limiting the color scheme, you will avoid too many colors confusing the picture.

4

Now that much of the painting is done, spend a few minutes studying the picture from a distance, and think carefully about what you have done so far. Remember that a lot of a painter's work goes on in the head. By thinking carefully before doing anything, you will be able to anticipate most of the questions that will come up as you paint.

Now get back to the canvas, and carry on working. Look for volumes, define forms and accentuate contrasts. If you spend a little time studying each flower, you will see that each petal is determined by the shadow of the others – by the tonal contrasts between the same color range. The shadows vary the intensity of the colors and tones (fig. 6). The artist models the texture and form of each flower with the tip of her brush. She exaggerates the plasticity of the leaves with thickly loaded brushstrokes, spreading the color widely and generously. In the leaves, she uses a dark green with a touch of white and dark carmine. She goes on to paint the pot with white and a little blue to show form (fig. 7). You should do the same.

5

6

Fig. 4. The direction of the strokes and texture of the surface highlight the vitality of the flowers.
Fig. 5. The colors get more intense and expressive. Tonal contrasts play an important role in such a beautifully balanced composition.
Fig. 6. The artist enriches the background texture. All the parts of the painting are just as important as the actual subject and must come into harmony with the foreground

27

TIPS

–When doing an exercise like this, try to use loose strokes, and don't feel that you always have make an exact copy of the model. A still life needs to be spontaneous and dynamic.

–Try not to go for a perfectly detailed image that lacks life. Flowers are open forms and need to be painted with a certain amount of freedom.

Fig. 7. As the painting progresses, the shadows are developed, forms are molded and everything takes on volume.

Fig. 8. Now is the time for those last pieces of detail that strengthen the result. Use a small, round sable brush for the task.

To finish the exercise, work on the details with a thin brush to produce more strength and expressiveness (fig. 8). And here is the finished painting. Notice how such a colorful treatment transmits so much freshness and vitality. You cannot fail to be impressed by the expressiveness of the piece, and it is the pastiness of the colors that has caused this effect. The artist's work shows how vivid thick, pasty oils can be. You have almost certainly painted all of the flowers in the same way, which is not the right way to go about things. If you look closely, you will see that the larger flowers were painted with pastes on wet, mixing the paint on the surface with the same strokes – what we could call grooved strokes. The daisies are much flatter and more uniform, having been painted with the opaque technique. However, in the centers of some of the flowers, there are small touches of thick paint, which have used all the paint that the brush can hold. The final impression of movement in the painting is associated to the direction and strength of the strokes, always from the center of the

9

flowers outwards. The fact that the background has been worked with darker, plainer colors also contributes to this, centering the interest of the spectator on the most brightly-lit part of the painting, the bunch of flowers (fig. 9).

You may well want to rectify things as you paint. It is very simple – use a spatula to take off any color from the painting surface and then paste over it. You can do this as many times as you like.

Fig. 9. Look at how the artist has kept the spontaneity of her first sketches without forgetting the harmonious effect that the delicacy of floral subjects preserves.

Painting a Still Life with Flowers in the Old Style

The artist Ester Llauder is going to paint a still life which offers particularly strong similarities to those which used to be painted in the baroque style. As you can see, the bouquet of flowers provides a profusion of earth colors, pinks and yellows which stand out even more when superimposed with the dark background, this completely lacking spatial references with regards to depth. Furthermore, it is lit by front-side lighting, the cause of the intense contrasts between light and shadow (fig. 1). In this way the strong lighting and marked contrasts create the sense of volume in the subject.

In this exercise, the content of the flower bouquet will be managed through chiaroscuro in the classic sense of the word. This means that the mod-

elling of the subject will be expressed through a successive gradation of color towards black or white.

Using a model with these characteristics, the best way to proceed is by producing a solid and accurate drawing. It must be linear and will have to indicate the position and specific shape of each of the flowers represented, in a way that will allow us to color each one of the elements more comfortably. The lines should be intense and visible so that they can serve as a guide during the course of the exercise (fig. 2).

Sketch the leaves sticking out from the flowers. Begin with these, using an earth color. The group of leaves shown with more of a tendency towards a reddish color is done with a little ochre, sienna and vermilion.

Those in the center have Payne gray in the mixture and in the upper part a large amount of burnt umber is used. As you get on with painting the leaves, add shadow and some details (such as folds and veins). The darkest parts of the shaded areas are generally achieved by mixing the local leaf color with a little burnt umber and Payne gray (fig. 3).

Now paint the falling greenish colored leaves, hanging or angled over the edge of the vase with washes of emerald green in the clearest places and the same green deepened by Payne gray to highlight the darkest areas. When you have finished this operation it is the appropriate moment to begin working on the vase. This is made of ceramic, although the dark patina is bronze col-

1

3

2

Fig. 1. As you can see, the subject is reminiscent of a baroque composition with earth and pink colors, all in all, an elaborate work which accentuates the chiaroscuro effects.

Fig. 2. The drawing must be precise given that it will be greatly used to correctly paint each one of the elements represented. Mark the lines heavily with a pencil because they must remain visible until the work is finished.

Fig. 3. Begin painting those leaves which share the same chromatic and textural qualities.

ored. For the moment apply a uniform wash with burnt umber earth mixed with a little Payne gray to identify both its volume and profile, on what is still a white background (fig.4). The characteristic features of the flowers are painted with a small brush using the dry paint technique and which is managed with various mixtures of yellow ochre, natural umber, a purplish color, cadmium yellow and crimson. This is done in such a way that the different shapes are distinct from each other and not confused. The washes are left to stand for a moment and when they seem to be virtually dry add new features and paint to bring the work closer in accuracy to the subject, making it much more realistic and detailed (fig. 5). Observe how the artist has first painted those flowers which have a less striking chromatic tendency, and in fact are more similar to the colors of the leaves. He adds other flowers, this time more colorful, those which with their colors add a lot more life to the bouquet. As you can see working with the paintbrush is not as free and uninhibited as was the case in the previous exercise. Instead it is much more controlled, precise and methodical. Pay attention to the small details, such as the orange flower in the upper part which show a variety of petals going from a vermilion red color to the most intense of oranges and then to cadmium yellow (fig. 6). As you will see for yourself painting flowers is a laborious process which requires a lot of ability with regards to skills of observation and patience.

Leave the work on the flowers for a moment to paint the background. In this way you will avoid making mistakes brought on by contrasting the col-

Fig. 4. In contrast to what has been explained up to now, painting this work involves working with fragments instead of a collection of parts, and as such means that an elaborate drawing is of great importance.

Fig. 5. With patience and a small paintbrush work with the flowers individually, endeavouring to maintain the chromatic harmony of the whole.

Fig. 6. You will have moments in which flowers similar to these will require good powers of observation from you, and ability, allowing you to translate the visual image onto paper.

ors of the flowers with the white of the background. Take a wide brush and start to cover the background from the bottom up. The painting of the background is done with various mixtures of ultramarine blue, Payne Gray and a little burnt umber, these giving this so characteristic blackish color. Leave some flowers white, these to be painted later on (fig. 7).

Continue covering the background until you reach the upper part. Now leave the brush to the side and take a small one. With this now paint the spaces between the flowers the same color, in such a way that the white background is completely covered. After this operation you will, perhaps surprisingly, discover that the brightness of the flowers has been intensified. This is based on the fact that the color displayed by a body depends in great measure on the color surrounding it (fig. 8).

From this point finishing off the work is simple. When the background color has dried only the white spaces left on the inside of the bouquet need to be painted and finished. In other words, only those flowers which still remain. This exercise is a very positive one,

7

Fig. 7. Work on the background by applying washes with the blackish color. This avoids having the contrast of the flower colors against the white of the paper.
Fig. 8. Painting the background dark makes the colors of the bouquet brighter and the form of the flowers more precise and profiled.

8

TIPS

- If you are working on the painting and see that it is not doing so well try not to loose your motivation. Keep on painting and you will see that there are solutions for many of the problems. It was Renoir who said that "For a painting to be good it has to go through bad moments".
- Do not paint this work in only one day because it is a complicated subject which requires precision and patience. This way you will not allow your rush to overcome patience and therefore lead to making mistakes.

9

given that it is something of a challenge for you, with the need to work with fragments and deal with real details. It is the complete opposite of the majority of pictorial methods which first advise that the main features of the compo-sition should be set out and the details worked on later. Despite the fact that the second method is the most advisable and usual, I recommend that you forget about this for the moment because once in a while giving up this kind of method for exercises such as this one are very useful. These types of exercises offer new challenges and new ways of working and I am sure that you

will learn much from them (fig. 9). When you work on these flowers avoid drowning the painting with gray colors, taking into consideration that painting shadows does not mean adding gray to every single flower. Deal with the colors in a more creative way: darken the flowers with ochre, with carmine, with umber earth or, if you like, also use some blue (according to some impressionists shadows were blue colored). In addition, be patient and do not start painting when the earlier wash is still wet because this work requires a great deal of accuracy and painting on wet surfaces can lead to the

color expanding and therefore leaving the edges without any profile. I do not advise this. I have often recommended in other books that you should not be excessively careful about painting the delicate and lovely forms of flowers. However, we have to make an exception in this exercise because here it is better to get lost in the details and their delicate shapes and changing tones.

Fig. 9. The final result is this excellent watercolor painted by Ester Llaudet, presenting a subject painted in meticulous detail, with patience and showing the marked effects of chiaroscuro.

33

Painting Flowerpots with Different Colors

After painting a bouquet of flowers inside a house, why don't you try to paint the flowers in a more natural setting, such as this terrace. The artist Óscar Sanchís is going to do exactly this, painting a terrace full of flowerpots with flowers of different shapes and colors. What this means is that it is important to be conscious of the composition, to take good note of the shapes and the textures of the plants and to work with intense contrasts between light and shade.

The exercise begins with a simple enough sketch of the interior, in this case showing those architectural elements which limit the terrace, these being the walls, the door, the windows and the bench (the last of which can be found in the center of the composition- see fig. 1).

The window, which acts as a backdrop, is the first to be painted after the initial sketch is completed. First give the shutters a wash of medium intensity burnt umber and then work on the vegetation with cadmium green, painting on wet and *alla prima*. You will paint the glass later on, so for the moment leave it white.

With a medium-sized round paintbrush continue working on the vegetation. Paint the green mass below the window with permanent green and a little yellow. Try to leave a white space in the area between the stems and flowers of the plant at the front, the aim being to silhouette them better. With the same permanent green and Payne gray paint the shaded area of the right shutter. With Prussian blue and emerald green paint the elongated leaves of the exuberant plant in the center. Look at how working on wet means that the colors mix on the paper and therefore make it unnecessary to be done on a palette (fig. 2).

Now take a small paintbrush and continue the task of painting the vegetation. Continue going down the paper painting the flowerpots to the left with only two colors, enough to give the desired sensation of volume. Now paint the group of red flowers: treat them as undefined monochrome colors keeping the center circle of the flower white, which will be painted with a yellow wash. Finish this phase

Fig. 1. Just like any step by step exercise this should be started with a sketch of the model.

Fig. 2. When beginning a watercolor it is preferable to start from those perspectives furthest away and to then move down the painting from the upper to the lower part.

Fig. 3. Paint the plants and flowerpots with some washes applied on wet and alla prima, this meaning without superimposing other layers.

by painting the flowerpot to the right with an ultramarine blue. It is important to always work with clean colors, because in this way the paint will come across in shining terms and with a chromatic energy which really stands out (fig. 3, earlier page).

Take the medium paintbrush and prepare a wash with Payne gray and medium intensity natural umber. With this paint the background, this being the floor and walls of the house wherever the vegetation allows this to be visible. The wash should be spread in a gradated way, from top to bottom, such that the closer it gets to the windows the darker it gets. Alternatively, the closer it gets to the lower part of the paper, the lighter it gets. When this wash has dried, draw lines on the floor with a small paintbrush to show the tiles coming together (fig. 4).

Now begin to paint the gaps. First, paint the window frame to the right with a purplish wash. With the wash still wet superimpose a little gray and natural umber, this allowing the mixture of the three colors to diffuse in the way you can see in figure 5.

Once you have finished the background continue with the perspectives closest to the viewer. See how the plants to the right should be painted, these being dealt with by using more grayish shades (emerald green and Payne gray). As with the earlier cases keep the white spaces occupied by the flowers for later when you will add pale pink washes (fig. 6). With ultra-marine blue apply an uneven wash to the bench in the center of the scene.

4

Fig. 4. Work on the details of the window glass and contrasts the shapes by adding more substance.

Fig. 5. Paint the window frame to the right **alla prima** *and work with three colors: violet, natural earth umber and Payne gray, allowing the washes to shade off and settle on the surface of the paper.*

5

6

Fig. 6. Begin highlighting the flowers with washes of carmine diluted with water. Similarly, do the bench in the center with an ultra-marine blue wash and the walls with gradations in color.

As you can see the main plants and flowerpots have been painted. Now it is time to paint the flowers (fig. 7). The watering can sitting on the bench is painted a blister green color, but do it carefully to portray its volume. To do this a purplish wash is applied to the left side of the can to give it more of a cylindrical appearance. The flowers recently painted are made up of pink, ochre, and carmine colors in the clear parts of the painting, whereas the colors of the darker parts are obtained with emerald green and Payne gray. It is important to take into consideration the morphology of each of the plants so that once painted they are easily identifiable (fig. 8).

This is now the best moment to paint the bench. Take a small paintbrush and with an intense ultra-marine blue paint parallel lines to represent the horizontal strips running up and down the length of the bench. With the mixture of ultra-marine blue and burnt umber earth paint the shaded spaces between the stems, leaves and flowers with a more intense color. After doing this the watercolor will have taken on a much greater contrast (fig. 9).

Fig. 7. After leaving the earlier washes to dry, and given that this operation should be carried out on a dry surface, detail the contrasts of light and shadow in the group of plants to the right.

Fig. 8. Continue detailing this first part, but paying attention to each of the plants' shapes and textures.

Fig. 9. With a small paintbrush add the details of the texture to the bench and darken the spaces between the leaves and the flowers to allow them to stand out from the darker background.

TIPS

- Something which should always be taken into consideration by any beginner is the need to try and enrich the tonality, this meaning the enrichment of areas which are not made up of different colors.

- The small white spaces, the small holes, which are usually left by many professional artists when painting watercolors, give a kind of vibrancy to the color and form which accentuates the vitality and realism of the subject. They also give the work a spontaneous and fresh finishing touch.

10

If you compare the final state with how it was just one step before you will see that the watercolor has changed. The foreground now offers us more detail, the result of more attention going into the form and texture of the plants and flowers. As a result the center of the painting has gained more light and emphasis.

Possibly, you have made the mistake of working with colors which are excessively dense. Imitate Oscar Sanchís who, like the majority of watercolor artists, leaves small holes (such as those in the floor tiles in the foreground) when painting large areas with blends of similar colors. Through these small, unpainted holes it is possible to see the previous layer

or the white of the paper. As such, avoid as much as possible covering all of the watercolor with uniform and flat washes. The different gaps left in the pictorial layers give a more spontaneous quality and offer some variation in the textures obtained. In addition it is a mistake to put too much detail into the doors and windows of the house because this brings the background much closer. Representing three dimensions in this type of work is managed thanks to the accentuated contrast in shade and colors of the vegetation in the foreground with respect to the more uniform colors and less detailed forms in the background.

Fig. 10. This is the final result which is shown with a general retouching of the vegetation and the center bench, now painted. As you can see the visual result of the combination of elements is splendid.

Painting a Flowerpot of Oleanders

Josep Antoni Domingo is an artist well disposed to explain to us how interesting his creative process can be, based on the technique of painting with velaturas (glazes).

The subject you are going to paint has already been indicated in the title, this being a flowerpot of oleanders, a shrub which flowers in August and which is made up of small flowers. You are working with one of the most popular garden plants in the Mediterranean.

Josep Antoni does not normally work with a pencil sketch because it is enough for him to take a small brush and highlight some areas of interest which can be used as a reference for constructing the painting. If you like, you can do the same, but of course if you feel more confident working with a sketch do not hesitate to do so. Highlight the background with a little ultramarine blue; the flowerpot with sienna; the vegetation, or the plant leaves with cadmium & emerald green and finally working on the group of flowers with magenta diluted in water (fig. 1).

Continue defining the different areas with small strokes of different colors and with some life. Apply a second coat of pink color in the flower groups adorning the plant and with short brushstrokes paint the long leaves so characteristic of oleanders an emerald green color. With the sienna-ochre color you have used for the plantpot, although somewhat more intense, draw the horizontal lines adorning it (fig. 2).

Continue being careful with the paper surface. First of all, add another transparent ultra-marine blue & cadmium green wash to the background. With a somewhat more intense ultra-marine blue and a mixture of emerald green natural umber earth begin to darken the shadowy spaces between the leaves of the plant (fig. 3). As you can see you are using colors which are virtually the same as those recently taken from the tube, in a pure state, without any changes or mixtures. As you are going through the drawing, notice how the initial colors are being transformed by continually superimposing glazes, giving way to new colors and a rich harmonization of the work.

Gradually, the indeterminate paint-work done in the earlier stages is mak-

Fig. 1. Josep Antoni Domingo does not use a pencil, but draws the first parts by painting with colors, using his paintbrush.
Fig. 2. The second wash complements the earlier one and gives more of a picture of what the final motif is going to be.
Fig. 3. Using emerald green with a little ultra-marine blue and natural umber gives the model more volume.

ing more and more sense, this meaning that the harmonization of diluted washes, which produced a certain kind of abstract painting, are being transformed. It is becoming a work where you can begin to guess the shape of the flowers, the different textures, the shadows, and to a great extent the volume. Notice, for example, that the position of the fully composed flowers have now been set and that some areas now have two or three different features (fig. 4).

Now is the moment to detail the leaves, beginning with those to be found in the upper part of the plant. Apply cadmium green, ultra-marine blue and blister green brushstrokes to these and model them in such a way that the leaves are presented in an elongated style. Do not hesitate to work on the volume by adding two other different colors and paint the hollows with more intense colors so that the profile of the foliage stands out better. If you compare this with the earlier state you will see how the intensity of the background color has been progressively increased and darkened (fig. 5).

Now take a sponge and add the greenish paint which appears at the left side of the foreground. With a small paintbrush work on the colors and shapes of the flowers in more detail, in such a way that the bouquet has more contrast. If you look closely at the chromatic range of the flowers you will see that ultra-marine blue has been has been included in the most shaded areas and vermilion in the lightest, and in this way greater variation is achieved. To paint flowers which have a kind of monochrome appearance does not mean that other colors cannot be used in the mixture. A better way, which I recommend, would be to always use what you can, this often being necessary to prevent the painting from becoming monotonous, monochromatic and boring (fig. 6, on the next page).

Continue detailing the grass on the left in the foreground and darken the flowerpot with ochre colored washes, leaving a small vertical band which will help us to represent the reflection and

4

Fig. 4. Continue painting new glazes on top of the previous colors which have now dried, adding more substance to the initial flat wash.
Fig. 5. By showing the contrasts and painting with intense colors the spaces between the leaves take on a greater sensation of volume.

5

where the earlier wash can breathe. With a small paintbrush lightly bring out the lines of the floor tiles the flowerpot is sitting on. In this way you are introducing a spatial reference to the work, albeit it in a fairly minimum sense.

Now go back and work on the irregular forms of the plant. See how it is gradually gaining in intensity and contrast. Given that the colors have been intensified in the rest of the work, changes must also be made to the flowers (fig. 7). As you can see working with the velatura technique does not mean that we are dealing with the painting of fragments, or working *alla prima* with the vegetation, but instead

means that we are doing it all at the same time and allowing the work to emerge in the same way as a photograph when it is being developed.

As you can see the technique used means taking full advantage of the transparency of the watercolor to put across the brightness of the subject. The details which are going to be added next are those which will finish off the work. Look at how the flowerpot has been given an effect, using a delicate Prussian blue wash, which increases the sense of volume. The floor has also had more work done to it, having been given different touches, but without the modification of any of

the basic structures (fig. 8, next page). In this last stage alternate the washes with heavier colors, until the watercolor is left with a much heavier feel.

The work you have done possibly includes colors which are much dirtier and not as bright as the original painted by Josep Antoni Domingo. This may be due to not having let the previous washes dry properly before applying the next glaze and as a result the colors have mixed together. The painting must be worked on through a series of washes, and it is not until the end of the work that a heavier type of paint is used to define the textures and details. It is also probable that on

Fig. 6. Stain the area to the left with a sponge soaked in emerald green.
Fig. 7. Now is the moment to obtain textures, detailing the form of the vegetation with thicker paint and a small paintbrush.

6

7

TIPS

- Paint the branches of the shrub, preferably with a no.6 round paintbrush. This is a very flexible brush with very long strands and a fine point. It works very well because it allows fast hand movements.
- If you like you can paint false shadows and contrasts to enhance the shapes of the model.
- To accentuate textural effects open up white areas in the vegetation with a cutter.

8

examining the finished work you will realize that the subject looks as if it has taken on too much. This may be due to the fact that you have put too many details into the plant, the flowers and the floor tiles, or it may be that you have wanted to show too many things in the painting. The drawn, white floor is what we call a relief area, a space which every work needs for spectators to have a more relaxed view of the

subject. Because of this, the way in which the artist has done the painting is worthy of respect. The painting should be worked on with washes without the introduction of an excessive number of brushstrokes, colors or textures.

Fig. 8. Here we have the finished painting. A complete lesson on water-color painting using the technique of working with glazes and showing how to work with the painting as a whole.

Landscape with the Pointillist Technique

For this exercise, we are going to be working with the artist Grau Carod, who is going to use pointillism to paint a scene with a waterfall in the midst of a wood. This technique involves applying unmixed paint in short, brightly colored strokes. The exercise will not be done with traditional oil paints, but with water soluble ones. This is a good way of experimenting with new colors, and studying how they tint and dry. If you do not have any, you can still do the exercise with ordinary paints. The artist uses a limited palette: permanent green, emerald green, ultramarine blue, cadmium yellow, cadmium red, carmine, ochre and raw umber (as well as black and white). The artist is going to base his work on this pretty illustration of a waterfall in a wood near Revel in France (fig. 1).

As you can see, the artist is going to work on a dry, tonal background. Do the same. Start by drawing the model with burnt umber and a small brush. You needn't be too precise, but make sure you position the waterfall correctly, along with a few traces of vegetation and the building in the top, right corner (fig. 2). Now take a small brush and start applying small touches of opaque color to the surface of the painting. Start with the sky and the water tumbling over the waterfall. You need to partially cover the vegetation at the edges with white and permanent green dots mixed with a little yellow, and use raw umber and black where the shadows are more intense (fig. 4) As you can see, the artist works on the whole painting at the same time – he mixes one color, applies a few dots and then moves on to a new part of the painting.

Little by little, white disappears from the picture. With a little raw umber, paint the tree trunks and branches and enrich the vegetation with new greens (fig. 5).

Adjacent colors are only mixed in the spectator's eyes when the picture is seen from a distance, so you should keep stepping back a few feet to see how your work is developing. You need to paint in a certain rhythm that always involves checking how everything is coming on. You can elaborate the foreground by spreading new emerald green dots mixed with white, ultramarine blue and violet to represent the water in the stream. The lower part of the painting is comple-

1

3

2

4

mented with a few irregular ochre lines mixed with a little white (fig. 6).

The waterfall has been developed a little more, and the way the water flows is now clearly shown. New blue dots are gradually starting to suggest the thickness of the vegetation. Small ultramarine blue pastes can be seen in the sky (fig. 7). The colors follow progressively, and as he starts work on details, the artist now uses thinner brushes. Consequently, the chromatic combinations are increasingly richer and more precise. There are touches of two or three colors of very

Fig. 1. The model is this peaceful woodland scene near the French town of Revel.

Fig. 2. The artist constructs the outline sketch with a brush over a tonal background.

Fig. 3. At first, the piece does not look particularly accurate, covered with apparently meaningless dots.

Fig. 4. As his work progresses, the artist adds new values to those of before.

5

6

7

similar hues next to each other, which mix in the spectator's eyes as completely new ones (fig. 8).

At this stage, the picture as a whole, seen from a certain distance, transmits chromatic sparkles and a shiny, vivacious landscape. The artist has made the foreground denser to show how it differs to the more distant planes. He has done this by combining blues, oranges, reds and ochres in the water of the stream (fig. 9).

Now all that remains is to take a final look over the piece, and as long as you are happy with what you see, you can consider your work finished.

To work with the daring colors of Divisionism, you need a well developed sense of color, but don't feel intimidated. As you try out new combinations and superimpositions, you will find that pointillism is a very easy and satisfying procedure.

TIPS

–You sometimes need to exaggerate or reduce colors and forms to make your painting look unified.
–The smaller the dots are, the more surprising the chromatic effects of your paintings will be.

8

Fig. 8. As the painting nears completion, the artist uses smaller brushes.
Fig. 9. The finished painting shows the kind of complex optical mixtures that can be achieved by superimposing different colors.

Fig. 5. At this early stage, the artist has used a medium brush to cover the surface of the painting quickly.

Fig. 6. As you can see, work with pure, clean colors makes pointillist painting extremely bright and gives them a chromatically strident effect.

Fig. 7. After a few hours' work, the painting looks like this. The successions of dots now suggest where the piece is heading.

9

Painting with the Washing Technique

In this exercise we will work with washes and glazes. Josep Antoni Domingo, an expert in the art of painting with acrylics, will be our guide in this step-by-step exercise. The technique of velatura, or painting with glazes, is done quite similarly with acrylics as it is with watercolors, although the colors are a bit more opaque and when they dry they appear a bit shinier. Let's begin. To do this exercise with acrylics you will need several flat hog bristle brushes and a round sable brush for the details. In addition to this, you will need a palette with hollows, to put the paint in.

The model for this exercise is this beautiful view of Toulouse seen from the Saint Michel bridge. We have a contrasting foreground, rich in gradations of blue and green, and further in the distance we can make out a bridge and the outlines of the buildings of this old city in the south of France (fig. 1).

After fixing the paper onto the rigid support, use a soft brush on watercolor paper, starting with light washes of cadmium green and cerulean blue. As you can see in the image (fig. 2), the artist has avoided doing a preparatory sketch in pencil and tackles the theme directly with the confidence that comes from years of experience. Now paint the water of the river using horizontal strokes of cerulean blue (mixed with a bit of gray) (fig. 3). Start from above and move down the surface of the paper. When you get to the bottom of the sheet, you will find that an excess of paint has accumulated there. Get rid of it with a rinsed paintbrush or with a sponge. If you do not do this, the paint will dry forming pools of paint which will ruin the washes. Remember that once they have dried, acrylics cannot be modified as is the case with watercolors.

Fig. 1. This step-by step exercise is based on the splendid view from the Saint Michel bridge across the Garonne river as it flows through the city of Toulouse (France).

Fig. 2. The artist starts by suggesting, with light washes, the location of the trees and the bridge, obtaining a very soft and gentle effect.

Fig. 3. Working initially with only two colors, the artist establishes the outline of the composition and marks the tonal key.

Now work on the arches of the bridge that appears at the top of the image using a little Venetian red (if you don't have this color you can use sienna instead) and Prussian blue so that the painting as a whole acquires a certain violet-like tendency, due to the cold colors adopted by the bodies as they withdraw into the background (fig. 4). This is an optical illusion caused by the water vapor and the dust particles in the air, that make the distant shapes and colors grayer.

Now apply some paint in a more concentrated form mixed with a little mat medium. Spread the greenish wash over the surface of the water to simulate the reflection of the vegetation. It is worthwhile to remember that the reflections are almost always darker than that which is reflected, in this case the branches of the trees (fig. 5).

Continue darkening the foliage of the vegetation by laying on new shades (ochre, terre-verte, and sap green). In this manner, the strokes of sap green will blend with the previous applications of yellow and cadmium green giving the impression of a delicate shade in the leaves (fig. 6). With a small brush dipped in burnt sienna and red, draw the thin branches of the veg-etation that invades the central part of the composition. A succession of washes should also be applied to the sky, so that it becomes progressively darker as the colors of the painting are intensified.

Work on the foreground first, that is to say, on the vegetation. The paint should be applied smoothly onto the paper with a round sable brush, following the method used in modeling and allowing the previous washes of brighter colors to filter through. Acrylic paint possesses more of a physical presence than watercolor and for this reason the objects appear to be brought closer.

5

4

6

Fig. 5. The artist applies one color on top of the other, using the paint as if it were watercolor.

Fig. 6. The subtlety of the superimposed second tonal appraisal makes the color under-neath the glaze shine through, giving the painting a bril-liant effect.

Fig. 4. The water has been painted with horizontal strokes, using the technique known as wet on wet.

45

This allows us not only to portray detail and give it texture but also to stress space (fig. 7). In this way, the deep blue of the foreground brings the area forward in space. Continue working on the texture and shape of the big branch that crosses the center of the painting (fig. 8). Darken the blue of the sky with highly-diluted washes so that it has a clear tonal gradation. Continue by beginning to build up the shapes of the buildings in the background, which still appear a bit faded. This task will be completed in the next stage, we'll leave it for the final finish. Finally apply a yellowish wash onto the water in the lower part of the painting in order to reproduce the reflection of the vegetation on the crystalline surface of the calm waters of the river. It is interesting to note that some colors, like yellow, appear more solid when they are used on top of darker colors (fig. 9).

To finish the painting, darken the blue of the lower area, add more details to the vegetation in the foreground and also to the buildings in the distance. In order to do this, use a small sable brush. Also add some shades of green to the water, add detail to the reflections and add textural effects to the foliage of the vegetation and the bark of the branches of the trees (fig. 10). The effect produced by the technique of velatura, or adding successive layers of glazes to a painting, is very peculiar. The colors are perceived as filtering through other colors and the effect is one of subtle and luminous mixtures. This can be seen especially in the leaves of the trees and the shadows that they project onto the surface of the water. Surely you have worried too much about finding the definitive colors for your painting on your palette, when this operation should have been carried out on the surface of the painting which is where the colors should be mixed and modified through this technique of superposing washes.

7

8

9

Fig. 7. The warm patches of vegetation make the foreground stick out, while the hazy grays and violets of the buildings in the background, make them seem to withdraw into the distance.

Fig. 8. The brush gives the water a sensation of calm movement, which is evoked by the light and reflections which are constantly moving.

Fig. 9. The rippling on the surface of the water is just enough to tone down the reflections of the trees, which have been painted with horizontal brushstrokes in order to contrast with the more energetic strokes used on the leaves.

TIPS

—The use of mat medium for paintings done with the glazes is quite common, since it makes the paint become more transparent.
—For extensive washes, palettes with individual ceramic or porcelain cavities are very useful.
—Acrylics can also be used together with watercolors, and perhaps this is one of the most satisfying ways of working with them, since it makes it possible to make the most of both.

10

Velatura makes it possible, also, to paint over and unify some areas without having to repaint them entirely. You may also have had problems in detailing the reflections on the water. The water, just like the sky, is an tricky theme, the effects of which are rather transitory and therefore difficult to capture without losing the sensation of movement. My advice would be to try to freeze the instant, making a couple of strokes with moderation in order to achieve a sensation of movement and fluidity.

Fig. 9. In the finished work, you will notice that the colors have a shine that can only be obtained in this way. Green painted on top of an area of more solid greens and blues will be richer and more intense. If, on the other hand, it is painted on top of a luminous yellow it will be more defined and clearer.

Painting a Mountainous Landscape with Veils

In the following exercise, we are going to be using the veiling technique. We shall be working with the artist and illustrator Josep Antoni Domingo. As you already know, veiling involves painting transparent or translucent layers over what has been painted earlier. To manipulate the paint and make the transparency effect stronger, you need to mix it with a veiling medium such as polymerized oil, opium oil or linseed oil thickened in the sun and diluted with turpentine. The color on the palette should be like a glass laminate. That said, we can move on to the exercise.

The model that the artist is going to paint is this mountain landscape dominated by soft tones and sweet contrasts of light and shadow (fig. 1). It is an ideal subject for painting with veils. First of all, the general distribution and basic outlines need to be established. You need to define how everything fits, using a small rounded brush and a grayish color diluted in a little thinners to scribble the main forms of the model.

Now take a large, flat brush and cover the sky and part of the cliff with a first layer of a gray that you have heavily diluted with thinners. The shadowed parts of the intermediate plane are painted with similar ultramarine blue washes, and the foreground should include a hint of violet. Use wide, heavy brushstrokes for doing all of this (fig. 3)

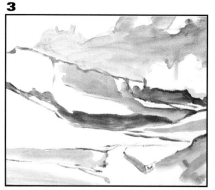

In a landscape, it is always a good idea to start with the sky. The layer of sky is painted over the pencil drawing, which should now be hidden by these first colors. To paint the sky and the rock faces, a series of plain washes is applied, getting progressively darker to form a light degradation. The rocky mountain is painted with a large, round brush, using a mixture of burnt sienna, ultramarine blue and burnt umber. The strokes are applied upwards and downwards so that they blend into each other. For the sky, you need to make a mixture of cobalt blue, ultramarine blue and titanium white. As there is a lot of sky, it can be painted quickly with either a large, flat brush or a large, rounded one. Pay a lot of attention to the outlines of the clouds, making sure that they blend naturally into the surrounding atmosphere (fig. 4).

You will see that the canvas is now completely covered with thin layers of color. The whole painting is full of light and the white of the paper can still be seen through the soft veils. For the greens in the foreground, emerald green, permanent green, yellow and cobalt blue have been used. Volume and values have been added through the use of several semi-

Fig. 1. The subject, a magnificent valley in Huesca, Spain, is dominated by a mountain range with vertical, rocky faces. The clouds project interesting patterns of light and shadow.

Fig. 2. The preparatory sketch is drawn with a brush loaded with paint diluted in a little thinners. The tonality is neutral.

Fig. 3. With a large, flat brush, the artist starts coloring the paper with generous portions of diluted color that, for the time being, can be quite abstract.

Fig. 4. Remembering that the artist uses transparency so that the colors below mix with the washes applied over them, you can see how important tonal effects are in the first washes.

transparent layers of color. The thin touches of darker color are now added to suggest the texture of the rocky mountain (fig. 5).

At this point, it is a good idea to leave the paint to dry for a few hours. You should really leave it overnight, or even for several days. Remember that whenever you paint with veils, you need to let each layer dry before you paint another over it. If you don't, the colors will mix and destroy the clean lighting effects of the piece.

When enough time has passed, you are free to carry on where you left off. You need to work a little more on the contrasts. The artist uses his skill to create an illusion of bright, shining light. One way to do this is to mix the warm, sun-soaked colors that cover the landscape (light greens, ochres, and yellows) with cool blues, grays and violets. Warm colors should look more intense through careful use of contrast. Bear this in mind as you copy the artist (fig. 6).

Now work on the rock faces of the mountains in the background. The texture of the rocks is painted with layers of plain washes. Each wash includes a series of horizontal strokes, one on top of the other. If you look closely, you will notice how the strokes are slightly superimposed over others. So that each stroke stays wet and can be mixed into the next, you need to work fast (fig. 7). With a medium brush, intensify the violets in the foreground to increase the sense of depth in the painting. With the painting almost complete, apply the point of a small brush with darker touches to reinforce the volume and texture of the rocky mountains. This is the best moment for adding details such as the

cracks in the rocks (fig. 8). Dark strokes are applied to the mounds of grass in the middle and foreground, darkening and highlighting the relief and the plays of light. Strengthen the violet near the rocks in the foreground and touch up the edges of the stream. At this final stage, before you can consider the painting finished, your work must be meticulous and a lot will

5

6

7

Fig. 5. For the moment, you do not need to make your work look too finished, because you still have to cover the hills with more washes.

Fig. 6. The artist has worked on all of the areas of color with veils. The interaction between layers produces a particularly soft, suggestive effect.

Fig. 7. This illustration clearly shows how subtle merging and blurring effects soften the edges of the different areas of color.

49

depend on your observations and the amount of definition that you want there to be in the picture (fig. 9).

Each veil modifies the color of the one before and creates subtle harmony between each tone. Painting veils with a medium like oils, which can involve such long drying times, can be a laborious process because you need to wait for each layer to dry before you can add another. But if you don't observe this basic rule, the colors will mix and the finished painting will look dirty.

If you add a veil, but then feel that it is too intense, take a fanned brush, hold it vertically, and brush short strokes over the surface. This will get rid of the excess paint and leave a softer, brighter veil, through which the color beneath will be visible. Another worthwhile alternative is to correct mistakes with a shaving brush or any similar type of brush with thick bristles. You can also use a piece of cotton or blotting paper. If areas painted with a uniform veil still need modification, such as clearing areas for touches of light,

8

TIPS

–For making veils, it is usually a good idea to choose the largest brush that you can possibly use for each task. This will make the strokes wider and freer.

–To save time, you can paint veils of oil over a background that you have pre-painted with egg tempera, casein, acrylics or non-liquid colors that dry in minutes rather than days.

–Veils should contain paint that is diluted in a special veiling medium to increase its fluidity and transparency.

9

10

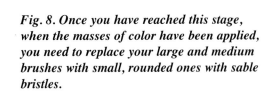

Fig. 8. Once you have reached this stage, when the masses of color have been applied, you need to replace your large and medium brushes with small, rounded ones with sable bristles.

Fig. 9. Now it is time for the small, rounded brush to come into play for the final details and to highlight the texture of the rock faces.

Fig. 10. Although work with veils produces a flat effect, its appearance is richer and brighter than when colors are mixed on the palette.

11

work on these parts with smaller brushes. The contours and edges of the different areas of color can also be a problem. Different colored veils can be applied to adjoining areas, and they can then be softened and merged to level up the tones and avoid the formation of silhouettes or, to put it a different way, outlines that are too linear or defined (fig. 11).

Fig. 11. The fascinating brightness of the finished piece explains why oil painters are so attracted to the use of veils for painting the effects of outdoor light and atmosphere.

Seascape with the Wet on Wet Technique

The wet on wet technique is ideal for outdoor work. It is quite a fast way of painting, with everything being completed in just one session, and paint being applied while that below it is still damp. The direct painting method is technically very safe. Paintings like this, which do not involve any preliminary painting, have an intimacy and freshness that the spectator responds to directly and spontaneously.

We shall start by studying the chosen model – a small cove on the Costa Brava in Spain (fig. 1). Beaches and coves are a great source of inspiration to our invited artist, Teresa Trol. If want to copy her, you should use guide sheet number three at the back of this book.

Once again, the landscape is outlined in the form of a simple drawing – enough to situate the mass of trees, the houses and the beach. The preparatory sketch does not have to be complete, but it should indicate all of the main features (fig. 2).

If you are painting outdoors, you need to mark out every shadow because they are going to change as the day goes by and spoil everything that you have planned to do. Take a large brush for the task, apply a raw sienna wash and indicate where all of the shadows lie. Notice that the initial wash is very free and there are several clear sections where the white of the support is visible, simulating the brightest areas of sun. This way, the image looks three-dimensional. From this simple prelimi-

nary sketch, Teresa elaborates the structure of the piece (fig. 3).

Now it is time to establish the first tonal values. Use a little emerald green for the vegetation, ultramarine blue

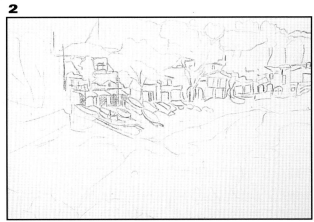

and cadmium green for the sea, and violet for the shadowed rocks to the left. The artist applies colors to the canvas one on top of the other, diluting them in a little thinners, as if they were

Fig. 1. Teresa Trol is going to paint this model, a view of Cala Salguer, a picturesque fishing cove near Palamós, a town on the Spanish Costa Brava.

Fig. 2. The preliminary pencil sketch outlines the forms of the houses and beach.

Fig. 3. A brownish color is used to suggest the positions of the shadows. You will often need to do this when you paint outdoors.

watercolors. As she works, she changes the position of the board to increase or decrease the flow of paint (fig. 4). As you can see, the preparatory sketch is still visible at this stage.

Now work on the group of houses with a small, rounded brush. The doors and windows are painted with two or three superimposed strokes that contrast with the whitewashed walls. The skill of observing an image and translating it to canvas normally only comes with a great deal of practice and almost always involves highly schematic painting methods (fig. 5).

When you paint the houses, you should differentiate the walls by varying the colors and lighting. Use a few strokes of a neutral white, with a little ochre, violet or cobalt blue. Work alla prima, in other words, hardly mix colors on your palette at all, instead letting the wet paints mix on the support itself (fig. 6).

Go around the shadowed area on the left, mixing violet and burnt umber directly on the canvas. In the same way, paint the boats on the sand alla prima. Painting wet on wet in this way is not only technically difficult, but your strokes will intensify any insecurity. But this can actually be used to your advantage, for example when you form the boats, you can make them rough and imprecise. With a small brush, paint the trees between the houses in a similarly imprecise way, using two colors (permanent green and ochre).

The surface of the water is painted with different mixtures of colors – violet and white for the area nearest to the rocks; emerald green, permanent green and cadmium yellow for the central strip; and ultramarine blue and white on the right. Notice that this is not a uniform wash, but several different mixtures and spirited strokes that are superimposed on wet.

4

5

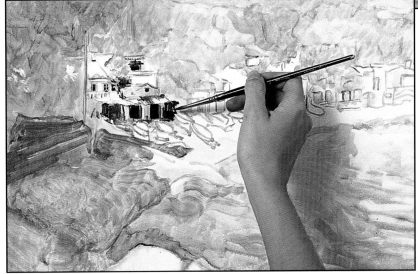

Fig. 4. Successively, the artist fits the composition with the first tonal values painted with very diluted colors.

Fig. 5. With a small brush and thick, dense paint, start detailing the openings in the fishermen's houses.

Fig. 6. Now use a small brush to make intense colors, just as they come from the tube, to paint the openings in the fishing huts.

6

7

The color needs to be a bit thick and not diluted too much, or the painting will run too easily. It needs to look slightly pasty (fig. 7). Notice that the strong color of the sea is lighter as it approaches the sunny part of the beach (fig. 8). Remember that when you apply a thick color over another wet one, the brush should be well loaded with paint. If not, all it will do is dirty the color. The foliage adopts an increasingly green color, often with a few yellow and ochre tones. The brushstrokes are overlapped and superimposed. In mid-summer trees look leafier than ever, and the foliage tends to be dark and intense.

8

Fig. 7. Now work on the dark parts of the rocks on the left. The mixture is made up of cadmium red, ultramarine blue and burnt umber.

Fig. 8. To paint the bright reflections on the surface of the sea, the artist applies short strokes with a large, round brush.

Fig. 9. While the paint is still wet, scratch a few light lines with the reverse end of your brush.

9

TIPS

–The darker brushes contain burnt sienna, and the warmer colors contain more ochre and yellow.
–It is better to mix colors on the palette and paint in zones. Mixtures on the canvas must be meditated to keep the colors clean.
–Some procedures dramatically reduce the strength of some contrasts. One of these is merging wet layers of paint with your finger.

10

Taking advantage of the fact that the surface of the canvas is still wet, it is fun to scratch the paint with the reverse end of the brush, making the little twigs that can be seen amongst the green vegetation (fig. 9).

The finished piece has attempted to combine strong contrasts of light in soft harmony. The solidity of the rocks and their structured forms contrast with the continuous movement of the water (fig. 10). It is sometimes hard to capture such changeable effects without losing the sensation of movement. I advise you not to try to freeze the moment, but to make a few measured lines and strokes that produce the impression of movement and fluidity on the surface of the water. I suggest that you do exercises like these in the open air, rather than just copying a photo. This way, although you need to

work quickly to capture the moving effects of light, this sense of urgency will inevitably lead to more vitality in the painting.

When you paint wet on wet, your colors may get altered or dirtied on the surface of the painting. It is not a good idea to manipulate the paint too much once it has been applied. To stop your colors getting muddy, the paint should be on the tip of your brush and your strokes need to be solid and homogenous, the brush held over the damp paint at right angles to the canvas. If you have made a mistake in any one particular area, you can scratch the paint away with a knife, taking out the color and then repainting it while it is still wet. Many artists do this, and what may look spontaneous and flowing may actually be the result of a third or fourth attempt.

Fig. 10. Seascapes like this are extremely popular with artists. Not only do they have a unique quality of light, but there are also just as many pictorial themes as one would find inland.

Flowers Using the Technique of Painting on Dry

Going through the two following exercises you are going to paint the same motif with different techniques : with the technique of painting on dry and with that of painting wet into wet. The first of these exercises (on pages 56 and 57) presents a more colorful tendency. I would ask you to pay a lot of attention to the two step by step exercises about to be explained because I am sure that you will learn many advantageous things from them. These could then be later applied to your compositions. The model which we are going to use for these two exercises is a basket with a well-lit, varied bouquet of flowers with the warm colors dominating it (fig. 1). The first exercise is going to be carried out by Ester Llaudet. I invite you to practice it with her.

First of all, begin drawing the model in detail (fig. 2). Work on the painting with a heavy brush and start concentrating on the bas-ket. Use a diluted ochre and a combination of the same ochre with Payne gray for the darker base of the basket. Next paint the center of the sunflowers with burnt umber earth (fig. 3). Continue pain-ting the rest of the flowers. With cad-mium yellow and ochre paint the sun-flowers' crown of petals and with a lit-tle diluted carmine do the group of pink flowers. With this same carmine mixed with a little ultra-marine blue paint the purplish flowers in the upper part (fig. 4). All of this is done on dry which means leaving the earlier wash to dry to then superimpose new was-hes and new colors. From this point change the heavy paintbrush which you have been using since the begin-ning (to work on large color areas) for a smaller one to allow you to carry out work on more detailed parts.

Paint the irregular branches sticking out between the flowers with permanent green and a little umber. It will be necessary to paint the leaves with two or three colors. Each one of the elements making up the still life are progressively enriched with new details, these giving the sensation of volume (fig. 5).

Fig. 1. This basket of flowers will be the model for carrying out the two following exercises.
Fig. 2. Painting in this style means that the drawing pro-duced beforehand takes on special significance, given that it is an indispensable gui-de throughout the exercise.

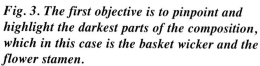

Fig. 3. The first objective is to pinpoint and highlight the darkest parts of the composition, which in this case is the basket wicker and the flower stamen.
Fig. 4. Draw and paint thoroughly, consi-dering the small details and following the exact shapes of the petals.

Now work on the background and make the mixture of colors colder by introducing a Payne gray wash. Concentrate on making sure the background is not uniform: it is a wash of gradated grays where the shadow from the model will be projected (fig. 6). Look for special qualities through small details here and there, layer after layer, image after image, until the painting acquires its definitive appearance. Strengthen and highlight the green of the leaves, and intensify the pinks of the flowers in such a way that the yellow flowers stand out better, as well as having areas of light and shade.

To finish, paint the structure or geometric fabric of the flower basket. For this take a small paintbrush, be patient and work on reproducing the shapes, the hollows and the wicker texture. Use two different browns, not only because one of these is lighter, but also for the composition- one with ochre and the other with more gray, doing so in such a way that they are in harmony with the tonal qualities of the painting and with the background color.

As you can see in the finished work, the artist has not taken a lot of liberty with respect to the final color. The painting has been dealt with in a realism style, meaning that it reflects the colors of the composition in a realistic way and without risking chromatic variations. Above all, the importance of the modelling must be pointed out, the result of which is the construction of shapes and the creation of volume (fig. 7).

Fig. 5. The watercolor is trans-parent and allows the mixture of colors or the superimposing of one color onto another, as in this case, where the different flowers of the bouquet are painted one by one.

Fig. 6. In this state the drawing, color, contrast and harmonization are practically complete. The missing parts are the small details these being the last features to be worked on.

Fig. 7. Barely, four hours have been necessary for Llaudet to finish her flower painting. Painting on dry needs a lot more time than painting on wet, because it is necessary in this method to let previous washes dry out before continuing.

5

6

7

TIPS

- Do not confuse the technique of painting on dry with that of using a dry brush because the first of these consists of superimposing washes when the previous one has dried, therefore preventing the colors from blending together and becoming mixed. On the other hand, the technique of using a dry brush is one which means working with a brush loaded with paint and hardly any water, in such a way that rubbing the brush leaves a rough texture on the paper.

Flowers Using the Wet into Wet Technique

I would now like to invite you to paint the same motif as the earlier exercise, although this time it will involve using a different technique: that of painting on wet.

This concerns a treatment of the model which is more colorful, more lively, cleaner, and brighter. Painting on wet consists of painting on a area or layer recently moistened with water or recently painted and still wet, with the wetness being controlled depending on the effect that you want to create. In this way the mixture and fusion of the colors is carried out on the surface of the paper and not, as in the previous case, something which happens on the artist's palette. The author of this exercise will be the experimentational watercolor artist Óscar Sanchís.

Now you can begin . With a medium paintbrush dipped into cadmium yellow paint the sunflower's petals. Without hardly a rest and using an ochre colour wash, highlight the effects of light and shade. With umber and sienna paint the center part of the flower. As you can see working on wet allows the edges of the colors to merge together at the same time as giving the painting a more spontaneous effect (fig. 1).

The painting on wet technique does not allow for working on the whole model at the same time, going from less to more. Instead it should be worked on in parts, in fragments, and painted from the beginning while the watercolor is wet (fig. 2). This said, paint the two purplish flowers in the upper part in such a way that the green, to be blended with the pink, forms free-flowing washes with irregular shapes and profiles.

Now paint the pink flowers in the center of the basket, first concentrating on the center of the flower and spreading the wash radially until completing the shape of each one of them (fig. 3). Next paint the stems for the leaves which have been added to complement the bouquet. If you look closely you will see that the green used to paint these contains a multitude of different colors which have merged together in a gradated way (violet, green, yellow and orange– fig. 4 of the following page).

Having reached this point the still life has taken on a lot of volume. Notice how, having always worked with light colors, the still life has gained a visual center and brightness in comparison with the previous exercise, where the grays and earth colors were present more. However, also notice how the shades have been accentuated by using purples, yellows and oranges, all of which mean that the painting has taken on something of a more colorful tendency.

1

Fig. 1. This time begin by painting the brightest parts. Paint the yellow flowers, in only a few seconds filling out the shape and color, modelling by superimposing the colors on wet.

2

Fig. 2. Do the same with the purplish flowers, blending green and magenta colours in the same wash, this process being one which gives rich textures.

3

Fig. 3. In the third stage of the painting you can see that the center part of the composition is nearly complete. This is due to the fact that the technique of painting on wet allows work to be done at a faster pace.

Now paint the basket's wickerwork and its characteristic texture with touches of ochre tinted with a little orange, burnt umber and little touches of ultramarine blue. Work on the wet colors giving them small straight strokes with blue and burnt umber in a way which makes the shadow vibrant. Given that this is not uniform the basket picks up a lot of emphasis (fig. 5). At this point the flower basket has such an intensity of color and texture that it has taken on an appearance which at many times is offered by oil paintings.

Take a medium brush and finish painting the background with purplish-greyish washes. If you want you can use the side of your hand to join or spread the still wet wash to achieve a sensation of translucence, taking advantage of the spontaneous fusion of the wet colors. Next paint with the same color, but somewhat more intense, the right side of the bunch to show the shadow and the contact of the model with the white surface. As you can see in the already finished watercolor, Óscar Sanchís has produced the bouquet with some vibrancy, with great brightness and light in a way which creates a balance between color and volume (fig. 6). He has left a lot of white areas for the painting to breathe, while he has covered other parts with transparent colors. Note the background washes which smoothly blend into the paper, and the trimmed profiles of the flowers to the right which show us where the areas of light and shadow begin and end.

4

Fig. 4. Now paint the branches, complete with their irregular array of leaves, which complement the composition. To do this mix green-yellow, orange and blue or violet such that these washes do not appear uniform , but instead are gradated.

5

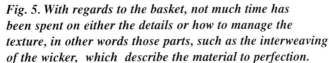

Fig. 5. With regards to the basket, not much time has been spent on either the details or how to manage the texture, in other words those parts, such as the interweaving of the wicker, which describe the material to perfection.

TIPS

- When you apply colors you must take into account the fact that a watercolor loses 10% of its intensity on drying.

- To control the spreading of the paint across the paper surface well, I recommend that you carry out this exercise on a board which is slightly angled. Do not work on a flat surface, because the excesses of water, instead of dripping down the paper will remain stuck and form small pools which on drying could badly effect the final result of the painting.

6

Fig. 6. Here we have the flowers of Óscar Sanchís in an original painting, with a particular conception and style, following the technique of painting on wet. As you can see the last step in finishing off the work has involved applying a very diluted grayto the background with the aim of spatially locating the bouquet.

Painting a Seascape with Spattered Paint

1

As we have said before, spattering, or spraying, is an excellent way of suggesting certain textures although it is also used to give livelihood to a painting with too many plain colored areas. So let's experiment with this technique and see how this curious method of applying paint can develop out of a seascape done in the technique of painting on wet. To carry out this exercise we have with us once again Óscar Sanchís.

The model is the view of some rocky cliffs of the Catalan coast. Those in the foreground have very definite shapes and colors, while in the background there are several planes of vegetation and rocky formations (fig. 1). To begin, sketch the main lines of the composition lightly with a number 2 pencil on a tensed sheet of paper. This will allow you to modify the drawing with an eraser without any difficulties (fig. 2). If take a used toothbrush and start to spatter different areas of the surface with orange and blue paint. By using this tool you will achieve a rather controlled spraying made up of numerous small drops of paint (fig. 3A). The way to carry out the spraying is as follows: First wet the toothbrush in paint until the bristles are well-covered. Then shake it carefully trying to get rid of any excess water. Next, hold it over the surface of the painting rubbing the bristles with your thumb, which will produce a spraying effect. The paint should be moist but not too watery. If you are going to work on large surfaces, you can also fill a bottle with paint and spray it on using a spraying device, or you could recycle a plastic spray bottle like those used for cleaning windows (fig. 3B).

2

3B

3A

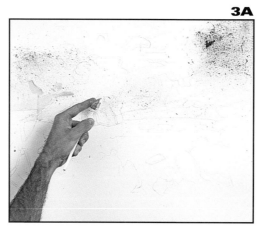

Fig. 1. We are going to paint this beautiful summer print of a rocky cove on the Costa Brava.
Fig. 2. The draft of the rocks in this seascape has been done in quite a bit of detail. You should also pay special attention to the shapes of the boats.
Fig. 3A. Instead of starting by applying washes, the first appraisal should be carried out by spraying on different colors.
Fig. 3B. In case you want to spray large surfaces, it's best to use a pulverizer like the kind we use to clean the house.

4

Then cover the bushes in the foreground with a semi-transparent yellowish wash and do the same for the water using ultramarine blue. Notice how the bluish wash brings out the outline of the vegetation in the foreground. This is known as contrasting complementary colors (fig. 4). The different applications of spattered paint (done with burnt umber, orange, green and ochre) should be applied freely, without worrying too much about coherence, covering the foreground and effectively transmitting the disorganized disposition of the leaves on the nearby bushes. The lighter tones of the rocks are painted with a mixture of ochre, cadmium orange and yellow (fig. 5). The first glazes should be very transparent. The colors will be intensified as the work progresses.

When these light colors have dried, tones of medium intensity, such as burnt sienna and burnt umber, are added and new applications of spattered paint (done with black, brown, green and gray) are applied onto the vegetation that covers the tops of the rocky cliffs as well as the foreground (fig. 6). Pay close attention to this spraying and you will see that this time the spattering is more violent and the dots are bigger. To achieve the rough textures of the rocks on the right you can use a small round brush.

Notice how both the trees and the rocks have been simplified and treated as large areas of color. The pictorial structure of the cliffs is almost abstract, but it retains sufficient detail for us to be able to identify the relief. The best way to achieve effects like those in the painting is to work on wet.

Spray the vegetation in the lower part of the image again using new colors (burnt umber, burnt sienna and violet). Since the bushes are closer we suggest using a bristle brush to spatter on the paint.

5

6

Fig. 4. The method the artist uses consists in spraying the basic areas with paint and then completing the process of building up the shapes with washes and using the wet on wet technique.

Fig. 5. The chromatic dynamism that the work will have can already be made out at this stage and the perfect communion between spraying and washes can also be seen.

Fig. 6. In order to paint the cliffs, the artist has concentrated his attention on the structure of the angular shapes that can be made out in the play between light and shadow.

In this way the drops will be coarser and larger, which will make the work more expressive (fig. 7). With a small brush add more spots to the vegetation, since the trees have noticeable and varied textures which provide us with a fascinating wealth of detail and shades of color. When you are about to finish the painting, it's a good idea to move a few steps back to decide what still needs to be done to unify the composition. It is important to vary the consistency of the paint and create attractive textures. To give life to the work, paint in some details with thick colors that will contrast with the diluted and faded tones of the washes. The spots where the white of the paper shows through correspond to the boats, which will be defined later (fig. 8).

As a finishing touch the vegetation on the tops of the cliffs in the background should be sprayed again using various colors (like violet, Hooker green, yellow, manganese blue and pink). And the dots are then redirected with a small brush. Finish by giving depth to the painting by contrasting and outlining the foreground. A few touches of more intense color on the water should be enough (fig. 9). At this stage, the sea has, in addition to different textures (areas treated with extensive washes, with spattered paint, with dense colors, etc.) an amalgam of colors (ochre, emerald green, ultramarine blue, indigo, sienna and pink) which defy the erroneous idea that many artists have of a smooth solid-colored surface with hardly any variations. With a small brush very carefully paint in the detail of the boats.

TIPS

—If you want to, you can reserve white spaces by covering up the parts of the canvas you want to keep free of paint.

—The nearer the brush is to the surface of the painting, the bigger the drops of paint will be.

—Both the shapes and the value planes are important in this context. The eye is always attracted to strong tonal contrasts, so the trees and the rocks that stick out in a seascape naturally become the focal point of the painting.

7

Fig. 7. Observe the variety of strokes and colors that have been used to define the copse at the top of the cliffs.

8

Fig. 8. Now, the saturated blue of the water contrasts with the brown colors of the cliffs and the adjacent vegetation, constituting the center of interest of this attractive seascape.

9

Fig. 9. The artist has enhanced the sensation of light in the foreground, increasing the contrast between the vegetation and the water.

As you will surely have noticed, the spraying technique is rather haphazard (which might have caused you some problems) since it's not possible to control exactly where the drops of paint will fall. However, it is a technique which offers a surprising finish and texture and is therefore worth mastering. Your colors might have gotten mixed as you sprayed them onto the paper, that is, some dots of different colors may have blended to form bigger dots. If this happened it's because, first of all, you were working with excessively thin paint, and in the second place, because you should have waited for one color to dry before spraying on another color on top of the first. In this way, the dots will follow each other creating glazes and the effect that will be produced will be similar to that produced in divisionism or pointillism.

When we find ourselves faced with a landscape as rich in motifs as this one, it is easy to be seduced by detail. You should avoid this. In order to do so, I advise you to deliberately use big brushes so as not to paint in an excessively detailed fashion. You will find this tactic useful when you want to give a painting a free and audacious air. A common mistake is to go over the painting too much, for thereby you lose the sense of fluidity.

You will also notice that this painting has a logical movement, that is to say, the rocks repeat a series of angular shapes, the water contains reflections and should be dealt with in horizontal strokes, whereas the strokes used on the vegetation should be made with scribbling movements. Try to make your strokes into the shape of these movements in order to keep it from looking static.

Fig. 10. Here is the elaborate texture of the finished work. Since acrylics dry quickly, it is possible to create a surface with a large amount of spattered paint in very little time, without running the risk of the colors mixing.

Painting a Sunset with Impasto

One of the most attractive aspects of painting is the possibility of giving volume to the surface of a work. This characteristic was not sufficiently exploited by the old masters, who tried to obtain a smooth uniform finish by combining glazes and scraped on paint, saving impasto for touches of light. But with the arrival of acrylic and mediums capable of giving paint more volume, a new field of possibilities has been opened. Currently, impasto is used quite assiduously to create works with vigorous colors and a strong expressionist effect.

Once again, with the help of Óscar Sanchís, you will learn how a work of these characteristics is to be carried out and which problems this may entail.

Before you begin painting, you will need to find a model with characteristics suitable for being depicted using impastos. It must be textured, contain sharp contrasts of light and little detail. We have found all of this in a beautiful sunset on one of the many beaches of Guardalavaca, on the island of Cuba. (fig. 1)

The artist has not made a preliminary drawing, but has started to paint right away using the palette knife to lay on the paint as it comes out of the tube, because he wanted the painting to develop out of its own momentum (fig. 2). After a few minutes of work, you will quickly see that it is the vertical chromatic emphasis brought about by the sun and its reflections on the water

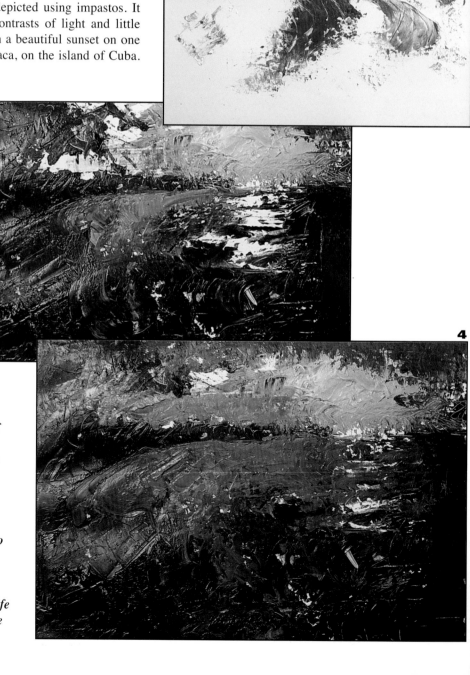

Fig. 1. The model is a beautiful sunset on the beaches of Guardalavaca (Cuba).

Fig. 2. Here are the first patches of color. The surface of the paper has been worked on with scarcely three or four shades which are mixed directly on the support.

Fig. 3. Once the main outline has been made, the artist can proceed to identify the shapes.

Fig. 4. Make your impastos more dynamic by scraping the palette knife over the surface of the paper to give more vitality to your compositions.

5

which should be the prevailing aspect of the composition. Use the following colors for the first stages of the process: flesh color, ultramarine blue, cadmium red, cadmium yellow and ochre. Now is the moment to add thickening medium to the color mixtures. When mixing paint with relief paste, this increases the volume without changing the color and it can be applied directly onto the support (fig. 3).

The large masses of color, as you can see, have been painted very rapidly so that the artist can go back over some specific aspects without becoming too obsessed with the details or interfering with the basic design. Some of the shapes and local colors of the photograph on the previous page can begin to be discerned. Try to get to the same stage, by copying the process followed by the artist (fig. 4). Add a bigger and bigger proportion of modeling paste, as your work progresses.

Little by little, the violet hues become more prevalent in the sky (which is covered in a shade of violet toned down with white), on the coastline and the sea (here the violet hues have a certain indigo tendency) and in the lower area where the reflections are found (in these there is a larger proportion of cadmium red). The water of the bay, on the other hand, has been obtained by scraping on successive layers of ultramarine blue, cobalt blue and gray with a round-tipped palette knife. The paint can be manipulated in different ways. It is even possible to apply or remove it with the fingers. In figure 5 you can see how the artist uses his hand as a work instrument in order to finish off some details. Highly textured landscapes with expressive and extraordinarily subtle colors can be created in this way. At this stage, the strokes of the impasto, which imitate those of the landscape, stick out for their precision and the marks of the palette knife and the fingers emulate the marks of the terrain (fig. 6). Notice how, on the one hand, the sparkling of the light on the surface of the water acquires more volume and relief than any other part of the painting.

The artist continues to work with the paints. Here he is using a rounded palette knife to scrape on some layers of color before painting the outline of

the tree on the left. You should do the same. You need to work the impasto with your wrist, molding and guiding the paint so that the texture of the work forms the shapes of the landscape. As you can see, this technique owes a great deal to the art of sculpture (fig. 7).

Now work on the darker areas of the painting, which need to be given a little more life and some more

Fig. 5. In some areas the fingers have been used to model the thick edges of the paint and achieve subtle tonal gradations.

Fig. 6. A few minutes later, it becomes obvious that the powerful reflections of the sun on the surface of the water will become the focal point of this composition.

6

7

Fig. 7. The movement of the water of the sea and the rocking of the branches of the trees are depicted using the palette knife to scrape on the paint.

65

light. To this effect, apply light colors inside the darker ones, especially on the waves of the sea that break against the shore. Use a small triangular palette knife for this task. The effect of the sea foam and the touches of light on the waves have been done by scraping the palette knife against the still moist paint in order to get a bit of white (fig. 9).

Using the same palette knife and a violet-like color tending towards black, draw the branches of the tree on the right. Saturate the rest of the surface of the water with small black spots, in such a way that they mix with the other colors. Now look at the contrast between the different textures of the surface of the sea, with thick curls of paint in some places and the effects of graffito on the branches of the tree on the left. Impasto does not consist merely in accumulating paint, it also involves distributing and guiding it as if we were working with low relief (fig. 8).

Add some more tou-

ches of light gray in the area where the waves break against the sand, and darken the central area even more, so that the sparkling reflection of the sun on the turbulent surface of the sea appears more luminous by contrast. Some of the areas of the painting are now already finished. The large quantity of paint that has been accumulated produces a disconcerting effect, giving a basically flat surface a three dimensional quality. Seen from a certain distance, the intense chromatic sparkling creates a radiant and vivacious seascape and an optic mixture of colors that surprises the spectator with its chromatic spectacularity.

This work painted by Óscar Sanchís shows how the palette knife and the impasto technique should be used as an expressive medium. Looking at the

8

9

TIPS

—It is advisable to mix colors before adding modeling paste.
—When the paint has dried, the colors stick out less than when it was moist. This is because the paste is white, but when it dries it becomes transparent.
—Hold the palette knife at different angles, vary the amount of pressure exerted on the blade and use different parts of it to obtain different types of lines and effects.

10

Fig. 8. Try to include as many textures as possible in your painting, but do it following a selective criterion so that they will enhance the beauty of the painting as a whole.
Fig. 9. One of the characteristics of this painting is precisely the variety of textures that are produced with the palette knife.
Fig. 10. As you can see, the definition of the light and dark areas contributes to the attractiveness of the painting just as much as the textures.
Fig. 11. After the intense work with mixtures and impastos, here is the finished work. The scratching done with the palette knife and the relief of the pictorial layer contribute even more to the expressiveness of this work.

11

finished work, you can see how the physical presence of the thick paint brings it forward in space, bringing it closer (speaking in terms of perspective) to the spectator, while the relief and the chromatic combinations make the painting more tangible and more expressionistic. Comparing the painting to the natural model shows that, despite the free treatment it was given, the painting is very true to the theme. Try to avoid being one of those painters who works slowly and hesitantly. This could cause you problems, not only because of the drying time but also in terms of the concept of the

work. Do not be afraid to work rapidly on the support. Establish the main traits of the composition and the relationships between colors immediately. Painting with impasto should be bold and spontaneous, not slow and stiff. The sensation of movement transmitted by the painting depends on the energy and impact of the strokes. One thick stroke on its own tends to transmit stasis but a series of free and fluid impastos will give life to the movement of the trees or the backward and forward motion of the waves. Do not try to produce a photographic copy. This is impossible when working with

impasto since impasto does not allow detail. Let your hand follow the contours of the landscape instinctively, so that the movements of the palette knife transmit the effect of fluidity of the water, the direction of the branches and the movement of the waves. Obviously, you will not obtain a "finished" image, but you will learn a lot about how landscapes using impasto work. Finally, I would advise you not to be misled. Although paintings with a lot of impasto give the impression of more freedom and improvisation, the truth is that they require a careful planning.

Painting a Landscape with a Palette Knife

Acrylics are a very flexible procedure which can be used in light washes, in a way similar to watercolors, or in impastos applied with a palette knife, as in the procedures reminiscent of the traditional techniques of oil painting. In order to do this exercise, we are going to use the second of the methods described.

Painting with a palette knife is an impasto technique. In this step-by-step exercise we count with the collaboration of Josep Antoni Domingo, who has already worked with us on previous exercises. In order to do this exercise, you will need two or three palette knives of different shapes and sizes. This technique requires patience and a steady hand. The method is laborious, so it is best not to begin with an excessively large painting. A 12 inch wide panel will do.

You can see the model in figure 0. It is a view of Uçhisar, a small village of the Capadocia, in the heart of Turkey, in the hours just before sunset.

The less experienced painter would have to do a preliminary drawing as a guide for the first applications of paint. But Josep Antoni Domingo goes directly to the building up of the main shapes using soft color washes. Try to place the fundamental shapes of the landscape as well, by making a first appraisal with hardly perceptible washes. This will allow you to make modifications if you make a mistake. (fig. 2).

When the initial pre-painting has dried, continue, still working with the brush, using thicker and more opaque paint to intensify the colors of the composition. Use ochre for the blades of grass in the foreground, emerald green, English red and ultramarine blue and violet in the middle ground and burnt umber, emerald green and cadmium green for the objects in the distance. Keep the colors as clean and pure as they are in the image, letting each area of color be clearly distinguishable on the canvas, and trying to keep them from mixing with the previous ones. Paint the sky with broad brushstrokes of cobalt blue, using a somewhat darker shade in the upper part of the canvas (fig. 3).

Fig. 1. The model for this exercise is a rural view of a village in central Turkey. It has pronounced contrasts of light and shade due to the fact that the sun is about to set.

Fig. 2. Without making a preliminary drawing, the artist starts outlining large areas with highly diluted paint that will act as a base for the successive layers.

Fig. 3. More tones have been added here, establishing a more specific color key.

4

Add a little emerald green to the sky, thereby suggesting the relief of the clouds that although inexistent in the model, the artist has considered would give the blue of the sky more variety. By pressing down lightly on the palette knife as you use it to move the paint across the paper, small irregular scratch marks will be produced that give the landscape a much richer texture (fig. 4).

Continue working on the painting with a small hog bristle brush, adding various shades to the background: emerald green and Hooker green for the vegetation, and bluish hues for the group of mountains on the right. Complete the shape of the houses using the palette knife to add new applications of paint that complement the initial shades (fig. 5)

Before applying a second appraisal, let the previous layer dry slightly. The artist spreads the paint onto the surface with a triangular palette knife, using the paint as it comes out of the tube, thereby making the red of the roof of the mosque more intense, adding new sha-

5

des to the intense blue that shapes the ravine on the left, projecting the violet shadows of the houses and applying new touches to the vegetation in the fields in the background (fig. 6). You should do the same.

The artist's palette knife flattens the paint against the surface of the support and leaves behind it a series of thin impastos with a slight relief where the application of color comes to an end. In this way, the color of the grass in the foreground is given even more life, by applying a thicker and creamier yellow which can be obtained by mixing ochre, white and a little bit of burnt umber.

Fig. 4. Mix a certain amount of thick paint, load the palette knife and spread the paint onto the surface of the paper.

Fig. 5. Consider the possibility of bringing out the color of the sky with the help of the palette knife. All you have to do is comb the paint in order to flatten it and obtain a richer and more textured effect.

6

Fig. 6. In this illustration you can see the effects obtained though successive mixtures of paint.

Normally impasto is saved for the details in the foreground, but in this case the distant fields have not been outlined in order to bring out the group of houses that are lit up by the setting sun, houses whose shadows are usually represented with a group of scarce thick solid-colored spots applied with a small palette knife (fig. 7).

Go back to the foreground in order to add new shades, this time using brown that has been toned down with white for the blades of grass in order to rein- force the linear element. Do this with the tip of the triangular palette knife (triangular palette knives are able to achieve effects of surprising precision) Continue building up the details of the vegetation in the background using different greens and browns. Touch up some of the details like the openings of the houses, the chimneys and the fine strokes that run vertically up and down the minaret, which have been done using the edge of a palette knife loaded with paint and pressing down onto the surface (fig. 8). As a colophon the artist added some strokes of paint applied with a small round brush to finish off the definition of some tex- tures and some details that could not be done with the palette knife.

Here is the finished work (fig. 9) Surely it is not what you expected. You may have imagined that paintings done with a palette knife produced

7

TIPS

—If you have problems with the drying process, either because the impasto you have applied is too thick or because the atmospheric conditions you are painting in are excessively humid, it would be convenient to dispose of a hair drier.

—A palette knife with an undulat- ed blade is ideal for achieving dif- ferent effects. Use the tip of the blade to add details or to dot the surface with incisions. Use the flat part of the blade to modify large areas and the edge to make lines.

—If you have overdone it with the impasto technique, you can elimi- nate some of the excessively thick layers of paint by using the flat part of the palette knife to scrape it off.

Fig. 7. The intense vio- let color of the shadows provides a sense of balance with the blues of the ravine and the warmer colors of the facades of the houses which are illuminated by the sunlight.

8

Fig. 8. The richness of the colors has been obtained by spreading one layer of paint after another, dark on light or vice versa.

vibrant works, with little definition and coarse impastos. But well-defined compositions like this one can also be achieved.

You may have let yourself be dominated too much by a desire to be effectist and that consequently your work has turned out excessively textured. You should learn to combine areas of flat color with denser impastos. Otherwise your work will appear too packed. As you can see in the painting done by Josep Antoni Domingo, the impastos have hardly any relief. If, on the contrary, the impastos have dried too quickly and this has made the posterior superposition of new colors difficult, what you have to do is add retardant medium to the mixture. In that way, the

drying time will be lengthened and the paint that is applied will be able to be manipulated again on the support, even a couple of hours after being applied. It is not necessary to work quickly. What matters is the result.

Surely painting with a palette knife must have seemed more complicated than painting with a brush, at least at first. Don't worry. After this exercise work on it until you have acquired the necessary practice.

Fig. 9. The use of a palette knife for painting is usually associated with thick impastos, but the truth is that it can also be used to produce works like this one, full of delicate effects and detail.

Landscape with Marble Powder

In this next exercise, we are going to see how the artist Grau Carod goes about painting with the technique of creating textures with marble powder. It will also help you to understand how a fatty medium, such as oil painting, can be mixed with a more acrylic procedure, such as marble powder.

To do this step by step exercise, as well as oil paints, you will need about 250 grams of latex and 300 grams of marble powder. Pour both elements onto a plastic plate or a piece of glass and mix them with a little water to make a paste with a consistency similar to that of cement.

Now study the model. It is a pretty view of Miravet, near Tarragona in Spain, which combines fields and trees, highly appropriate for creating interesting textural effects (fig. 1). Decide how you are going to represent the relief. Do as the artist does: take a spatula and start molding the surface of the support with the paste (the support should be laid out flat on a table) (fig. 2). Try to represent the relief of the vegetation on the mountains with small pastes. Leave one side white, without texture, for the sky and the groups of hills in the distance (fig. 3). Before you start painting, leave the mixture to dry for at least a day.

After that time has passed, pass your hand over the surface to check that it has dried properly and that, consequently, the support is ready to be painted on.

Start painting the sky and the distant hills with ultramarine blue washes with a touch of carmine. The color should be slightly diluted with thinners so that the paint is deposited in the creases and irregularities of the surface. Also, add ochre and permanent green to the more distant planes (fig. 4).

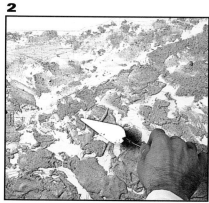

Fig. 1. The model is this pretty view of Miravet, a little village near Tarragona, Spain. Its orography is just right for working with marble powder.

Fig. 2. Use a spatula to apply the marble powder directly onto the support in the right shapes and patterns.

Fig. 3. Compare this image to the original photo and you will see that the relief and pastes of texture are just the same as those in the model.

Fig. 4. Start covering the sky and distant hills in different colors and add the first greens to the vegetation.

With just three or four colors, the artist establishes the compositional layout and sets out the color key. Do the same. Spread more color over the rough surface so that brown and green colors dominate. Permanent green and ochre, in particular, will play an important role in the finished piece. At this point, the artist uses deliberately large strokes to avoid details. This is a useful tactic if you want the paint to have a wide, daring conception (fig. 5).

Here are the first tonal values. They may not be the definitive colors, but they will serve to eliminate the intrusive white of the support. The color has been applied with irregular, slightly blurred outlines. Both the houses and vegetation have been simplified and painted with large areas of color (fig. 6). At this point, the pictorial structure of the painting is almost abstract. A background painted beforehand in relatively plain colors serves as a base onto which successive layers of merged colors can be added.

After these first stages where the paint has been diluted with thinners, start painting more densely colored layers. Touch up the mountains in the background with a little Prussian blue, making sure that their outlines contrast enough with the blue of the sky. The outlines must be clear so that they are not confused with the vegetation. With more neutral colors, and in particular ochre, work on the mountainsides by adding new layers of vegetation (fig. 7).

The object of this exercise is not to make too detailed a reproduction of the landscape, so the roof can be painted with a layer of plain red and the walls of the houses are lighter to highlight them more clearly against the green-ochre landscape in the background. We can make out a few details, such as the windows, doors and chimneys.

5

6

7

Fig. 5. Keep elaborating the middle ground with an irregular range of colors that increase the textured effect of the dense foliage on the mountainsides.

Fig. 6. As you can see, the artist's method involves coloring basic areas and then building them up with shorter strokes.

Fig. 7. Notice how the paint is spread softly over the surface to create the effect of lightness in the vegetation on the hillsides.

73

8

Trying to detail the houses any more would be an error, because the textured background that we are working on does not allow for too much elegance (fig. 8). Now, we work a little more on the rocks in the foreground, which give a greater sense of depth to the landscape, and darken the vegetation in the middle ground even more, so that they contrast better with the more distant planes. This somewhat blurred and imprecise treatment of the different areas of color lend a certain sense of movement, light and color to the picture (fig. 9).

At this stage, you should use horsehair bristles, be they flat or rounded. The color has thickened as the piece has progressed, even becoming a paste at this final stage (fig. 10).

Although there is not much detail or accuracy, the painting portrays the scene's strength of character. If you try to make the vegetation or the buildings more detailed, you will not find it an easy task because marble powder is a rough, coarse material that does not lend itself very well to meticulous work. You should use a lot of modeling and merging for this painting. The paint is usually applied with the light, rubbing movements of a hard brush. When working on a marble powder background,

9

TIPS

–When working on a surface textured with marble powder, you need brushes with resistant bristles, such as horsehair. If you use softer bristles, you will be dismayed at how quickly they get worn. This is because the grainy surface of marble powder is highly erosive when it is rubbed upon.

–If you want to modify the initial texture, try to do it while the paste is still wet. Once it is dry, the paste gets hard, and your only option is to paste another layer on top.

Fig. 8. Detail needs to be minimal, because a textured background is not suitable for highly elaborate work.

Fig. 9. The set of houses has been painted geometrically to contrast with an imprecise background in which colors are superimposed over others with little apparent meaning.

10

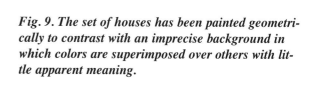

Fig. 10. If we darken the vegetation in the middle ground and add detail to the rocks in the foreground, the composition looks deeper.

11

bear in mind that the texture of the paste will help you to neutralize the color (fig. 11).

You will have almost certainly wondered how you are supposed to go about correcting a mistake when painting on a surface like this. You obviously cannot take the color off with a spatula and paint over it again, as you would do if you were working on a flat surface, but there is a solution. You should get a cloth (blotting paper is no good because it would tear) and dampen it with a little thinners. Rub it over the area in question and try to get rid of any unwanted paint. Keep rubbing with the cloth until you get the gray color of the marble powder back. Now you can repaint the section.

Fig. 11. Despite the difficulties of working on a marble paste background, the paint in its final state has a remarkable textural and chromatic richness. The combination of oil paints and marble powder is one of the most popular mixed techniques in art today.

Painting a Lake in Acrylics and Oils

Yet again we are counting on Josep A.Domingo's skills to help us with this exercise. He will be painting a scene in acrylics and oils. The subject is a peaceful view of a lake in Catalonia on a summer afternoon (fig.1). This scene in acrylics you will need the following colors, Burnt Umber, Chrome Green, Cadmium Yellow, Cobalt Blue, Ultramarine Blue, Golden Ochre, Olive Green, Emerald Green, Raw Umber, Vermilion and Titanium White. You will also need a selection of flat bristle brushes and a sable brush for details.

First add some delicate touches in Ultramarine Blue to the darkest areas where the color is most intense. Some artists always paint in the shadows in a violet color particularly in the open air as the light conditions can change rapidly (fig.3).

Continue by adding the main themes of the landscape with a mixture of Golden Ochre and a little Olive Green with Ultramarine Blue. At this stage the colors should be applied in a diluted form, making cautious progress to avoid covering the entire sketch with opaque paint. These dilute colors serve as a base for the following washes (fig.4).

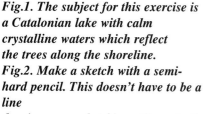

Fig.1. The subject for this exercise is a Catalonian lake with calm crystalline waters which reflect the trees along the shoreline.
Fig.2. Make a sketch with a semi-hard pencil. This doesn't have to be a line
drawing as any sketching will eventually be covered by opaque paint.
Fig.3. Paint delicately at first then with increasing boldness, first introducing washes of blue in the clear patches of sky, the distant hills and the lake.
Fig.4. Continue adding washes and toning down the white of the paper. You will notice that at this stage the washes are transparent, applied in a similar manner to watercolors.

Add a little orange in the middle ground and some Olive Green and Cobalt Blue in the lower half of the picture. What you have to do now is keep adding further layers over the initial washes. Reproduce the colors of the vegetation, upside down on the surface of the water, to create the reflections. Start to sculpt the clouds in soft pinks and blues, painting them using delicate layers of paint, overlaying the colors to create an atmospheric effect (fig.5).

Keep working, complete the deep blue hills and the clouds gathered in the sky, then move on to the foreground and middle ground. Observe how, as the more intense colors are introduced (the violet in the sky, the oranges in the vegetation), the painting gains volume, depth and intensity (fig.6).

Now turn your attention to the surface of the lake. See how the artist has painted the reflections of the trees along the far margins of the lake. He uses a range of colors similar to those used for the trees but the range is darker and colder. You will also notice that where the house is reflected, the artist has left a white space which projects vertically over the crystalline surface of the lake. All these reflections are painted with strong vertical brushstrokes. The foreground is still roughly defined, the washes are uneven and of varying thickness. Try to imitate this effect (fig.7).

5

Fig.5. Add the first contrasts and color gradations to the initial washes. In this way the image progressively develops using the colors taken from the original.

6

7

8

Fig.6. Work on the image as a whole, developing a richer blend of colors so that the clouds and the middle ground are intensified.

Fig.7. See how the reflections in the water recreate the same shapes and colors of the vegetation on the margin of the water. This can be achieved by simply extending the strips of color vertically downwards.

Fig.8. With a fine sable brush, develop the distant reflections and the ripples that appear on the water's surface in the foreground.

The next part of the exercise is more complex and requires all your powers of observation. To paint the ripples on the water's surface in the foreground you need to look carefully at how they are created. In order to reproduce them take up a fine sable brush, a little sky blue, and patiently trace the radiating ripples.

With the same brush, using a darker Olive Green, continue working on the ripples by adding little patches with a series of parallel lines of irregular lengths (fig. 8 previous page).

Continue by adding details in the middle ground with hints of Olive Green, oranges, yellows and reds. For this, use a fine bristle brush. The brilliant dashes of orange bring out the middle ground, while the blues and pinks of the clouds on the horizon make them recede. In this respect, colors are another important factor when it comes to creating depth in a composition (fig. 9). Bear in mind that any alterations of color that you make to the vegetation need to be imitated in the reflections on the water's surface.

Look closely at the clouds, their initial sketchy appearance has been refined, the distant hills are clearly defined.

Fig 9. If you want to highlight the house all you need do is intensify the colors of the vegetation surrounding it and it will stand out because of the increased contrasts.

Fig.10. This is the result of the work in acrylics. From this point we will work on the texture of the composition using oil paints.

Fig.11. Work an impasto across the clouds with a flat brush, giving them more body.
Fig.12. Do the same with the vegetation in the middle ground. The texture of the crowns of the trees works well and is complimented by the brilliant colors of the oil paints.

TIPS

- Paint some of the details with dense colors to contrast with areas of diluted and subdued tone. This will bring the composition to life.
- Before applying oils to the acrylic paints be sure that the acrylics are completely dry, if they are damp it is highly likely that the surface will start cracking in a few days.
- Remember that oil is always applied to acrylics and never the other way round. Acrylics do not have enough hold to be painted over oils and after a few days they will start to peel off.

The sharp profile of the hills has the effect of projecting them towards us, however, this effect is contradicted by the smooth texture of this plane (fig.10 earlier page).

Now you can leave the acrylics and take up the oils. By applying an impasto of colors, you can create textures that enrich the composition by adding relief and depth. It is vital to vary the paint's consistency to create interesting textures. To do this, the artist takes a small flat brush and adds some initial layers of impasto to increase the body of the clouds (fig.11 previous page). As you will see, oil paints have a more brilliant appearance than acrylics.

The abundant use of oil impasto applied in the middle ground has the effect that the trees are projected towards the viewer, they become the focal point of the composition. The use of oils also allows you to liven up the colors of the middle ground by adding irregular brushstrokes to the vegetation. If you look closely at the detail (fig.12 previous page) you will see

how distinct the two media are from one another.

You may well have had problems creat-ing the reflections in the lake and the ripples in the foreground. Unfortunately it is hard to advise you further as there are no specific rules that make these effects easier to capture. All I can suggest is that you look carefully at the way in which the artist has combined and applied the colors and that you endeavour to do likewise.

If you find yourself struggling with a similar difficulty when painting outdoors, you must rely on meticulous observation and attempt to transfer the information that you see directly onto the paper. Turning to the combination of oils and acrylics, you shouldn't have any problems with these two media as, despite their different consistency, they are not dissimilar in terms of the way they should be handled and applied. Perhaps the only drawback that you may come across is the speed at which the acrylics dry, you are under pressure to work swiftly, you may be pushed for time if you want to mix colors on wet.

Fig.13. This is the finished composition, which skillfully combines the qualities of the two media: the quick drying and excellent covering power of acrylics and the freshness, texture and brilliance of the oil paints.

13

View of a Town with Acrylics

We will begin with a very easy exercise. In consists in painting the view of a town with acrylics, first using glazes and then adding detail to the houses with a small brush in more intense, contrasting colors. This first exercise is going to be carried out by the Aragonese painter and engraver, Teresa Trol, who is an expert in acrylics, having painted numerous works using this medium throughout her career.

The model is an aerial view of Begur, a village on the Catalan coast (fig. 1). The first step is making a draft, although you should limit yourself to drawing the motif in just a few lines. Do not try for a finished drawing, but make the sketch as simple as possible. Use charcoal for this first step (fig. 2).

Once you have made a draft of the composition, wipe the surface with a rag in order to remove any remaining charcoal. You will see that after rubbing it out, you will still be able to make out the outlines of the drawing on the paper although these will be fainter. Take a medium-size paintbrush and apply soft washes of cadmium green for the vegetation and chrome oxide green on the roofs of some houses (fig. 3). Now, with a little ochre, burnt sienna and raw umber and using semi-transparent washes, paint the roofs of the nearest houses. At this point, only the most important traits of the painting will be outlined, the paint being applied as diluted as possible. The base of the areas which are to remain light in the finished painting, must remain white (fig. 4).

The basic shapes of the composition have been set using washes and now it is time to continue working with a small brush adding contrast between light and dark tones to the painting to indicate the shape and tone of the houses and the vegetation in the foreground. Now paint the pronounced outlines and the textures and relief of the roofs and the facades of the houses.

Fig. 1. The model is an aerial view of Begur, a village on the Costa Brava.

Fig. 2. The composition has been sketched with charcoal, combining thin lines with more intense ones.

Fig. 3. A general transparent wash is gently applied, which will act as a base on which we will begin applying more paint.

Fig. 4. At this point, the outlines of some of the houses have been sketched in using glazes.

5

As you can see, the new paint that is added easily covers what has already been painted (fig. 5).

Little by little the image of the village takes shape. Continue building it up. Take the dark alley that leads to the church as a point of reference. Starting there, work on each of the houses along the way individually. Start with the foreground, drawing parallel lines that simulate the placement of the roof tiles. Intensify the vegetation in the foreground with sap green and paint the openings, that is, the doors and windows, of the group of houses, black. You need to move upwards, over the surface of the paper, until you get to the church (fig. 6). Do not forget to decrease the intensity of the colors as the brush moves upwards or, in other words, as you move further into the background and away from the spectator. At this point, finish outlining the houses more precisely, using a thin brush, and then try to accent the contrast between the lighter areas (roofs of the houses) and darker ones (openings and narrow streets).

6

Towards the end, the composition already has a powerful sense of space, which comes not only from the typical style of the houses, but also from the colors and light effects (fig. 7). To finish, apply an ultramarine blue wash to the background to give the painting more depth and to make the outline of the church tower and the roofs of the village houses stand out.

7

Use the same shade of ultramarine blue that you used for the vegetation in the background on the facades and roofs of the houses in order to achieve a greater unity of color in the painting. Shadows contain a great deal of blue. Make it visible. And here is the result (fig. 8): the view of a town built up using a combination of lines and glazes.

Fig. 5. In the foreground, the more intense lines, which have been made with a small brush, complement the previous washes.

Fig. 6. Once again using the small brush, the artist adds detail to the textures of the roofs, marks the openings of the houses and paints in the location of the dark alleys.

Fig. 7. As we move up the painting, the houses should not be as well-defined as those in the foreground. This will make them appear to be further away.

Fig. 8. The finished work is a good example of how washes can be combined with a meticulous and detailed finish.

TIPS

—Beginning painters tend to avoid landscapes with an excessive agglomeration of houses. However, this exercise shows that it can be a stimulating theme with considerable possibilities.

—Do not leave small brushes, especially the one used in this exercise, in a jar with water for too long, since the bristles tend to lose their shape as a result of their contact with the bottom of the jar.

8

Urban Landscape with Fusion Techniques

Markets, cafes and streets are interesting subjects to paint, because they offer us a wide range of effects, textures and forms. And that is exactly what Carlant is going to do in this exercise, paint a street with pedestrians using fusion techniques. Although one of the main effects of oil paintings is the use of heavy brushstrokes, another of its most characteristic aspects is that brush marks can be hidden by mixing and softening.

For this step by step exercise, the subject is going to be a street in the old quarter of Bern, Switzerland (fig. 1). As you can see, the subject offers a powerful sense of space, not only derived from the point of view or the typical style of houses, but also the rainy weather, which appears in the image in the form of grays, ochres and violets that contrast with the warmer appearance of the sky.

Let's start. For painting with such a strong tonal structure, a sketch with dark, gray colors can be very effective. Do as the artist does and start off with a brush drawing (fig. 2).

Pre-paint with gray, opaque tones, which will give you the chance to concentrate on the forms and tonal values of the subject before having to make any decisions with regard to color. Work on the sky in the same way. Use two degraded colors for this - Naples yellow and a little carmine. The presence of carmine should be more evident as you approach the horizon (fig. 3).

Fig. 1. Carlant is going to paint this picture of a wide street in the old town quarter of Bern in Switzerland.

Fig. 2. If you plan to paint a picture with a lot of merging and blending, it is a good idea to make a sketch with the lines drawn with a brush.

With somewhat more intense colors, sketch the figure with his back turned and the fountain in the foreground.

At this early stage, the artist is using just as much diluted paint as thick paint, and sometimes merges very diluted colors over thicker layers. With a small brush and a touch of ochre and raw umber, he has sketched the sculpted figure that appears on the left-hand facade. In a similar way, he has added this color to other parts of the painting, such as the hair of the person with his back turned and one of the cars on the right (fig. 4).

Fig. 3. The subject is constructed with light grays over which thicker colors are superimposed. A mixture of carmine and Naples yellow is used for the sky.

Fig. 4. After a short while, the white of the paper is covered with the first values of rather dull colors.

As you can see, the artist constructs the forms by merging the colors with the layers below. Merging, softening and blending techniques make the surface look smoother and rid the picture of the presence and immediacy of straight lines, replacing them with a softer, more global treatment (fig. 5). You should do the same.

The arches and windows of the facades have been painted using merging, brushing thin layers of opaque paint over another color that remains visible in places and plays an important role in the appearance of the painting. The limits between one color and another are not so clear, they are rather imprecise and blurred (fig. 6).

The figures have been painted with the minimum of detail but the results are convincing enough because of the care that has gone into their postures, clothes and movements (fig. 7). To get these results, work with a small brush.

If you paint the picture in just one session, you will find it easier to get the progressive graduations of color and tone right. This is because the painting stays damp long enough for a larger series of colors and tones to be spread. You will see that the windows in the facades are less detailed and more blurred the further away they are. To do this, use a fanned brush like a feather duster to flatten or blend the colors.

5

6

7

Fig. 5. The depth of color in the facades of the streets has been created with a series of superimposed, merged colors that produce subtle degradations.

Fig. 6. The way of harmonizing the different areas of gray and violet colors is the unifying factor of space in the painting.

Fig. 7. This illustration shows how the outlines of the groups of people have been blended into the surrounding tones. Different brushes have been used for the task.

83

Used like this, the brush merges the colors together but keeps them separate (fig. 8).

Once the effect of depth, or perspective, has been established, paint the details of the fountain in the foreground. Use more intense colors that will show up against the other tones in the picture. If necessary, you now have to create more contrasts so that the painting looks more three-dimensional.

This is when we stop to analyze the development of the painting. You can see how the artist has used low key colors, to create a rather dull, but more delicate and subtle, chromatic tendency. The colors are not saturated, but neutral and reduced (fig. 9).

And here is the finished painting (fig. 10). You may have had problems constructing the depth of the image. For a subject like this, you need to think carefully about the perspective of the buildings. It is not difficult if we remember the basic rule that the parallel lines will always join on the horizon. If the perspective is wrong, a building or view of a street can look rather unconvincing. Proportion is just as important. The windows in the facades, the sizes of the people – they all need to look right in relation to each other. The width and height of a

8

Fig. 8. One can often capture the atmosphere of a place through the use of color and texture, with neutralized colors for a rainy scene like this.

Fig. 9. The overall neutrality gives an extraordinary force to the dull colors of an overcast day.

TIPS

–Normally, paintings like this are based on sketches or the combination of studies and photographs because people are never going to stay in the same place long enough for you to paint them from nature.

–All city streets have a characteristic atmosphere. So, when you decide to paint an urban landscape, try to recapture that atmosphere and find the essential elements that portray the character and feeling of the place.

–If you want to soften your tones even more, you can use a sable brush on the surface of the painting, following along the borders of different colors.

9

10

building must relate to each other properly, and check the sizes of the doors and arches. The painting may look too floury, which means there is too much white. You need to realize that adding a color does not have to mean adding white too. Colors can also be lightened with (among others)

Naples yellow, ochre, cadmium yellow or sky blue. If you have been merging, the result may look too uniform, with too few contrasts and therefore, too little relief. After softening, the most normal thing to do is to mark the darker and lighter tones and repaint them during the final stage.

Fig. 10. Inexpert painters try to avoid urban landscapes, but the exercise on these pages shows just how stimulating the many possibilities of this subject can be.

Painting Roofs with the *Anticerne* Effect

1

Now we are going to do a more creative exercise, in which contrasts of color play a fundamental role. We are going to be painting the rooftops of a pretty seaside town using the *anticerne* effect. This is an alternative technique that uses colored backgrounds so that colored strokes appear isolated and surrounded by the color of the background. For this exercise, we are going to be working with the renowned artist Óscar Sanchís.

First, let's look at the model. It is a view of several rows of picturesque rooftops in the Croatian town of Rovinj (fig. 1). The painting is going to use a daring range of colors that play on the contrast between warm colors lit by a bright sun and the cool colors of the buildings in the shadows, shaded by brushstrokes that represent the warm reflections.

We start by covering the background with a light orange color (fig. 2). On colored backgrounds, the image has more body and volume than when it appears on white, even at the preparatory stage. These backgrounds serve to provide a global hue for the superimposed colors and lays out a semi-light color base over which both dark and light colors can be painted. The background color that you are going to paint on needs to be completely dry

2

before you spread any more paint over it, so it might be a good idea to leave the canvas to dry for a few days before you start work. If you like, you can paint the background with acrylic paints because they only take about half an hour to dry. With a small brush loaded with an intense blue, start working on the outline sketch. As you can see, this is a linear drawing, without any coloring in or degradations (fig. 3) (Óscar Sanchís often likes to paint directly, without bothering with any preparatory work, but this time it seems like he has preferred to lay out a few basic outlines). For the preparatory sketch, the artist has used blue because it is orange's complementary color, in other words, the one that will contrast most on an orange background (fig. 4). Start painting the vegetation with dense, opaque colors, using a medium, flat brush. Just a few directional lines, with the bristles well loaded with color, should be enough (fig. 5). Tonal backgrounds like this require opaque painting methods. Veiling is no good here, because white cannot be reflected.

3

4

Fig. 1. The model is this pretty aerial view of rooftops in the tourist resort of Rovinj, on the Croatian coast.

Fig. 2. Painters who are used to painting on white are always surprised by the excellent chromatic possibilities of painting over a differently colored background.

Fig. 4. This is the preliminary sketch. Ultramarine blue is used to contrast the strokes with the orange background, both colors being complementary to each other.

Fig. 3. The artist gets straight down to work on the outline sketch, establishing the positions of each of the main compositional elements.

5

Now paint the facades of the nearest houses by combining flesh colors such as pink, ochre, and heavily whitened yellows (fig. 6). Apply small but thick touches of paint, hardly mixing or manipulating them in any way and make sure that each line is established from the very start. On an opaque background like this, the painter bases his work around the creation of lighter tones on the opacity of superimposed pigments.

The darkest and lightest colors are the first to be completed, because the artist's method involves working on the most contrasted colors first and then concentrating on the more subtle, intermediate tones.

6

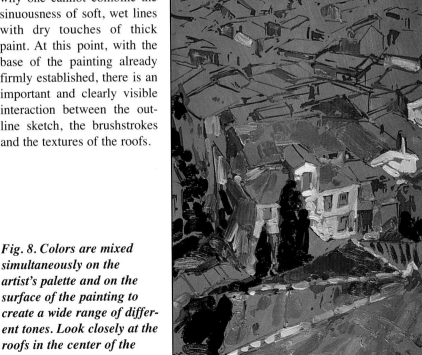

As you can see, the different colors are applied with very little mixing at all, in pure primary and secondary tones, producing a bright, shiny and fresh quality. In this way, paint the roof in the foreground with burnt sienna, yellows and reds; the illuminated facades of the buildings with flesh colors; and the shadowed areas with different blues and burnt sienna (fig. 7). With the painting at this stage, notice how the artist does not cover the lines of the preparatory sketch completely. These lines are integrated into the brushstrokes as a central element of the painting (fig. 8). The fluidity, dexterity and vigor of each stroke put a special feeling of freshness into the piece. There is no reason why one cannot combine the sinuousness of soft, wet lines with dry touches of thick paint. At this point, with the base of the painting already firmly established, there is an important and clearly visible interaction between the outline sketch, the brushstrokes and the textures of the roofs.

7

8

Fig. 5. We start working on the masses of dark color with a medium brush. The colors are completely opaque, although gaps are left where the background color shows through.

Fig. 6. The first lines are direct and abrupt, using as much paint as our brush can hold.

Fig. 7. We move to the foreground, always important in both natural and urban landscapes, because it needs to guide the artist's eyes towards the center of the piece and raise an interest in the colors.

Fig. 8. Colors are mixed simultaneously on the artist's palette and on the surface of the painting to create a wide range of different tones. Look closely at the roofs in the center of the painting.

9

Fig. 9. Spontaneity and dexterity with the brush are the keys to compositions like this. You need to forget about the real colors of each item and let your imagination come up with new interpretations.

Fig. 10. Colors mixed so freely on the support suggest the different brushmarks and make the painting look far more interesting.

10

11

Fig. 11. This illustration shows how expressive strokes can be when both thick and opaque oils are combined.

12

Fig. 12. The subject has been painted in a daring range that plays on the contrast between brightly sunlit warm colors and the cool appearance of the walls in the shadows.

The superimposition of the strokes is tremendous, and the colors appear to be mixed (fig. 9). However, even more definition is needed in the middle and background. Notice how the background color modifies the temperature and atmosphere of the painting, and if you look closely, you will see how the artist has freely mixed two or more colors with the tip of his brush, making each stroke look extremely vivid. The grooved colors reproduce the bristle marks (fig. 11).

With cobalt blue and titanium white, the artist paints the small area of sea with flowing, overlapping strokes that cover (though not in a uniform way) the top section of the painting.

When confronting a painting like this, you need to synthesize the rhythm of the composition by using color, movement and brushstrokes. Notice how the background color appears between the areas of color, provoking contrasts of tone and color. The greatest contrast is between saturated complementary colors. To work with contrast, you need to understand and apply the laws and characteristics of complementary colors (fig. 12).

In the finished painting, you can easily see how, using the anticerne effect, the color and tone of a background influence the appearance of a painting. The background color forms an integral part of the piece as a transition

13

Fig. 13. The finished piece is full of vivid, expressive lines. It has all the immediacy of an alla prima painting, but every aspect has, in fact, been carefully elaborated.

between the different areas of color and to provide glimpses of a neutral shade where the opaque one is just a dry stroke or a very soft veil. The painting may look aggressive at first sight because of the use of so many pure and complementary colors. If you have been practicing alongside the artist, you may have found it difficult to decide how to reorganize the color and forms of the model in your picture, particularly because we have done

away with the more tonal effects of local colors. Therefore, you need to avoid degrading colors, mixing or using your fingers to merge thick colors and produce different areas of paint. Your colors must be applied opaquely, as pastes and with the limits of each area of color clearly defined. It is a question of developing your sense of the abstract, which involves selecting the colors and elements of the visual world to create a certain effect, with-

out worrying about representation in the normal sense of the word. What you can never forget when painting with the anticerne method is that, when surrounded by orange, each color is visible in all of its purity and brightness. If you want, try painting the same picture with a white background, and you will see how different the result is. When placed next to orange, colors shine. Next to white, they have deeper tones.

Painting a Recently Cut Bouquet

Now Josep Antoni Domingo is going to show us his technique for painting a beautiful floral composition consisting of a basket with a varied assortment of flowers, adorned with ferns and stalks of oats. The recently cut flowers are presented in a bouquet sitting on a chair, in a beautiful corner of a garden. The scene presents a complementary element which is very much a part of summer, a hat which has been hung from the trunk of one of the two trees appearing in the middle distance.

Sketch without too many details, the shape of the chair and the tree trunks in the center with a sienna color and medium marten brush. Next extend a second application using burnt umber to the tree trunks and tint the position of the bouquet of flowers with cadmium green (fig. 1). As you can see the artist has done away with any references to pencils, but in any case if you believe it to be necessary make a sketch in pencil, although endeavouring not to press on it too much. It is important to try and make sure that the pencil line is not visible when the watercolor is finished. Continue filling out the spaces on the paper, always limiting the colors to flat tones. Paint the background with emerald green mixed with cadmium yellow and apply a transparent turquoise blue wash to the tree trunks. For the moment do not paint the area corresponding to the bouquet of flowers (fig. 2).

When the outline has been finished begin painting the different tonal areas and mix the colors according to what you see. Treat each tonal area as if it is an independent and flat figure. In this sense paint the hat hung to the right with a little cadmium yellow and ochre. Paint the shadow with a transparent ochre wash tinted with violet and project it in a descending direction, as if the sun is in a high position. With a medium paintbrush paint the flowers in a somewhat disordered way, without going into details on the flowers' forms. Use enough paint with successive colors: violets, Sienas, cadmium green and carmine (fig. 3).

Fig. 1. Begin sketching with a paintbrush.
Fig. 2. In the initial stages the motif is reduced to a few basic washes, although each one of these is divided into various shades and tones.

Fig. 3. In principle, if it is possible, you should endeavour to limit the colors that you are going to use on the flowers to only two or three different shades.

4

Through fine and transparent glazes, continue darkening the colors in the background and that of the chair. With diluted emerald green finish high-lighting the vegetation in the background and using cadmium green with a little natural umber paint the darker upper part of the image (fig. 4).

Leave the earlier washes to dry and continue adding new glazes slowly and progressively darkening the subject. With an ultramarine blue wash paint the shadows of the tree trunks and the base of the chair. With cadmium green and a little lemon yellow add another wash to the vegetation in the background (fig. 5). Now take a small paintbrush and simulate the tree trunk texture with broken lines which should be applied longitudinally with ultramarine blue.

To make the work more attractive, concentrate on darkening and strengthening the overall painting. Intensify the background colors in a way which defines the foreground and continue adding more color to improve the flowers and leaves, adding stronger tones where it is necessary (fig. 6). Apply purplish and dark colors to the vegetation surrounding the trunks to give an effect of greater depth and to allow contrasts without which the well lit part of the trunk would not be emphasized.

Fig. 4. When you are painting large areas with "flat" colors, dilute the paint before applying them, to give a fluid and transparent consistency.

5

6

Fig. 5. Once the main areas have been painted, carefully work on the smallest and most textured areas such as the rough tree trunk surfaces.
Fig. 6. To cover all of the work finish painting the background, then any part of the paper where there are still white spaces, including that occupied by the flowers.

Now is the moment to work on the leaves and petals with greater detail. Apply the colors, one next to the another so that they create their own mutual influence on each other, then superimpose the washes to give the work some new qualities (fig. 7). Treat the greenery of the leaves in the same way, with the aim of capturing their characteristics of light and transparency. Now the moment has arrived to distinguish the different tonal areas of the flowers by means of color forms. For the darker areas use the same color, but more heavily filled. For areas with an intermediate tone add enough transparent glazes in the same color or another which is similar. Do the same with the green colored leaves (fig. 8). Use chrome green with a drop of red for the dark areas. If dark and clear tones are used for each color it can create the sensation of three dimensional space on a flat surface. With the whole of the painting showing more intense tones, you should also add new washes to the hat so that it appears more defined, painting the ribbon with a medium intensity purplish wash. The finished painting is an example of a determined pictorial focus, using small glazes and small semi-transparent additions of color to constitute a realist picture. This work is an example of the flexibility of the procedure of painting with glazes, and of the skill necessary to get as much out of it as possible. When you are working with

TIPS

- Work on mixing the appropriate tone for each area, comparing it with the other tones on the palette, before applying it to the canvas.
- Keep the forms as simple as possible and do not be tempted to create shadows by using the method of painting darker colors on wet.
- Work quickly, applying the paint with the greatest possible transparency.

7

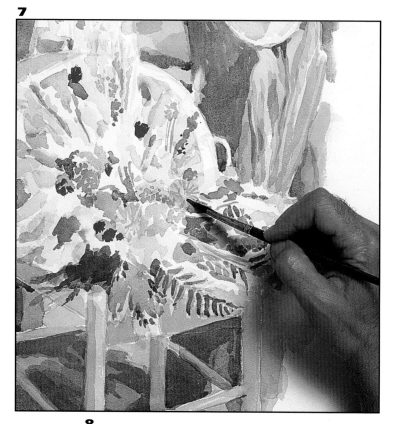

8

Fig. 7. Use a medium sized paintbrush to paint around the flowers and leaves and a small marten brush for the minuscule details.
Fig. 8. You should apply a combination of dark and light shades to both the flowers and leaves.

9

the glazing technique, you will surely be tempted to superimpose the colors and mix them. This will come from closely looking at the painting, with the lines between the different glazes appearing too well defined and the washes flat and monochrome. Do not be mistaken. Do not try to blend colors to make the work more realistic. Let the process follow its course and paint according to what has been indicated. You will see that as you move away from the painting the colors come together and achieve the desired effect (fig. 9). You will possibly have noticed that the washes you have done give a different watercolor in appearance to that painted by the artist. The appearance is the result of the type of paper used and the quality of the watercolors themselves. As such, for example, painting on paper with little substance means that the washes extend with great speed and little control, while those carried out on absorbent paper, with more substance, take on a smooth and mixed aspect when dry. Always leave earlier washes to dry and do not work on wet, because working on dry paper gives a sharper and fresher effect. There are also some artists who consider this to be a very safe method.

Fig. 9. This is the finished painting. To achieve a good reproduction it is necessary to study the existing relationships between colors, because shades and tones are altered by what surrounds them.

Painting a Basket of Dried Flowers

If you try to paint a floral scene in various sessions it will be better if you choose dried flowers for this task, because these will not droop and the leaves will not fall after a few hours. It would be difficult to find dried flowers which could offer such bright colors as that of a still life of natural flowers, however, despite this, the challenge in painting them is interesting with the artist obliged to use a broken range of colors. The artistic range of such colors, as you should already know, comes from mixing in unequal parts, two complementary colors with white.

Look at the model (fig. 1): it is a basket of dried flowers containing muted greens and ochres with a tendency towards a grayish color. I have chosen this model because the whole gives off a certain warmth, an orange harmonization which will make the final result of the work more attractive. For this exercise we are relying on the collaboration of the artist Grau Carod. I would ask you to work along with him, paying attention to each one of the steps which are explained next.

To arrive at the expected sketch first draw a vertical line in the center, then approximate and mark out the space which is going to be taken up by the basket and begin detailing the motif. As you can appreciate by looking at the sketch made by the artist, it has been decided that the basket should be lengthened so that it appears more stretched and less wide (fig. 2). You can do the same if you like, but it is not necessary. This depends on each individual's own interpretation.

Paint the background with an ochre colored wash with a little sienna and vermilion. Use a no. 18 round paintbrush with marten hair. Do these washes in an uneven way, allowing the colors to mix on the surface of the paper (fig. 3).

1

Fig. 1. The model is a luxuriant bouquet of dried flowers put together in a typical wicker basket.

2

3

Fig. 2. First of all, make a really detailed drawing on paper. Indicate the position of each one of the flowers and detail the textures of the bouquet.

Fig. 3. With a thick paintbrush, spread a mixture of yellow ochre, earth sienna and vermilion.

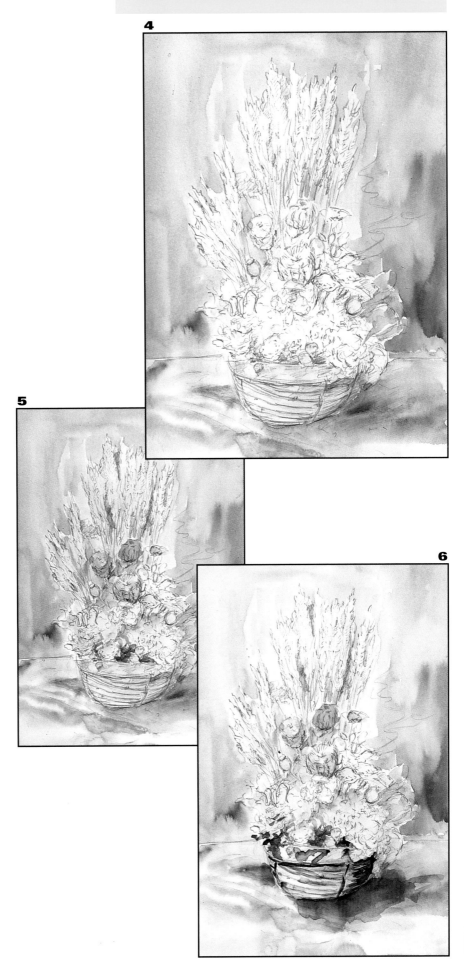

When the background has been painted apply color to the base, table or support the basket is sitting on. For this mix yellow ochre with burnt umber and add the color with thick and uneven brushstrokes, without moving into the space being kept for the bouquet. However, shade off the background a little with the model boundaries so that these boundaries are not hard, to prevent them from looking trimmed (fig. 4). With a very diluted wash with ochre, give the basket its first coloring. Now take a medium paintbrush and begin working on the bouquet. Give the pink flowers in the center their first coloring, with a Naples yellow for the buds and pink for the colored spikes (fig. 5), doing so with light brushstrokes. Now take a small paintbrush and continue. Paint the wicker basket's framework and the most intense shadows at the base of the bouquet with Payne gray washes. With a semi-transparent Payne gray wash and natural umber show the shadow projected by the model at the base of the basket (fig. 6). The darker, bottom part of the basket enhances the lower part of the bouquet and additionally, introduces new qualities to the dominating orange color of the model.

Fig. 4. Apply brushstrokes to the background in an uneven way, such that the different colors are mixed on the paper's surface, forming washes.
Fig. 5. Apply color to the center of the bouquet and begin painting some light and shadows.
Fig. 6. In this stage of the still life define the shapes using various paintbrushes which you will have to change continually, choosing them as a result of the desired brushstroke.

Endeavour to cover the whites of the flowers, adding shapes and colors, intensifying all the nuances, keeping some white areas, const-ructing, inventing or transforming flowers which do not exist in the model and which appear in the painting through as if by magic (fig. 7). With the aim of understanding better the progressive work involved in painting look at the process developed by Grau Carod through the pictures (fig. 5, 6 and 7). On finishing this stage we can see that the center of the bouquet is well covered by different colors. The top third part, however, remains as it was at the beginning. The work for this part is done very quickly, although without any need for rushing it. Alternate the strokes on the painting in an almost automatic way,   contemplating the motif quickly, which although it shouldn't be   broadcast as such, does act as a constant stimulant.

With a small paintbrush detail the model even more and superimpose new strokes which enrich the earlier work, so that the flowers in the lower part of the bouquet take on more importance, this resulting in an amalgam of superimposed strokes which have also been worked with in an energetic and impulsive style (fig. 8).

With regards to this point the artist believes that it is opportune to leave the painting as it is, and if the work needs it, to add a few touches after a few days when it is dry. This is a practice which I recommend, because all recently painted work needs to be left for two or three days. After this period come back to it and if you believe it necessary, add some new touches. However, if you believe that it does not need any modifications sign it and consider it finished. It is worthwhile highlighting this fact, so that the still life does not loose the freshness and spontaneity derived from the earlier work.

8

Fig. 7. Now the color has been added to nearly all of the paper's surface. Until this moment the artist has suggested working across all of the painting, leaving the shading work for a later stage when it will be worked on area by area.

Fig. 8. Continue painting with what appear to be loose, unworried strokes, which in addition to stressing the profiles, will also give volume to each of the elements in the bouquet.

TIPS

- All of the painting needs to be worked on at the same time, it is necessary to see the work as a whole, without concen- trating on one small part. If the latter is done it can make us lose sight of the overall painting.
- The fact that you began to paint the background before the model will save you some worries. Establishing the tone for the larger areas of the painting right from the beginning means that you do not run the type of risks which exist when the individual elements of the still life are painted first. This is due to the fact that a color is lighter or darker as a result of the surrounding background color.

9

Studying the process and the final result, as shown in the finished painting in figure 9, will allow you to see that this work has been carried out by using somewhat specific brushstrokes. First of all, virtually right from the beginning you have been using a small paintbrush, this allowing the work on the painting to be more expressive, super-imposing one stroke on top of the other. This has been done with the construction of small brushstrokes, in a broken up way, such that when the viewer contemplates

the work from an adequate distance the colors come together, producing gradations and richness in texture. Secondly, at no time have you worked with pure colors and only a few times with clean colors, in other words with colors directly from the tablet . As a result of this the colors ended up being harmonized with something of an orange colored bias. Consider these two factors mentioned: the expression and control of the brushstrokes and the harmonic range of the colors.

Fig. 9. After some days you will have to confront the work with the aim of incorporating some new details and modifications.

Painting a Garden with Spatulas

Paint applied with a brush can be diluted, concentrated or of medium consistency, but when it is applied with a spatula it always has to be thick to form crests and gaps onto which light and shadow can play. In the next exercise, we shall be finding out how to paint with this strange instrument, and to do so, we shall be working with the sculptor and painter Carlant. Feel free to use guide sheet number four and follow each of the following steps carefully.

We are going to paint the garden of a pretty cottage in Winchester, a town on the outskirts of London. We are not only interested in the texture of the vegetation, but also in the strong contrast between light and shadow (fig. 1).

Before starting, do as the artist does, and draw a simple sketch that outlines the fit and composition. When you are going to use opaque techniques and less delicate treatments, it is best to sketch with charcoal. When you have covered the whole support with thick paint, there is no danger of any of the lines showing through the paint (fig. 2).

On the palette, we start mixing a little ultramarine blue with carmine and plenty of white. This mixture, made in unequal proportions, will be used for the sky, and will have a certain violet appearance. With green and a touch of indigo, roughly color the vegetation in the foreground, worrying more about the color than the form of the undergrowth (fig. 3).

For the vibrant colors of the sky, make short spatula strokes as if you were using a trowel, and to create the clouds, you need to make a rough texture where the colors mix. Do this by moving the tip of the blade energetically, and be generous with the paint, applying enough to fill in the texture of the canvas (fig. 4). At this early stage, it is important to cover all of the white of the paper to avoid simultaneous contrast. White in the background makes it harder to appreciate the colors within the context of the piece, so you need to eliminate it as soon as possible. The first colors need to be wide and generous, with short, irregular strokes that can be applied with a pear-shaped spatula. This way, three or four different tones can

Fig. 1. The artist has chosen this scene of a house and garden on the outskirts of London.

Fig. 2. All oil paintings that use an opaque technique need a preparatory sketch to situate the composition and fit.

Fig. 3. First, you have to color the sky and the vegetation in the foreground, without worrying too much about details.

Fig. 4. Painting with a spatula can, in principle, be more complicated than using a brush, so you will need a lot of practice before you feel comfortable.

5

Fig. 5. Look at the differences in the way the sky (smoother and less degradations) and the vegetation in the foreground (rougher, pastier and less precise) have been treated.

Fig. 6. Start with a thin background and gradually move on to applying thicker layers.

Fig. 7. The directions of the strokes vary, as does the amount of paint applied.

7

6

already be seen in the green of the garden, and they will soon start configuring the patterns of light and shadow (fig. 4).

Hold the spatula at different angles, vary the pressure you apply and use different parts of it to produce different lines and effects. The pastes should follow the directions of the blades from the very start, in other words, the textures and forms of the elements. Therefore, the walls of the house will need to be flatter and the profiles much less irregular than those of the trees and plants in the garden (fig. 6).

The shadowed parts of the building have been painted with a mixture of dark grays and gray-violets. The green blanket that covers the garden is also nearing completion. In a painting like this, painted entirely with a spatula, the flat and rough parts of the grass in the garden reflect light in different ways and create an interesting and highly complex surface (fig. 7). Bearing this in mind, study the leaves of the tree on the left, in which violet shades can be seen in the shadowed areas, along with cinnabar green, cadmium green and permanent green mixed with ochre and other dark gray colors.

The roof of the house is painted with a touch of ochre and English red; the sunny facades with ochre, sienna and a little white; and the doors and windows with small pastes of mixed colors. For the more subtle effects in the forms of the windows and doors of the house, hold the spatula as you would hold a bow to a violin, supporting the plastic part of the blade with your index finger and pressing the tip onto the surface of the painting, thus applying the paint more meticulously.

Look at the color of the walls of the house, more uniform compared to the rest of the more freely and vigorously painted garden (fig. 8). When you paint the vegetation, you do not only have to use the flat part of the spatula; you can also create sharp, accurate lines with the edge.

Now try to expose the more brightly-lit sections of the foreground. To do this, spread thick, ochre, compound green and emerald green pastes mixed with a little white. Similarly, put more shape into the shadows with the use of violets, blue-grays and English red. Spatulas are useful for applying color to the wet surface of the garden without dirtying the color beneath. To do this, load the blade with color and press

few strokes and then adds the few touches of detail that he feels are necessary for the painting to be comprehensible. The overall balance between synthesis and shade that the artist puts into his painting generally boils down to the artist's own personal feelings. Be clear about what you are aiming for before you start painting, and always work with these intentions in mind (fig. 10).

You may have made the mistake of trying to add an oily medium to the paint. As in any pasting method, you should never mix the paint with a diluting agent or medium. If you do, you run the risk of losing the right consistency to conserve the spatula marks. Just as color loses its intensity when it is over-mixed on the palette, directly applied paint loses its freshness if it is rubbed too much against the canvas or

8

TIPS

–The flexible steel point can be used with a certain accuracy for adding color to details, for touches of light and for textural effects.
–You should not confuse painting spatulas with knife-shaped ones. The latter are only to be used for moving and mixing paint on the palette.
–As thickly applied layers of paint can take some time to dry, you have plenty of time to manipulate the paint on the actual support.

Fig. 8. The voluminous pastes used for the vegetation in the foreground add depth to the piece.

lightly on the spatula as you work. The artist makes the tip scrape the paint, thus combining spatula painting with a kind of graffito technique.

Finish off by covering the white of the support and defining the forms better, although you do not need to aim for too much realism. Spatula work does not lend itself very well to highly detailed painting.

The artist keeps moving in just two directions: aiming for synthesis and shade, and alternating between the two. In other words, he paints the most essential of what he sees with just a

9

Fig. 9. The wavy forms, with their energetic textures, were made with the spatula held flatly, while the straight lines were made with its point.

10

if it is applied thoughtlessly. So, don't move the spatula back and forwards. Hold it steadily against the canvas and spread the paint in a single, deliberate movement, lifting the spatula cleanly when the line is finished. There is a danger that each new paste mixes with the one before, which can dirty the colors and blur shapes. Don't be fooled into thinking that paintings made with pastes are more suited to improvisation and free, uninhibited styles. This is anything but the case, and they actually need to be planned very carefully.

Fig. 10. Paintings made with a spatula tend to look irregular and pasty, and because of the flat edges that most blades have, their strokes present a certain geometric distribution.

View of a Lake with the Scraping Technique

Now practice using the scraping technique. As has already been explained before, scraping consists in rubbing paint onto the surface of the work with a palette knife or plastic card, so that it is extended forming a smooth layer. The thickness of the layer depends on how much pressure is exerted. In this way, semi-transparent layers can be obtained as well as textured opaque impastos.

Grau Carod will carry out this step-by-step exercise and I would ask you to follow its development closely. The exercise that we propose is to paint a beautiful illustration of the Austrian lake known as the Attersee, a surface that reflects the light of the sky with pale blue or silver sparkles. The forms of the landscape and the movement of the water are rendered not only through the scraping movements, but also through the motifs that will be taken into consideration (fig. 1).

The support for this work will be a piece of Bristol board fixed with masking tape onto a panel that is resting on a table. When working in the scraping technique never use coarse-grained paper or other types of paper with an excessively wrinkled or engraved surface.

Mix the colors on the palette with a palette knife. When the paint has a semi-thick consistency move the paint over the

surface with a plastic card to form a thin layer. It is not necessary to draw anything before you begin. A preliminary painting done in relatively flat colors serves as a draft or base, situating the forms that make up the model (fig. 2).

After a few minutes, the base of the

composition will be fixed. The surface of the lake appears cerulean blue, the middle ground has been done in ochre and terre-verte, the mountain on the right with cadmium green and emerald green and the one on the left with violet (cerulean blue and carmine, fig. 3). The violet color of the mountain can be explained by the law of contrast and atmosphere according to which bodies tend to present a gray or violet hue as they get further away from the spectator. In this first appraisal the colors have not been applied in a flat way but present an effect of broken color which makes it possible for the white of the paper to filter through.

Fig. 1. The model is a panoramic view of the waters of lake Attersee, near Salzburg, in Austria.
Fig. 2. When opaque techniques and less delicate treatments are used, it is not necessary to make a preliminary sketch. You can tackle the theme directly with paints.
Fig. 3. These are the basic colors: cerulean blue for the water and the sky, emerald green and violet for the mountains in the distance.

Although the consistency of the paint is that of paint as it comes out of the tube, the layer of paint is spread so thin that the color underneath shows through, creating an effect very similar to that of velatura. Continue applying new colors, one layer after another. Dip the card in a more intense shade of blue and work both on the middle ground and on the foreground, that is, on the surface of the water. Press down moving the card from top to bottom until you have achieved a veil of color simulating the reflections (fig. 4). Notice how the green of the vegetation is repeated as a reflection on the surface of the lake. Continue livening up the surface of the lake with new impastos of color, and I use the term impasto because each time you go through this process you should press down less on the palette knife and apply the paint more thickly. If you compare the resolution of the middle ground with that of the sky or the mountains in the distance, you will notice how the thin glazes of color contrast with the light impastos and bold contours (fig. 5). Until now the artist has worked with a card that was about 3 1/2 inches wide. As the work progresses, smaller and smaller cards will be needed which will allow us to make the forms more explicit, enriching the planes by scraping the surface with somewhat more precision. Most of the scraping movements will be done from top to bottom so the lines will have a horizontal tendency. We will correct this tendency by changing the position of the panel in order to direct and control the application of the scraping, that is, we will turn the panel in order to adjust the stroke to the shapes found in nature (fig. 6).

4

Fig. 4. Here you have an example of the superimposition of color that can be obtained with a plastic card. In a way they have a certain likeliness with small impastos.

Fig. 5. Whatever the consistency of the paint may be, try to get the scraping movement to mirror the movement of the surface of the lake from the very beginning, in order to keep the painting from having a static appearance.

5

6

Fig. 6. The application of paint gives rise to a texture, obtained through a series of small scraping movements or veiled impastos that give the surface of the painting a vibrant and effectist appearance.

103

With a little ochre, yellow and cadmium red, suggest the rocky formations of the mountain on the left and also add more volume to the vegetation on this mountain, once again with ochre, terre-verte and chrome oxide green. Move down the surface of the painting. Add scraped on layers of titan white in the central area of the lake, in order to define the direct reflections of the sun. Finally work, once again with the wide card, on the foreground. Superimpose new impastos in more intense cerulean blue mixed with a dash of white. The foreground is always important in a landscape, be it natural or urban, since it has to lead the spectator's gaze towards the interior of the work and awaken an interest for the colors, forms or textures (fig. 7).

The rock formations and the vegetation on the opposite shore of the lake have been defined by using thicker layers. In this way, the hill in the background already has, as you can see in figure 8, an extraordinary chromatic vividness. The scraping technique provides a mixture, or better yet blending, of colors reminiscent of the sfumato technique, although the resolution is in this case coarser and less pure.

At this stage, it is time to apply some final effects: intensify the shadow that the raft projects, darken the vegetation on the mountains even more, go over the reflections near the opposite shore and add some precise linear effects. In order to achieve them, it is necessary to move the plastic card longitudinally over the pictorial surface (fig. 9).

8

Fig. 6. The artist applies one scraped on layer of paint on top of another, using the paint as if he were working with impasto.

Fig. 7. In this detail, you can see how the mountains on the opposite shore of the lake are built up.

Fig. 8. The directional scraping movements create an immense

9

TIPS

—When you paint the water, you will see that there is a logic to its movements, which are repeated. The waves of the sea curl, the waves of a stream flow around a central point and the surface of a lake always presents the same type of ripples.

—You can also work with a scraper. However, being more rigid, the applications it produces are thicker and more irregular.

—If you want to work with the scraping technique on wet, you can use a retardant, which will make it possible to manipulate the paint for a much longer period of time.

The finished work shows a rich variety of effects which are impossible to obtain with any other instrument of the pictorial tradition. The practice of scraping may seem a bit archaic since it does not allow the artist to produce lots of filigrees, that is, depict details, but, despite these hindrances, the final result obtained with the technique is surprising and effectist and has a great textural richness. Although there are no well-defined elements and the landscape has not been given the precision that is usually associated with drawings and paintings, the work transmits the strength and character of the place (fig. 10).

One common mistake is to work the paint too much, thereby losing the sensation of fluidity that it should render. When painting a work with such textural richness, you must consider leaving some rest areas, that is, areas that are not as overloaded, with less pictorial information, so that the spectator can find a place to rest his eyes when looking at the work. Otherwise the painting will seem too saturated with elements. This function is fulfilled perfectly by the sky. If you look at it closely you will see that it is composed of subdued layers of scraped on paint, done in just one color in the manner of tonal gradations. Another common mistake is to lay on too much paint. We mustn't forget that we are scraping or moving the paint over the surface of the painting and not laying on paint (although in some areas of the painting this could be the case). To scrape on paint it is necessary to press down with the palette knife or plastic card so that the edge scratches the surface depositing the paint in the form of a thin semitransparent film.

Fig. 10. In the finished painting we can see an animated combination of shapes and textures. The scraping technique gives the image a wonderful pictorial quality.

Painting with Acrylic and *Collage*

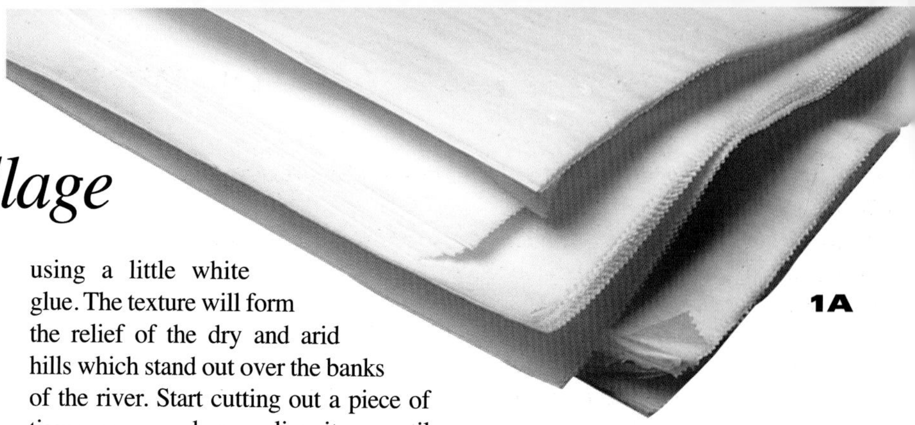

In this step-by-step exercise we are going to combine two of the most flexible and expressive procedures: collage and acrylic paint. We are not going to be working with colored papers, but with textures, for paper that is crumpled up and stuck onto the surface can create a pictorial base with surprising relief effects. It will be up to you to decide how to make the most of it. For this exercise you will need two sheets of tissue paper or Japanese paper (fig. 1A). Óscar Sanchís is the artist we have chosen to paint the theme that you can see in the adjoining photograph. It's a view of the banks of the Nile River with the Pantheon of Aga Kan standing out above it (fig. 1B). The support we are going to use is watercolor paper of medium grain, onto which the artist will stick, for example, tissue paper

using a little white glue. The texture will form the relief of the dry and arid hills which stand out over the banks of the river. Start cutting out a piece of tissue paper and crumpling it up until you have formed a small ball. Unfold it and glue it onto the support, pressing firmly with your fingers so that it sticks well. Here the artist has used latex to fix the material to the paper. However, if you like you can also use a medium, due to its adhesive power (fig. 2).

In this way the upper half of the paper will be covered with a texture full of creases and wrinkles which will be used as the background, to give the representation of the sand hills that surround the banks of the river more richness. As soon as you can see that the glue has dried, take a flat hog bris-

tle brush and paint the sky, forming a slight tonal gradation. Add white, violet and pink to the ultramarine of the sky, more as you move down towards the line where the hills begin (fig. 3). As you can see, all the colors are diluted. However, they have a clear sfumato effect, which is normally used to make big flat areas more interesting like the sand or the sky, as well as making the surface more shiny. Do the same and blend the colors together by softly rubbing the different shades of ochre in the contours of the hills to make them appear to join the sky.

Fig. 1A. Tissue paper, if it is wrinkled before you stick it on, is very appropriate for bringing out textures using the collage technique.

Fig. 1B. Before you begin, you should choose a model that has certain textural characteristics which make it appropriate to be represented using the collage technique, such as this view of the Nile.

Fig. 2. In this exercise, the artist has started by gluing a big piece of wrinkled tissue paper onto the pictorial support.

Fig. 3. Once the basic structure has been situated, that is, by putting the paper in its place, the artist begins to paint the sky.

4

In this way you will achieve a better integration of the different planes (fig. 4).

At this point, the background has already been sketched. The sfumato effect of these first washes makes the tones more subdued in some parts of the composition, making some areas look softer and also giving them more light and freshness. With a little bit of cobalt yellow and a wide brush. Project some vertical lines onto the water. These will aid us in reproducing the reflections of the banks on the surface of the river (fig. 5). Once you have defined the colors and big shapes, continue working on the painting with more fluid and intense paint. Liven up the middle ground with loose touches of dark green (sap green, olive green and ochre), representing the clear line of the vegetation. In order to depict the foliage of the trees your strokes should be irregular, as if you were scribbling (fig. 6).

Now move on to the lower part of the image. Deal with the reflections on the water by projecting spots vertically from the bank, using brownish tones instead of green. When the water is spotted cover it with superimposed thick layers of light blue paint, moving the brush from left to right and vice versa, so that the new horizontal strokes of the water mix with the colors of the previous wash. As a result, the shapes will be attenuated, loose their definition and become more abstract. The reflections should be clearer and more intense the closer you move towards the shore (fig. 7).

The reason why the surface of the water has been dealt with in this way

5

should be clear, namely, to give it a sensation of movement, a special vibration, in order to give a composition that is apparently calm and static a sense of rhythm.

Using thicker gray paint and a little carmine toned down with ochre, continue modeling the relief of the hills so that, in the areas where the paper is crumpled or wrinkled, the paint only sticks to the salient parts, creating a curious effect.

6

Fig. 4. Paint the sky and the outline of the hills trying for a sfumato effect, in order to obtain a speckled and broken color, with pink spots that are applied on top of the previous blue ones.

Fig. 5. At this point, the applications of acrylic paint give the work a sense of depth and connect the different planes of the composition.

Fig. 6. As you can see, the vegetation is painted in an intense shade of green, while the sky has a clear sfumato effect.

Fig. 7. The branches of the trees are depicted by means of rough strokes and nervous sgraffito.

7

8

Take a small brush and start giving volume to the white building located near the bank of the river and the pantheon that can be seen on top of the hill. At first work with merely two shades: white and ochre for the illuminated parts of the house and the pantheon respectively and a violet-gray for the darker facades (fig. 8).

The detail in figure 9 shows the variety of color and textural effects that can be obtained by gluing wrinkled tissue paper onto the surface of the support. Superimposing color washes onto the wrinkles in the paper brings about fantastic organic forms that enrich the textural variety of the work, creating effects that are related to the aridity of the landscape.

9

Fig. 8. Now is the moment to sketch the buildings using scarcely two shades, these corresponding to light and shadow.

Fig. 9. By simply passing a brush with undiluted paint over the wrinkles and folds in the paper, more details and textures can be added to the hillsides.

Fig. 10. Use a smaller brush for the small details on the buildings and the boat on the right.

Now it's time to add the finishing touches, adding some final details. In order to do this, you will have to use a small flat brush and with a bit thicker paint detail the architectural characteristics of the pantheon. Also paint the openings in the building on the left, near the shore, and define the sail boat on the right (fig. 10).

What makes a collage really good is not the quality of the materials but the way in which they have been used and wor-

TIPS

—Acrylic paint is highly adhesive and this property makes it especially suitable to be used together with collage techniques.

—It is also possible to combine collage with a paste that makes it possible to create textures with thick impastos, onto which effects can be created in relief.

—One very important point that should be kept in mind when using paper as the main material is whether you are going to cut or tear it, since the contrast between the edge of cut and torn paper can be very effective (torn paper is usually more expressive and suggestive).

ked on with a certain base. A material as simple as crumpled tissue paper can produce a tremendously gratifying experience for the artist.

Your work may not have the textural effects that we indicate here. This could be because you have watered it down too much, or because you have applied too many or too thick layers of impasto. If the former is the case, the cause is that you have worked with paint that has been excessively thinned down in water. Dry brush strokes provide better results than glazes when applied on a textured surface like the one in this work, for the paint is deposited in the folds and wrinkles that the paper forms. The biggest difficulty you

may have encountered is the painting of the reflections on the water. It's a question of interpretation. However, here are some tips: do not try to reproduce the shape of the reflected body, for it should appear blurred, like a hazy spot and, if necessary, a bit deformed by the rippled surface on which it is reflected. The reflected colors should be a bit dimmer than the original ones. The direction of the strokes should also be kept in mind. They should integrate with each other in a harmonious fashion, without too much detail and without trying to paint a specific shape, simply as a set of spots that form an abstract composition (fig. 11).

Fig. 11. The art of collage is extremely flexible and can be oriented in many different directions. Therefore, it would be a good idea for you to continue experimenting and composing works like this one.

A Footpath with Oil Pastels and Turpentine

In this next exercise, we will be mixing oil pastel with turpentine essence that dilutes, blends colors and creates interesting picturesque effects that will remind you of oil paintings. The artist Grau Carod will help by illustrating the process.

First of all, study the picture of the subject material, a footpath between fields of crops with a heavy mass of vegetation on the left (fig. 1). Having studied the composition and chosen the right range of harmony for the theme, draw a rough sketch on paper with a number 2 pencil. Alternatively, if you prefer, use the third guide sheet at the back of this book. To paint this composition, use a more limited range of colors than you did for the last exercise, namely white, cadmium yellow, orange, red, carmine, violet, cyan blue, ultramarine blue, permanent green, emerald green, yellow ochre, burnt sienna and black.

Once you have drawn the outline you are ready to start painting. See how it should be done by studying figures 2 and 3, in which the artist works on the gradation of the sky. Use the cyan and ultramarine blue sticks to paint the upper part of the sky in the same way as Grau has done in figure 2, using thick, parallel and super-imposed lines.

Now slightly dampen a brush in turpentine and use it over the sky to create a regular, uniform tone. You don't need to rub heavily, just lightly bring the hairs of the brush into contact with the surface and the color will dissolve (fig. 3).

Keep on adding more colors in the same way, first shading with the pastels and then going over them with the brush. You will see how the dissolved colors become washes that

Fig. 1. This is the subject that Grau Carod is going to paint. It is a footpath lined with vegetation.
Fig. 2. Using an ultra- marine blue stick, start shading areas of the sky.

Fig. 3. With a brush that you have dipped in turpentine, go over the lines you drew before so that they form washes like those that appear in watercolors.

produce the same kind of effect that a normal oil painting would (fig. 4). Use a little green and yellow to create the mass of vegetation on the left, use ochre and burnt sienna on the tree trunk and the fence and do the distant hills in permanent green, violet and cobalt blue.

Add a few colors that contrast with those that have gone on before. Use different shades of green over your original wash for the undergrowth and leaves and use your fingers to give them the right effect. Layer and mix colors with others, creating different hues that suggest the variety of vegetation. Although the colors may seem denser now, notice how the artist has diluted the original layer of color by brushing them with thinner (fig. 5).

Little by little cover the white of the paper with increasingly more contrasting strokes for the closest vegetation and more merging should be used in the center and background. Now paint on top of this first layer of diluted paint only using lines. But for the moment, don't press down too hard. Start off slowly and build things up as you go along (fig. 6).

Now you need to paste on more pastel, more material and more color. Work on the hills in the background with a little emerald green, ultramarine blue and violet to highlight the outline of the mountains more strongly. Use ochre and burnt sienna on the vegetation on the left hand side of the picture, and permanent green for the grass and weeds on the path (fig. 7).

Fig. 4. Paint warm colors in the foreground and use colder ones for the more distant features, and then spread the color with washes.
Fig. 5. At this stage, the picture looks like a preparatory sketch. The picture is gathering form within a wide range of colored patches.
Fig. 6. At this point, Grau Carod intends to cover the white of the paper quickly. You should not hesitate to use washes either.

111

Notice how aware the artist is of the directions of his lines. They are irregular at the edges of the path, they go upwards for the leaves of the trees, are vertical on his trunks and horizontal on the grass on the path. Grau Carod combines flat, wide lines with the point of the pastel. He also uses a knife and a cutter to open spaces in the layer of paint, for the branches, the tree trunk and the plantlife at the sides of the path (fig. 8).

Paint one area, then move on to the next as if you were carrying out a tireless general inspection. Stop whenever you feel it necessary to intensify a shadow and make sure that the foreground stands out properly from the background.

In the end, the artist has decided to use the white pastel pencil. Not to mask the color, but to reduce any excessive contrast or intensity. You should do likewise, because I think this is one of this pencil's most interesting effects.

7

8

112

Fig. 7. Now you need to stop using washes and work with the points of the sticks, drawing thick, less precise lines.

Fig. 8. Look at the contrast between the closer and more precise area to the right and the left-hand side that disguises every line with washes.

9

Once you have finished, the lines of the picture unite and the shades blend together to give a more uniform effect. This divisionist resolution gives character to the piece. The predominance of different blue and green hues stands out and protects the overall picture from any kind of excessive dispersion that would come from too much detail. You might have used too many layers of color in some areas, which would rather spoil the surface with too imprecise tones or too many undefined ones. To solve this problem, all you need to do is take a knife and scrape some of it off. When the surface is clean, rectify the colors, but be careful not to make the

same mistake again. Now look at the sky and the fields and hills in the distance. Check that they have all been produced with washes, in other words, that there is no trace of any lines, so that the right effects of contrast and atmosphere are achieved. Colours should always fade into the distance. If they don't, the picture won't look deep enough and will look like a flat confusion of lines, with too many textures and details on the surface that will not help at all to make your composition more comprehensible (fig. 9).

Fig. 9. The drawing reflects the disturbing intensity that Grau Carod puts into his paintings. The fact that he never stops watching, thinking and interpreting synthesises forms and colors with quick strokes and transparent washes.

Painting a Group of Musicians

In this exercise you can put everything that you have learned so far into practice as we take on a new theme, that of the human figure. The painting shows a group of moving people. If you want to produce paintings like this, you will find that this is a good place to start, with people who do not vary their posture very much. The painting is going to combine opaque techniques with veils. Once again, we are honored by the presence of the artist Josep Antoni Domingo.

As always, the artist first spends a few minutes observing his subject and thinking about which details he is going to concentrate on in particular. With a number 2 pencil, synthesize the general appearance of the group with just a few lines. As you observe and draw, keep each person's pose fixed in your mind. Notice how, although it is a synthetic drawing, the artist has found the proportions between the different figures and has applied a light shadow so that the patterns of light are clear from the very start. See how, with just a few lines, he has already suggested the texture of their clothes (fig. 2).

When you have accurately drawn the sketch, you can start painting. Like the artist, you should start by coloring the figure to the right. From the start, try to recreate the volume of the figures and reflect the areas of more or less light, superimposing layers of color. To get the right tone for painting skin, mix titanium white with ochre yellow and vermilion. With a thin brush, add more vermilion to the pinkest areas, and a touch of cobalt blue to the darker areas under the first person's chin. The same blue, mixed with burnt umber, is what you need to recreate the color and texture of the folds in his trousers. For his shirt, the artist has settled for using the white of the canvas. With a few simple, gray lines, he has

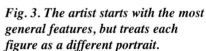

Fig. 1. This time we are going to paint this lively group of Irish musicians.

Fig. 2. Whenever we paint figures and portraits, we need a preparatory drawing. If not, you could easily make structural errors.

Fig. 3. The artist starts with the most general features, but treats each figure as a different portrait.

Fig. 4. As you can see, the background and figures are developed at the same time so as to create a sense of atmosphere.

defined the creases along his arm. A simple vermilion color should be enough for the second person's jersey. For his hair, the artist has used burnt umber, adding yellow to indicate the lighter parts. For the guitar, he has used light ochre with a touch of white, to which he has added burnt umber for the darker tones of the fretboard. As this is not a static, studio pose, the artist has used a background made up of impressionistic brushstrokes that seem to generate more atmosphere. At the top, he has made a degradation out of cobalt blue, yellow and white mixed with burnt umber and gray-green, and, at the bottom, cobalt blue (fig. 3).

As you can see, the artist has borne several things in mind up until this stage. The proximity between the real life colors and the ones that he has chosen has been achieved through synthetic applications of color and simultaneously dealing with the figures and the background.

Once you have started defining the colors of one figure, start thinking about the next. Just like in the previous phase, start by applying layers of color and then use a thinner brush to add specific details (fig. 4). The brownish mixtures that you made before can also be used for the jacket and hair. Notice how the artist, through the direction of his brushstrokes, recreates the textures and folds in the clothes and applies touches of light and shadow here and there as he searches for details in the foreground. Use the white of the canvas once again for the trousers, and shadow them with gray touches. Do

5

6

7

Fig. 5. The painting advances meticulously from left to right, gradually revealing the forms and postures of the people in the picture.

Fig. 6. The figures in the foreground need to be more detailed and better defined than those sitting further away.

Fig. 7. The picture is more colorful now, and we move on to the textures of the clothes and making each person look lifelike.

115

the same as the artist, and keep working on the background, adding a little yellow to the mixture as you add more detail to the figure at the back.

Keep on working, applying new values to the figures in the background and take advantage of the mixtures of color that you already have on your palette to paint the others. Volume can be created by representing the textures of skin and clothes (fig. 5). When an artist paints a human figure, he needs to study, within the limits of his chosen palette, the most appropriate range of flesh colors for that particular subject. For this picture, he has mixed different proportions of ochre, red, blue and white.

He works on each figure separately, but adds details to them all at the same time, thus creating a better sense of unity. An exercise like this requires experience and artistic mastery (figs. 6 and 7).

The artist takes a few moments to relax and think about how his painting is developing. You should take several such breaks as you work, as it will take several sessions to be completed.

Now it is time to work on the details that are going to produce the required effect. As the artist gets nearer to completing the painting, the figures have more body and their facial features are more defined. Look how he has reproduced the strings and the opening in the guitar, and try to copy his style (fig. 8).

The artist keeps working on the rest of the piece. He tries to get the right textures and volumes for each item of clothing, making the creases and folds even more detailed. Now, with a thin brush, shade the shadows on the white trousers, making the figure in the foreground more important. Notice how his shoes do not shine as much as his other clothes, which helps to recreate the texture of leather (fig. 9).

Fig. 8. Use a thinner brush for details. This is probably the task that puts your skills most to the test.

Fig. 9. Try to create the different clothing textures by superimposing more intense colors than the real life material.

10

And the exercise ends here (fig. 10). The artist has achieved a detailist result that, along with a richly shaded background, puts life and expressiveness into the exercise. Surely, when you try a similar exercise from nature, you will find it difficult to make your initial drawing accurate. Try to synthesize forms and pay attention to form rather than detail as you draw. For a general evaluation of contrasts between light and shadow, squint your eyes and you will see how the forms look clearer and darker. The most difficult aspect might be painting the facial features. Remember that in order to paint lifelike representations of human features you do not have to be a great drawer. If this aspect of your work is still not very well developed, leave the face quite

blurred and roughly-sketched without paying too much attention to detail. Another difficult factor is the different treatment of the textures and qualities of material, such as the folds in the clothes and the flat surface of some of the instruments. This not such an easy factor to avoid. If it seems complicated, try to practice painting objects wrapped in cloth or paint the folds in the clothing using veils, because that way the margin of error is not so wide. These are usually painted in the same color as the clothes in real life, but somewhat dirtier and more intense than the original color. Use short, deliberate strokes.
In principle, painting figures in movement is a complex process, but with enough practice, your results will certainly improve.

Fig. 10. The painting is finished. It transmits a sensation of action and movement as if time has been frozen for an instant. Don't feel too disappointed if your first attempt is somewhat unsatisfactory.

Painting a Pond with Water Lilies

Bibiana Crespo is going to paint a pool of water lilies in a creative style. This will allow you to see the technique and resources used by the artist, the ease of making the brushstrokes, the flow of the paint and the fresh way of working with a watercolor. This will result in a simple painting which maintains a momentary impression and covers a wide range of methods which could be considered as semi-abstract. I invite you to join the artist in this work and to learn new systems of working.

This is the model chosen: it is basically made up of lilies, many of them in bloom (fig. 1). As you can see the model has a specific enough frame, given that it does not give a depth of field. In the picture only the motif appears, the lilies and the water, without sky, hills or trees which act as a backdrop, this therefore allowing us to deal with some parts of the painting in a semi-abstract way.

The drawing which you have to begin the exercise with corresponds to a line sketch, this only dealing with the location of the different elements in the painting and with a geometric design (fig. 2). There is no intention of detailing, profiling or evaluating the work.

Fig. 1. This is the model: the sunny surface of a pool covered by lilies in bloom.

Before you begin painting, do what the artist does, which is to wet the paper with clean water, using a wide deer-hair brush to remove grease and help the technique where the colors blend in the watercolor. With this same brush apply the first colors to the still wet surface, trying to create right from the beginning a more spontaneous finish. If you look closely at figure 3, you will see that the first washes are not uniform. In this first stage, the presence of emerald green, Prussian blue and Payne graycan be made out in the painting. The spaces corresponding to the leaves and flowers must be kept white in the meantime.

Fig. 2. Begin drawing with a graphite stick, for a few seconds, making some strokes to act as a reference for beginning the work, and also to later allow you to paint with greater ease and less concern.

Fig. 3. With a brush do the background wash, the space corresponding to the water, with small variations of green, blue and grey.

With the paintbrush loaded with color and using energetic brushstrokes, profile the lily leaves, leaving the painting so that the strokes spread and merge with the previous wash (fig. 4). Continue with a flat brush loaded for a transparent wash and complete the color of the lily leaves in such a way that the white of the paper stops breathing. You will get the uneven green color, for painting the leaves, by mixing cadmium green, permanent green and a little burnt umber (fig. 5). The strokes should not be methodical, but instead have more expression. Learn to control the brushstrokes (fig. 6).

The use of expression, meaning the control of arm movement, can give the work an expressionist mood and a much more diffused treatment of colors. This needs an exercise in synthesis on the part of the artist, because it is necessary to sum up the shapes of the model in a number of strokes of color or in a large number of transparent brushstrokes. In this way the form of the painting is not constructed through a series of lines, but instead by applying strokes of color.

Fig. 4. The enhancement of the brushstrokes is clear at the beginning, but seconds later the color is stabilized, diluted and blended unevenly with the surrounding washes.

Fig. 5. Look at the synthesis of shapes and colors which make up the lilies in the composition. The transparency of the watercolor allows the mixture and composition of colors by superimposing some on top of others.

Fig. 6. In this image you are shown how the lily leaves are painted with a wide paintbrush. Look at how the wash applied is completely uniform and carried out in only one brushstroke.

119

instead by applying strokes of color. From time to time rinse the paint from the brush and dry it with a cloth, which should always be at hand, and with the brush half dry, use it to absorb excesses of water in different places. After a few minutes finish the background, the leaves and the reflections, harmonizing them with some cold shading. As you can see the work has been carried out with excessive simplicity and a poor color appearance (fig. 7). As such we are now going to brighten it up by painting the flowers.

Apply a magenta color to the wet surface, corresponding to the pink flowers of the lilies. Notice how the color is diluted as a result of the effects of the wet paper. With an oiled pastel stick of the same color define the shape of the flowers with quick and precise strokes. With a medium, paintbrush give the upper flower petals some touches of Prussian blue and paint some of the petals in the center an orange color, thereby giving greater variety and chromatic richness to each of the flowers. Again the colors on the surface of the paper are diluted because the paper is still slightly wet (figs. 8 and 9, the

7

Fig. 7. The leaves and the reflections on the water surface have been succinctly painted in the stage shown here.

8

Fig. 8. With the aim of showing the well-defined outline of the flowers correct their appearance by modifying them with a watercolor pastel stick in the same color that was used in the watercolor.

TIPS

- Consider the risk of large drops as a result of an excess of water in the brush. In the case of working with an angled table you must be careful. Alternatively, if you are using a flat board you have to take care not to soak the painting too much. To get rid of excess water use a cloth or absorbent paper as much as possible.
- If you like , you can work as many professionals do by spreading, rubbing or painting with the fingers.
- Do not do this in a step by step manner, using small sheets of paper, because this type of exercise needs you to work on large sheets.

latter shown on the following page).
As you have seen, this exercise has been dominated by a sensation of freedom, something which every artist should experiment with. Without doubt, in subjects such as this, you should find the ideal framework to give free rein to your spontaneity (fig. 9). The greatest danger with this type of technique is that you are left feeling unsatisfied with the result and end up detailing the work too much, believing that it is the best option to sort it out. Don't do it. This technique relies on suggesting the shapes instead of defining them. Given the speed of carrying out this exercise I advise you that for whatever situation do various watercolors consecutively, in only one ses-

sion, gradually entering this subject. Don't try to go over the mistakes and defects, but instead begin the painting another time, trying not to make more mistakes.
When establishing yourself in the work do not draw too much, in other words do not make a detailed drawing. Do not be carried along by the shapes, but instead deal with them in a way which is suggestive. A drawing which is too detailed could pre-condition the final result of the work.
Possibly, your rate of work will be slower than desired and the paper will dry out before finishing the wash. As a result the watercolor effects will not be the same as the painting obtained by Bibiana Crespo. The watercolor on

wet demands a lot of attention on the part of the painter, before putting paint to paper. The execution as such must be fast to take advantage of the level of wetness desired. If you are working quickly and the paper is still drying out, make sure that where you painting is not in the sun, next to a heater or in the middle of a stream of air.

9

10

Fig. 9. With magenta colored washes mixed on wet with a drop of Prussian blue and orange, paint the flowers.
Fig. 10. Looking at the final state of the painting and comparing it the earlier condition, anyone would say that the artist has worked a lot more. However, in reality the most important work was carried out with the previously done washes. The only new features are the appearance of three more flowers and the profiling of some details.

121

Painting Flowers with Watercolor Pastels

It is well known that the infinite variety of forms, colors and textures of floral painting offer the artist many opportunities for putting his skills into practice. The following exercise is an example of how to paint a floral composition with pastels or watercolor sticks.

This is the subject (fig. 1), a beautiful bunch of flowers in which the delicate variations of color and complex shapes of the flowers are good reasons for opting for watercolor pastels. To do this, the artist Óscar Sanchís will use a technique called alla prima, which involves painting each flower in one go, and then mixing the colors when they are still damp. He will focus his attention on color and precision, with a definite bias towards decorativeness.

Floral paintings require much fewer preparatory measures than other subjects, as there are not many essential lines that determine the positions of each flower on the page. This drawing can be done with a medium strength pencil (fig. 2).

Take the brown and violet watercolor sticks and add more characterization to the rough outline sketch, going over the pencil lines to show the different forms of the flowers and vase, and describing each of the petals. Rubbing with the side of the stick, highlight the shadows on the vase (fig. 3).

Now start painting. Look at what Óscar Sanchís does in these two illustrations (figs. 4 and 5, next page) that summarise how to apply color. The artist takes advantage of the qualities of the pencils. First, he draws and applies the colors with intense lines (fig. 4) and then goes on to highlight the flowers by softening some of the lines and strokes with water, creating a curious glossy effect that highlights

Fig. 1. The subject of this step by step exercise is a colorful bunch of flowers with several shades of orange, pink and ochre that contrast with the blue background.

Fig. 2. As in many cases, the linear drawing made with a graphite pencil is essential for working out the size of the composition, its position on the paper and the position of each of the flowers in relation to the others.

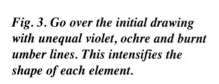

Fig. 3. Go over the initial drawing with unequal violet, ochre and burnt umber lines. This intensifies the shape of each element.

the velvety texture of the petals (fig. 5). This way he skilfully combines lines and washes, bring-ing more variety and textural richness to the image. You should do the same.

Move downwards through the bunch of flowers. Each flower, leaf and stalk is represented by two basic values that are blended in the same wash. So, for example, in the wide open flower, we can see a yellow tone in the central area of stamens, pink on the lit part of the petals and sepia in the most shadowy, intense areas (fig. 6).

Continue spreading colors until you have covered the whole bunch. To paint the roses you simply have draw the outline of the petals with red and fuchsia and dilute the lines with transparent washes. Make sure that you show the shadows by adding cold colors like blue, brown or green, and use transparent washes for the illuminated areas. Work down through the whole subject, dealing with each area in the same way. Be sure than you rest your hand on a dry area when painting in details so that you don't spoil recently painted areas (fig. 7).

Having reached this point, the bunch of flowers is almost finished. All that needs finishing off are the little branches with leaves, and you need to darken the inside of the bunch and the spaces between the flowers. Now paint the vase using the wet on wet technique, with a little sepia brown for the base and shadowed section, a green and yellow shade for the lit section and a little Prussian blue in the middle (fig. 8). As you can see, the artist has taken advantage of the strong forms of the composition and has left the decorative characteristics of the colors to dominate the image.

Figs. 4 and 5. With the point of the oil pastel, mark out the edge of the flower (fig. 4). Then, go straight on to diluting and spreading the line to create the rich textures of the petals (fig. 5).
Fig. 6. Continue down the bunch of flowers, elaborating each of the flowers as you go.

Fig. 7. Using different fast, delicate strokes and varied colors (pink, ochre, sienna, green) elaborate the bunch of flowers alla prima.

The figure and form subordinate the color, balancing the information supplied by each part of the painting. The picture as a whole has a spectacular appearance, but if we were to leave things at this stage the outline would be too obvious and the forms would stand out too much against the white background (fig. 9).

The background is made by rubbing the side of the watercolor stick over the surface of the paper, painting a series of granular shaded areas around the vase (fig. 10). When a damp brush is passed over the rich texture of this surface, the color will mitigate and expand. The effects soften into a tonal gradation. The background is completed by adding a little yellow and violet at the bottom, leaving a blank space around the base of the vase (fig. 11).

The ultramarine blue used in the background, as well as intensifying the colors of the subject, brings more depth to the picture as a whole. This background, treated with flat, transparent washes, contrasts with the dense agglomeration of stalks and flowers in the lower left section. The absence of any further information concerning the background does not weaken the impact of the picture in any way, but quite the contrary. It makes the central theme stand out even more. As you should know, there are many ways of working with watercolor pastels. I would say that the first application should be the main color of the flower, which should be kept light so that it combines with the lines that mark its

8

9

10

Fig. 8. The relationship that you establish between lines and washes is fundamental to this technique. It is a factor to bear in mind when bringing character to each element, as happens here with the pink colors that appear on either side of the bunch.

Fig. 9. When you finish working on the petals, stalks and leaves with different warm and cold hues, you will have finished this stage.

Fig. 10. Now the artist intends to quickly cover the surface of the paper by rubbing the background with a blue stick.

124

TIPS

-Fear of making mistakes can often damage the final appearance of a painting. The process demands decisiveness and determination when both drawing and using the brush.

-It is advisable to go up to the subject and study how the flowers are attached to their stalks, and the patterns of veins on their leaves.

11

outline. Don't use white pastel, it won't be of any use because the brightest light you need is that which the paper itself provides. If you want to open up spaces, you would be better off leaving areas unpainted. Using clear spaces and small openings between the colors is especially useful when painting bright, simple subjects like this one, which are more likely to be

used for a graphic interpretation than in a realistic representation. When you paint with watercolor pastels you should not hope to achieve the soft, transparent effects of normal watercolors, although with practice you will discover that you can create a wide range of attractive effects that can be used to make drawings like this.

Fig. 11. The effect of blue over gray in the background quickly comes through. This uniform background now helps to highlight the colors of the subject and avoids the excessive contrast between the theme and a plain, white background.

Painting Flowers in a Creative Style

Miguel Olivares is going to paint flowers creatively because once in a while it can be useful to try out other painting styles. In this way the workings and different characteristics of various methods and tech-niques can be learned, and if you decide that this way is not the one which could be most adapted to your style of painting, you will discover that you have acquired some techniques and that you have incorporated then in your normal style. If you never change the system you run the risk of becoming monoto-nous and boring. This time the artist has used a tempera, a painting which is deri-ved from watercolors, offering a more opaque and dense appearance.

As is normal to see in the paintings of Miguel Olivares he begins with the background color, which in this case is an irregular ochre wash. You should do the same.

Take a pencil and begin drawing the composition. Here the artist has used his imagination to develop the drawing (fig. 1). As you can see, this early drawing of the bunch of flowers has little to do with an academic governed represen-tation, being much more inspired by the nai-vety and purity of children's drawings. Take some time to bring out the forms of the flowers, the leaves and the vase, although in a way which is more synt-hetic (fig. 2).

Take a medium paintbrush and apply the first washes. Paint the leaves hanging from the lower part of the bunch with a fluid Payne gray and emerald green wash and the center of the flowers with burnt umber (fig. 3). A *gouache* is equally valid to carry out diluted and semi-transparent washes, these having a smooth and velvety texture when dry. Take a decorative piece of paper, like the kind used for wrapping presents, and after cutting it into a rectangular shape, stick it over the space destined for the vase in the *collage* style (fig. 4, next page). This will give the work a more colorful finish and introduce graphic variety to the mixture decora-ted with pieces and touches of opaque color. Continue sticking new pieces on the canvas. Cut pieces of yellow paper from a magazine to represent the petal corolla of the sunflowers. Now, again take the medium sized paintbrush and paint the center of the anemones with

Fig. 1. With a pencil draw the model with linear strokes and with a resolution which is not too detailed. It should have a naive appearance, reminding us of children's drawings.

Fig. 2. As you can see, the sketch shows a certain lack of concern in avoiding academic rules and is part of a style which is much more modern and creative.

Fig. 3. Gouache colors can be modified by adding water, which creates similar washes to those created by watercolors.

pink colored opaque washes and the roses with an intense red color. *Goua-che* is a type of opaque painting for which, in theory, clear colors can be applied on top of dark colors, including the covering of pencil marks (fig. 5). Finish painting the clear colors for the anemones, which from the previous stage appear next to the sunflowers as visual and light centers of the still life. Also, accentuate the cadmium green leaves surrounding the flowers which, because of the contrast, will give the group of flowers greater relevance and volume. Miguel Olivares declares that eagerness for perfectionism can be extremely boring, not only for the person who is painting, but also for the viewer.

The shadow projected over the flat surface by the vase (fig. 6) finally gives the relief necessary for this composition. Having achieved the final result of this exercise, I would like to conclude the book by wishing that you too will be creative, and not be stuck in what can be strictly academic painting. Practice in the same way as Miguel Olivares has, trying to look for new points of view, new processes and new ways of repre-senting the amazing world of flowers.

Fig. 4. Combine the tempera painting technique with a collage substituting the volume of the vase with a decorative paper.

Fig. 5. Cut out yellow paper from different magazines, with the aim of these representing the sunflowers' petals.

Fig. 6. This is the finished work of Miguel Olivares. He has not stopped to detail the forms of the still life, in fact he has done the complete opposite, creating a work with bright, attractive and decorative colors. It is a creative exercise which I recommend.

TIPS

- Avoid light paper because the film which makes up a gouache painting is thicker than that of a watercolor and can be broken if it is used on somewhat weak surfaces.
- If the *gouache* is applied when it is dry and thick it can completely cover a color, however this is not so recommendable, because it could consequently produce a broken picture surface .
- Leave previous layers to compl-etely dry before applying the next one.

Painting with the Wet White Technique

The method of painting with the wet white technique is based on the juxtaposition of small touches of relatively pure colors on a surface prepared with a thick coat of white paint, while it is still wet. This experimental technique results in an effective, vibrant painting. For this exercise, we are going to be working in collaboration with the painter and etcher Ester Llaudet.

We are going to use a small, wooden board, primed with latex and whiting. To do this exercise with us, you will need a board that is about a foot long. You can see the chosen model in figure 1. It is a view in the mountainous region in the Northeast of Cuba, near Santiago.

Before starting, the artist spreads a thick coat of lead white mixed with varnish resin over the surface of the support (fig. 2).

There is no preparatory sketch; the painting must be started immediately, while the white paint is still damp. Try to apply the paint in small strokes, modifying the color and tones by controlling and altering the mixture and density of your strokes. Doing this, start by applying ultramarine blue, emerald green, cadmium red and ochre to the bottom, right section of the painting (fig. 3). Keep your colors as pure and clean as you can and distinguish each stroke clearly and gently mix them into the white background.

Keep working on the landscape and draw the outline of the vegetation in the foreground with emerald green. Use ochre, orange and permanent green to complete the middle ground. Finally, use gray, burnt umber and a

Fig. 1. We are going to paint this view of steep mountains in the center of Cuba.

Fig. 2. The first thing you need to do is cover the painting surface with a thick layer of lead white mixed with varnish resin.

Fig. 3. Load a brush with paint (not too liquid) and apply it to the surface in short strokes.

128

4

Fig. 4. Let the colors mix on the canvas and not the palette.

5

Fig. 5. Notice how the colors get paler as they move into the distance.

6

little emerald green and ultramarine blue to insinuate the outline of the mountains in the distance (fig. 4). For these first applications of color, the contrast of complementary colors has been exploited, such as that between red and green in the foreground. For the lighter areas, the strokes contain less paint and have been mixed more heavily into the background white. They are based more on the background white than intense colors owing to the transparency of the pigments.

At this stage, there is a clearly neutral effect to the colors in general, produced by a series of superimposed colors that only partially cover the color below (in this case white). This is an optic combination of colors. The opacity of the color progressively darkens the overall tone, but thanks to the spaces between the strokes that the background white can be seen through, the surface stays bright (fig. 5).

Keep working until all of the initial values of the landscape are finished. Superimpose new strokes, but use more intense colors for the mountains in the distance, to put more detail into this morphology that is so typical of central Cuba. Look closely at how the artist has used shadows with quite unnatural colors like green, blue and turquoise, and has superimposed the grayish tones in the background. With a slightly smaller brush and a touch of burnt umber, the artist has darkened the vegetation in the middle ground. This takes a lot of the flatness out of the image, and gradually produces depth and relief (fig. 6).

The stokes may look small and insignificant, but it is impossible to apply a touch of color without it affecting the painting as a whole. For the areas of sky, apply a few light tones of ultramarine blue, letting the white coat beneath show through in the lightest areas. Keep

Fig. 6. In theory, you should only use primary colors, because these can be mixed to produce secondary and tertiary colors.

adding new contrasts to the intermediate zone and intensify the colors of the fields with a little yellow ochre (fig. 7).

Now go back to the vegetation in the foreground and superimpose new, irregularly distributed layers of yellow ochre, violet, ultramarine blue and emerald green. A more intense, contrasted foreground creates a more believable sense of space and perspective (fig. 8).

When the colors are seen from a distance, they mix optically to create subtle tonal and color gradations that serve to define the image. In the darker sections, such as the foreground, colors have been used in all their intensity.

To finish the painting, we complete a few details painting the vibrant color of the flowers in the foreground with cadmium red and lemon yellow. The branches of the tree that emerges in the middle of the painting are painted with burnt umber (fig. 9).

As you can see, the finished piece certainly shares many of the characteristics of pointillism. The white coat of paint that we have been painting over increases the effect of the lines and creates a freer, thicker style of painting that is dominated by more pastel-like chromatic ranges (fig. 10). The impact of this delightful painting owes itself, in part, to the mass of bright color. The colors have been carefully chosen to get the right general harmony and, at the same time, the odd touch of contrast. Ultramarine

TIPS

—When painting, always be selective. You sometimes need to exaggerate or reduce colors, contrasts and forms in order to balance the harmony of the piece.

—The paint will take a few days to dry, so you have plenty of time for modifications.

7

8

9

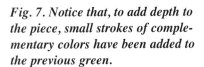

Fig. 7. Notice that, to add depth to the piece, small strokes of complementary colors have been added to the previous green.

Fig. 8. We intensify the foreground to give the piece a greater sense of depth.

Fig. 9. Although the idea is not to represent the trees particularly accurately, they are totally convincing.

10

blue and violet have been stretched from the background to the foreground to unite the composition.

Don't try complicated superimpositions of colors, and don't use too much paint at once, or the painting will look too pasty. Use separate brushstrokes and don't work too much on any one spot, or you will either take off the white from below or create a confused mess. To avoid errors, always have a piece of wood that is also covered in lead white handy. You will find it useful for testing out effects before using them on the painting itself.

Fig. 10. The white wet technique is a characteristic example of how to apply small touches of color to elaborate a painting. Seen from afar, the intense chromatic effects create a vividly shiny landscape.

Painting with Acrylics and Marble Powder

In the following step-by-step exercise, with the help of the artist Carlant, we will explain how to obtain interesting textures by mixing acrylic paint with marble powder. If you want to paint with marble powder you can chose one of two methods: the first is to apply a putty made of marble powder and latex to model and give volume to the pictorial surface before applying paint. A second possibility would be to add volume while you're working, by adding small quantities of marble powder to the paint mixtures thereby giving the paint the rough aspect that characterizes this technique. The artist has chosen the second of these options and is going to work painting directly with the palette knife instead of applying successive layers of paint with a brush in the traditional manner.

Carlant has decided to take as the model for his seascape, this corner of the Costa Brava, which is very suitable for achieving interesting textural effects thanks to the mobility of the surface of the water and the relief of the rocks (fig. 1). Before you begin prepare the following colors on your palette: burnt sienna, ultramarine blue, ochre, permanent violet, cadmium red and raw umber. This limited palette will be enough to obtain all the shades needed for this painting. The first step consists in drawing the model in pencil without paying too much attention to detail, since due to the fact that we will be working with opaque colors, the drawing will be covered by the pictorial matter (fig. 2).

I invite you to practice this exercise following the indications below.

First paint the background or areas of flat color. For the cape in the distance and the sea water, use a gray-violet base, the luminosity of which will be fundamental in creating the illusion of the light and the sun in this painting as will be seen further on. Paint using the base of the flat palette knife, extending the paint in a thick layer. In this way you will create a uniformly colored surface that will reflect the maximum amount of light possible (fig. 3A).

Fig. 1. We are going to paint a sunny corner of the Costa Brava. Clearly contrasting areas of light and shade can be seen on the rock formations.

Fig. 2. The draft provides the opportunity to appreciate how the main elements of the composition work, and to make sure that the painting is correctly balanced.

Fig. 3A. The drying properties of acrylics make it possible for the artist to build the background up rapidly, and apply new impastos after just a few minutes.

Fig. 3B. As you can see, the palette used by the artist is composed of burnt sienna, ultramarine blue, ochre, permanent violet, cadmium red and raw umber. In the center, which is white, you can see the marble powder.

4

The sky has been painted with even color. The sea, on the contrary, displays a tonal gradation that goes from the lighter areas at the top to the more intense shades of blue as you get closer to the foreground. Applying the paint with a palette knife may be slower and more complicated than using a brush, so you need to be patient and work on it until you have acquired the sufficient practice (fig. 4).

From here on, work on the painting using thick, opaque strokes. In order to represent the perpetual movement of the surface of the water and the waves, apply touches of different juxtaposed colors onto the water (cobalt blue, pinks, violet-like colors, greenish-yellows etc.). One color can be applied on top of another to obtain a greater relief or to enrich its tonality. To carry out this task, you should use a small palette knife (fig. 5).

5

To create small spots of color, hold the handle and press the metallic part down with your forefinger. This will make it easier to work in the smaller and more delicate areas. Also apply thick touches of paint onto the rocks. The best way to render the sea foam is by allowing the white of the support to show through on the edges of the rocky beach (fig. 6). The cape or headland that appears in the distance has been painted in grayish colors to emphasize the distance effect.

The artist continues moving down the painting, using the alla prima technique, that is, finishing off the areas of the painting as he covers them without going back over them. You should do the same. In order to capture the brightness and the quality of the light of the landscape use light colors with a pastel tendency for the sea and somewhat more intense colors on the rocks. In accordance with the laws of atmosphere in landscape, the color of the sea is lighter and has less contrast in the background than in the foreground. This effect also brings out the sunlight on the surface of the water (fig. 7).When painting the

6

Fig. 4. Until now, the artist has worked applying solid-colored layers of paint onto large areas.

Fig. 5. See how the small impastos of color follow the direction of the shapes and masses.

7

Fig. 6. The treatment of the surface of the water gives the painting as a whole an agitated and mobile appearance.

Fig. 7. With an energetic movement of the corner of the sheet of paper, you can achieve a rough and speckled texture just like the artist.

133

rocks, you should keep in mind that the water, in contact with the rocks, creates a dark band at their base. In addition, to represent the relief of the rock formations it will be necessary to contrast the tones (fig. 8), highlighting the unevenness and cracks on their surface, through dramatic light and shade effects, without forgetting the use of chiaroscuro, the contrast between the lighter and darker areas. Finally cover the stony cove in the foreground with flat thick layers of violet-gray paint (fig. 9).

The painting is almost finished now and creates an illusion of reflected light through numerous brushstrokes and touches of juxtaposed colors. The colors are optically mixed when they are observed from a certain distance, and in this way they appear more intense. It is now time to add some finishing touches, resolving some details. Use the tip of your palette knife energetically to obtain graffito effects on the pictorial surface layer. Observe how once the surface has dried, it is very easy to paint on it with a brush. Take a small one and add detail to the group of grasses that appear at the bottom of the image. A more contrasting foreground helps to project the space of the work towards the back, producing more of an effect of distance and depth (fig. 10).

Seen from a certain distance, the intense chromatic sparkling of Carlant's landscape creates a radiant and

8

9

Fig. 8. To give the rocks more volume, you must work on the different planes separately and highlight the contrast between light and shade as much as possible.

Fig. 9. At this stage, the impastos have an extraordinary chromatic variety, even though only a limited range of colors has been used.

Fig. 10. Small sgraffito are carried out by scratching the pictorial surface with the tip of a palette knife while it's still moist.

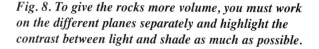

10

TIPS

—Be generous with the marble powder and apply enough of it so as to fill in the texture.

—It is better to use hog bristle brushes for this technique since they are the most resistant. Marble powder easily erodes the tips of brushes.

—If you want to practice the sgraffito technique or modify the pictorial surface you will have to work quickly, since once the paste with marble powder has dried, it will not be possible to modify the layer of paint.

dynamic seascape, a flickering painting that depicts the luminous effects that are found on the surface of the water and in the shadows and natural semitones of the rock formations. The artist has worked on this painting one area at a time. This might have caused you some problems. Since the artist had a very clear idea of what the finished work would look like as he applied each thick layer of paint, he could predict with reasonable certainty how each brushstroke would affect the entire painting. For this reason I would advise you to close your eyes and try to imagine what the work you are about to paint will look like before you begin. Thinking about the painting before doing the actual painting is a very good exercise. As you can see, the painting has a harmonious range of

blues and browns. Therefore, you should not make the mistake of using too many colors, for you can obtain many shades and varieties by mixing a limited range of colors. You will see how the colors tend to whiten when they are mixed with marble powder. Do not worry. Instead of fighting against this effect, try to make the most of it. Accept the fact that you are working with slightly pastel shades. If you have tried to add too much detail to an area of the painting, you will have noticed how this is a difficult task since marble powder is a very coarse material and not very suitable for this type of work since it does not allow a detailed rendering with lots of filigrees.

Fig. 11. Not a single fragment of this painting is flat. All the tones and colors have been built up through an intricate network of small strokes reminiscent of the impressionists.

Female Portrait

We are going to paint the portrait of a young girl with acrylic paint. We will once again be joined by the artist Josep Antoni Domingo, who will paint this portrait using soft, thin glazes, carefully superimposed to make out the forms of the face and the qualities of the skin of the model.

Before starting to paint, the artist should think about how to place the model, both in terms of the illumination and of the general structure of the forms. This is the result. The face of a young girl, in a three quarter profile, is seen in diffused light, without too many contrasts that highlight the factions, although this will favor the toning down of colors and shapes (fig. 1).

To paint this figure, start by drawing the contours of the head with a pencil. Then do a first rendering of the facial features, so that the sketch resembles the person it is meant to portray (fig. 2). Start painting the hair with flat and very diluted paint (remember that you will have the chance to add more details later on). Work on the background, applying a mixture of chrome oxide green, permanent green and white, making sure that you extend it all the way to the border of the silhouette (fig. 3).

Continue working on the whole figure, dividing the skin tones into areas of light and shadow. At this stage, keep the tones separate. Add touches of light, by painting areas with soft yellowish washes, while applying sienna washes in the darker areas. Paint the tones and colors of the face and figure, making the whole painting come into harmony with the background (fig. 4). Now continue with an appraisal of the rest of the skin areas, like the shoulder and the hand. The facial factions have become more rounded as a result of the artist's gradual modeling of the skin tones, which he has done by using subtle gradations to blend the different areas of color on the face. You should do the same. Then paint the mouth, without using too intense or pure a shade of pink. The lips should be related to the rest of the facial tones and be integrated into the whole of the composition.

Fig. 1. The model the artist has chosen for this exercise is a portrait of a young girl in a three quarter profile.

Fig. 2. The constant observation of the face of the model, accompanied by hours of study and practice, will make it possible for you to capture the predominant features in a preliminary sketch.

Fig. 3. Paint the hair and apply the background color carefully, until you have finished outlining the left side of the figure.

Fig. 4. Start with the skin tones. Do not mix the colors on the surface but blend the edges of the different colored areas carefully.

5

With a little burnt umber and a small brush, place the eyes, at first painting only the line of the eyelids, the eyelashes and a circle for the pupils. This painting is now at an intermediate stage of definition. Although they will still be modified somewhat, the colors and the tones already form a satisfactory base for the building up of details (fig. 5).

Once the basic tones of the skin have been applied, the moment to think about

6

Fig. 5. Think of the face as a series of planes and simple forms and do not try for a photographic reproduction of the model.

Fig. 6. After the first washes, the most important thing to do is check the location of the features over and over again.

Fig. 7. Once he has gotten the painting to resemble the model and has gotten the qualities of the skin right, the artist has to decide what degree of detail and definition his work should have.

7

details has come. This means paying close attention to each of the facial elements (eyes, nose, mouth) and trying to detail them, or adjust their shapes to that of the model. Each area is painted with glazes, so that the image appears little by little as the colors and the features are intensified. Try to get the right tone for the skin using titan white, ochre, Venetian red, cadmium red, raw umber, permanent green and cobalt yellow. Highlight the shadows around the eyelids and do the same with the chin and the nose. Work on the hair using successive washes of burnt sienna and a little ultramarine blue. Continue elaborating these features with even more intense strokes wherever you want to give a sensation of depth (behind the ear, the hairline, on the neck etc.) and leave the areas that have touches of light lighter (fig. 6).

With a small brush paint the teeth. The white should be the same color as the paper. Now work on the shadows on the face and hands, being careful to maintain a tonal balance between the face and the rest of the head (fig. 7).

Mark the darker areas of the cheek and the shadows on the neck adding a touch of permanent green to the skin color.

Try to paint with exactitude but using more fluid strokes for the areas around the hair, in order to maintain the character and shape of loose hair. Use a pure magenta to paint the strap of the shirt (fig. 8).

As you can see, the artist has used a simple chromatic range: the creamy warm colors of the skin contrast with the green of the background and the magenta of the shirt strap. Add some finishing touches to the skin tones, reiterating the background color in the skin areas. Be careful not to flatten the face and maintain the tonal contrast between the touches of light and shadow (fig. 9).

The finished painting reflects the subtle use of washes and shows the good results obtained with acrylic paint. The inexperienced artist may feel the temptation to draw with the brush instead of painting. Do not make the mistake of painting what you think should be there instead of what is really there. Study the face of the model meticulously and then go about coloring it. If you find this difficult, reduce the motif to simple planes and treat the facial features as if they were abstract objects.

If you work with thin layers of color instead of thick ones, the danger of covering the pictorial surface too quickly will be reduced, since thin layers can be modified and corrected more easily than thick ones. Be careful with the eyes, which are a trap for inexperienced painters. The natural tendency is to make them too big, due to the great importance they have on the face.

8

TIPS

—Your palette should contain a range of skin tones going from light ones to very dark ones.

—The color of skin is not pink, as some artists believe. Skin tones vary greatly and can include shades of blue, violet, pink, salmon, ochre, brown, yellow... It all depends on the illumination as well as the race and age of the person who is being painted.

—Take frequent breaks while painting in order to move away from your work to judge how the painting is going, especially in regards to the characterization of the model.

Fig. 8. Fairly diluted paint has been used. The colors of the skin have been built up with a series of super-imposed transparent color glazes.

9

Fig. 9. This detail clearly shows the method in which the artist works by superimposing glazes.

On the other hand, it is common that when you paint a portrait for the first time, the eyes are too elaborate and have too fixed a gaze, giving them as unnatural feel. The key to doing a good portrait is to make as exact a preliminary sketch as possible. If the features are not correctly placed from the beginning, there is little possibility of getting them right later. The artist will find him or herself, again and again, applying layer after layer of paint in order to correct the original painting.

Fig. 10. With a rather limited range of colors and based on a structure of modeled tonal surfaces, this beautiful image has been achieved, a figure portrayed in a rather realistic fashion.

Portrait of a Young Lady

Ester Llaudet, who has already worked with us on earlier exercises, is now going to paint a young lady's face. This can be one of the most difficult tasks that an amateur artist ever has to face. The model is this girl's smiling face (fig. 1). As you can see, her head is viewed frontally and her body is facing slightly to the right.

Before you put your brush to paper, study the model carefully. Make a mental note of the facial features, proportions, lights and colors that you see. After a few minutes' observation, you can start. To draw well, not only do you need skill and talent, but you also need to know how to observe.

Before anything, draw the symmetrical axis with charcoal, and then a square frame. Both of these will help to lay out the proportions and angle of her face. Now draw the girl's facial features synthetically, highlighting contrast with your charcoal stick and blurring the areas of shadow (fig. 2).

With the charcoal portrait complete, Ester now finds the colors that she will need for coloring the face. She mixes white, ochre and vermilion for the illuminated parts and burnt umber with a few touches of Prussian blue for the shadowed areas. Then she starts oil painting, superimposing different layers of color as she builds up the face (fig. 3).

Next, work on the eyes and lips by modeling the flesh of her skin with different intensities of flesh colors, making the contrasts of light and shadow more potent, as it is in them that the strength of the girl's expression resides (fig. 4).

Pay a great deal of attention to the lips and eyes, because these two facial elements are fundamental in making your painting look like the person. Once you have painted them, move on to the hair and eyebrows, using burnt umber mixed with ochre yellow and cadmium red to get the mahogany-like effect of the reflections in her hair (fig. 5). Paint her teeth with a watery burnt umber and a thin brush.

Notice how the tonality of the model's face changes. The pink color of her skin becomes less intense when it contrasts with the dark brown of her hair. The tonality of a color will always depend on the colors that surround it.

Take a break, and look at the painting globally, then keep working on the look in the girl's eyes until it is as similar as you can make it to the model's. Apply reflections of light to the pupils and with a mixture of the tone of the skin and burnt umber, define the outline of her eyes and the shadow of her eyelashes with a thin brush (fig. 6).

With the same brush, put more volume into her lips. Apply more intense colors on the right than on the left, where her lips are more brightly-lit. Construct the form of her nose by creating subtle variations of flesh color. To do this, mix unequal proportions of pink with ochre, burnt umber and raw sienna (fig. 7).

Fig. 1. The model is this girl's smiling face.
Fig. 2. Ester wants to capture the spontaneity of the model's expression, which requires a quick and skillfully drawn sketch.
Fig. 3. Without making the features too precise, Ester looks for a lifelike representation and the right facial proportions.
Fig. 4. The first areas of color establish the areas of light and shadow on the face. This is done by adding a little burnt umber to the original flesh color.
Fig. 5. Once the general picture is complete, concentrate on the lips and eyes, possibly the two most important aspects of the face.

Fig. 6. At this stage, the painting is starting look very similar to the model.

Fig. 7. The eyes are outlined with a thin brush, the nose is constructed and the lips are formed.

Fig. 8. Work the background with an ultramarine blue and titanium white background.

When you have finished painting the basic features of her face, try to make it more expressive by accentuating contrasts between light and shadow and defining volume.

Once this stage is over, Ester applies a degradation to the background, mixing ultramarine blue with white, highlighting the front of the figure. Use the same base color that you used on her face to color her cleavage (fig. 8). Follow these same steps and spend a little time getting the color of this part of her body right, along with her dress and a few final touches to the background. Before considering your painting complete, you should work a little more on the color of her flesh. Think about contrasts, degradations, anatomy and shadows (fig. 9). As you will have seen from the portrait, the model has been represented within a warm

color range. This way, the artist transmits the warm-hearted nature of the girl, and intensifies the rosy color of her skin and the mahogany-like reflections in her hair.

There is a good chance that, when you do a similar exercise, you forget that if you want coherent results, you need to develop the painting as a whole as you go along. If you do not do this, it will not be harmonized enough to look like the model.

Fig. 9. The finished piece is a valuable study of the female face, painted by the artist in less than a day.

Glossary

A

Acrylic. This paint has acrylic resin as a binder, which is made from a combination of chemicals or a derivant of pretoleum.

Agglutinate. Substance that is mixed with powdered pigment to make a medium of painting.

Alla prima. Direct painting technique that involves painting quickly in just one session and never going back over what one has painted.

B

Blending. Procedure that involves softening contours and areas of contact between colors to form gentle gradations.

C

Chiaroscuro. Rembrandt was a master of chiaroscuro. In his work, forms and colors are clearly visible despite being surrounded by intense shadows. In his books on painting, Parramón defines chiaroscuro as "the art of painting light over shadow".

Chromatic harmony. The balanced relationship of different colors within a painting.

Composition. The balanced and harmonized distribution of the different elements that appear in a picture. Composing involves bearing these factors in mind as one selects the best arrangements.

Covering capacity. The capacity that a color has to dominate other colors in mixtures and veils.

D

Degradation. Reducing the value of a tone, gradually making it more intense or softer, so that the transition is gradual rather than abrupt.

Dry brush. Painting technique that involves applying thick paint to the support, so that it sticks to both the pores in the canvas and the texture of the paint on the surface.

F

Film. Layer of paint or coating over the surface.

Fit. Preliminary drawing that establishes the basic structure of bodies as simple geometric forms (cubes, rectangles, prisms etc) that are often known as frames.

G

Genre. Classification of artistic techniques, such as still lives, landscapes, figures and interiors.

Gum arabic. Resin from the acacia plant which is used as a binder for watercolor and gouache.

I

Induction of complementaries. A phenomenon derived from simultaneous contrasts, which complies with the norm that states that "to modify a particular color, you simply need to change the color that surrounds it".

L

Local color. The genuine color of an object when it is not affected by shadow, reflections or other factors.

M

Medium. Liquid in which pigments are held, for example linseed oil is used for oil paints and acrylic resin for acrylics. Pastel sticks can be mixed or dampened in any of these mediums.

Merging. Technique that involves spreading or reducing one or more layers of color onto to a background layer, so that the lower layer is still visible through the superimposed one.

Mixed techniques. Using different painting procedures in the same picture, or using a combination of different supports.

Modeling. Although this is a sculptural term, it can also be applied to painting and drawing to refer to the way in which different tones are applied to create an illusion of the third dimension.

O

Opacity. The capacity that a gray shade or wash has for covering a layer below it. Opacity varies from pigment to pigment.

Opaque painting technique. Pastel technique that involves applying thick layers of color to create a textured surface with little or no merging.

P

Pasting. Technique that involves applying thick layers of color to create textured surfaces.

Perspective. Way of representing the three-dimensional world on a two-dimensional surface.

Pigments. Coloring agents in powdered form that are obtained from natural sources (although some are now made synthetically) that, when mixed with an agglutinate, create paint.

Pointillism. Painting technique that involves applying small dots to the canvas.

Pre-painting. Preliminary paint that the rest of the colors of a piece are painted over.

Preparatory sketch. The preliminary stage in the construction of a drawing or painting, from which the definitive piece can be derived. Several sketches might be made before the artist decides upon the idea he wants to work with.

Primer. Adhesive or gelatinous material that is applied to the canvas before it is painted, making the support less absorbent. It can also be used as an agglutinate in paint.

Proportion. The relationship of one part with the tonality of a piece.

S

Saturation. Value or chromatic degree of a color. Strength of a color that a surface can reflect.

Graffito. Technique that involves scraping a layer of color with a sharp instrument, so that the color of the support becomes visible.

Solvents. Liquids used for dissolving oil paints. The solvent for water based colors is water and for oil based products, turpentine essence, thinners and similar substances are used.

Stanley knife. Sharp knife used for cutting paper, made up of a metal blade inside a plastic handle.

Style. In sculpture, drawing and painting, this is the way that the task is approached. It can be agitated, brusque, delicate, slow, fast... It determines the manner of working of each individual artist.

Support. Surface used for painting or drawing, such a board, sheet of paper or canvas.

T

Tempera. Water based paint in which the pigment is mixed with glue extracts from animal or vegetable sources.

Texture. Tactile and visual quality of the surface of a drawing or painting. It can be smooth, granulated, rough or cracked.

Tonal background. Opaque coloring in which the color is mixed with white to spread the color in a uniform way. A tonal background can also be colored.

Tonal color. Color offered by the shadow of objects.

Tone. Term that has its origins in music that, when applied to art, refers to the strength and relief of all the parts of a painting with respect to light and color.

Transparency. Way of applying color so that light or the previous layer of color filters through.

V

Value. As much in drawing as painting, volume or modeling is obtained from the tonal values of the model. At the same time, it is achieved through the comparison and tonal resolution of effects of light and shadow.

Veils. Layers of transparent color that are superimposed over the preliminary color when it is dry.

Viscosity. Measure of the characteristic fluidity of a color or medium.

Volatility. Evaporation potential of a solution.

Volume. Three-dimensional effect of a model in the two-dimensional space of a painting.

W

Wash. Type of drawing/painting that dates back to the Renaissance period. It consists of a painting made with only one color, generally sepia, diluted in water. It can also refer to any watercolor, aniline color or chinese ink.

Wet on wet painting. Technique that involves painting over an area of recently applied paint while it is still damp. The level of dampness can be controlled, depending on the effect that the artist wishes to create.

Whiting. Ground, washed chalk that is used for priming cloth and in the composition of pastels.

Acknowledgements

The author would like to thank the following companies and people for their help with the publication of this book. Gabriel Martín Roig for his help with the texts and the general coordination of the book; Mónica Mosso for her help with the texts; Antonio Oromí for his photography; Vicenç Piera of the Piera company for his help and advice concerning painting and drawing materials and utensils; Manel Úbeda of Novasis for help with the publication and production of the photography and photostatting; the people who gave us permission to use certain photographs as a models for painting, and a special thanks to all the artists who provided the step-by-step exercices.